How to Manage a Successful Bar

Christopher Egerton-Thomas

John Wiley & Sons, Inc.
*New York / Chichester / Brisbane /
Toronto / Singapore*

Copyright © 1994 by John Wiley & Sons, Inc.

Library of Congress Cataloging-in-Publication Data:

Egerton-Thomas, Christopher.
    How to manage a successful bar / Christopher Egerton-Thomas.
      p. cm.
    Includes bibliographical references.
    ISBN 0-471-30461-1 (pbk. : alk. paper)
    1. Bars (Drinking establishments)—Management. I. Title.
  TX950.7.E35   1993
  647.95'068—dc20   93-6425

To Edwin Beckett,
whose sterling devotion to duty
has helped inspire my research;
and to Claire Thompson,
super-editor, with thanks.

CONTENTS

PREFACE

Consumer patterns may be changing, but reports of the death of the traditional bar are greatly exaggerated. Bars are often the focal points of restaurants, and the most profitable part of the operation. Often they help form a healthy element in the local neighborhood social fabric. A recent U.S. survey, in which people were asked what they did to relax, showed that 50 percent watched television, while 35 percent went to bars and restaurants.

Given a decent location and reasonable overheads, the only further ingredient required for success is good management. This book spells out exactly what that is. Since a bar manager is almost invariably a bartender too, a comprehensive coverage is essential. This book even tackles gray areas that many would rather not discuss.

The bartender is as much part of the social landscape today as the parish priest used to be, and often performs some of the same duties. He's also a folklore figure. Sometimes he's swarthy and sinister—the shifty guy in the western movie, who only serves "shots" downed in one gulp by the hero. He hastens to inform the local Baddie when Our Hero hits town. Sometimes she's understanding and motherly. Or young, glamorous, and unattainable but excellent dream fodder, as well as an efficient dispenser of alcoholic and other beverages.

Quite often nowadays the bartender is a dead ringer for a Hollywood idol, husky voice, designer stubble, and all. Whatever the image, the job is pretty much the same wherever you go. There isn't a lot to it—bartenders are not flying 747s in tricky cross-winds—but there are things a bartender needs to know. The better he knows the job, the easier it will be and the more money he and his employer will make. As Mr. Clausewitz said, "Train hard, fight easy." Admittedly he was discussing war, not business, but one hopes the point will be well taken! Preparation, set-up, and training are the keys to successful bar operation.

Most bartenders are never formally trained. Many "bartending schools" leave much to be desired, often making heavy weather of simple matters while ignoring important areas. Some schools place great emphasis on knowing how to make a large range of long-dead cocktails that will never be requested, from "Sazeracs" to "French 75s," at the expense of more useful skills. The range of requested cocktails is ever-shrinking, and at any given time a group of no more than a dozen will be fashionable. Naturally, as requests become regular, bartenders will need to learn their recipes. This book presents a useful list of drink recipes divided into "Must Know," "Should Know," and "Could Know" groups.

Techniques, organizational ability, and above all a knack for handling people are at least as important as mixology.

Traditionally, many students have worked their way through college by bartending. Flexible hours have enabled them to attend classes and earn money at the same time. Artists of all kinds, especially actors, have found bartending a useful alternative occupation while temporarily among Equity's almost constant 82 percent unemployed mass. It's a useful second career for those who retire early enough to want to do something else before they finally put their feet up. And to many more, it's a pleasant job with many useful perks and always, at least, a decent income. Sometimes bartending is a stepping stone to management and the dream-goal of owning one's own business.

In the performing arts, at a certain point, the artist must have so thoroughly absorbed the technicalities of his dance, theatrical part, or concerto, that he can devote most of his energy to interpretation and the thorough engagement of the audience. It's the same in the bar business. Practice makes perfect. After a while everything to do with managing the bar becomes automatic, and 90 percent of a bar manager and his staff's attention can be devoted to those very important people—the customers. A good bar staff will not wallow and fuss in how to cope with this situation, or how to make that cocktail, but will devote most of their energies to the customer, in the hope of making that person a *regular* customer.

But it is at that point that the greater challenge emerges, and finally this book will tell you how to avoid "burn-out"—every worker's enemy.

CHAPTER ONE

Introduction

Bar managers and their staffs can congratulate themselves on being members of one of the oldest professions. Their place in human society is almost as old as recorded history.

How It All Began

The consumption of alcohol began with civilization. (Some would say that civilization began with the discovery of alcohol.) Reconstituted debris from grave urns found in the valley of the rivers Tigris and Euphrates, where humankind first began the transition from hunter-gatherers to farmers, turns into a thick and nutritious vitamin B loaded beer—a far cry from most of the bottled beers of today. This may have been humankind's first manufactured food. One theory holds that part of the motive for settling down to farming, as opposed to endlessly wandering in search of food 10,000 years ago, was to raise crops that could be fermented into beer, cider, or wine. Rice, dates, palm leaves, cacti, fruits, cereals, flowers, and potatoes have all found fermentation somewhere. Spirits came later. Brandy was perhaps discovered in the Middle Ages at a medical school in Salerno. Another theory is that it was invented by a Dutch merchant who found he could transport the distilled liquid to the point of sale, where water could be added to turn it back into wine—only to discover that there was a good market for the spirit just the way it was.

The Old Testament contains references to wine; and Noah was one biblical character who had too much to drink on occasion. Pagans, Christians, and most other religious adherents embraced wine and beer heartily. Alcohol played a part in religious ritual from the Greek and Roman temples of the classical world ("a libation to the gods"), and is still used in African voodoo and modern Catholic Church rites.

Centuries ago water supply was often uncertain and alcoholic beverages earned a practical place as simple liquid refreshment apart from their other, quickly apparent, advantages. This benefit should not be too exaggerated. Wine and beer were often of poor quality, and complaints about beer that had deteriorated at sea are common in naval and merchant records. One of the reasons that the Pilgrim Fathers stopped in New England was because they had run out of drinkable beer and needed to make some more.

Until late in the 19th century the seamen of Her Britannic Majesty's Royal Navy were permitted a free daily allowance of either eight pints of beer, or two of spirits, which might be either rum or brandy. Since more than 60 percent of seamen were either convicts or "pressed men" (rounded up from taverns in naval base areas), it is not hard to see the role of alcohol in those delightful times. Many of the men must have spent their lives in a drunken stupor.

Accounts of battles on land at this time also betray an alcoholic presence. Barrels of rum and brandy were rolled into the infantry squares at Waterloo. Alcohol was used as an anesthetic for operations, particularly the amputations that were so enthusiastically undertaken in those days.

The word "alcohol" derives from the Arabic *al-kohl*, which originally referred to finely ground antimony eye-liner (still in use throughout Arabia today by both sexes), but eventually came to mean any kind of exotic essence.

It is perhaps ironic that alcohol is now forbidden throughout most of the Arab world by the dictates of Islam. Alcohol consumption in strict countries such as Saudi Arabia can be punishable by jail sentences or public caning. Many Westerners have come close to this fate, and rescue from it has strained diplomatic talent to the limit.

Though it cannot be denied that Islam has effectively imposed prohibition where others have failed, it is hard to imagine any French government that imposed a sentence of 50 lashes on anyone taking a glass of red wine with dinner surviving for long.

In other Moslem countries alcohol is sometimes tolerated, usually where a dependence on foreign tourism makes it desirable. In Egypt, for instance, it's available in hotels catering to tourists. The Sultan of Oman, having been educated at Sandhurst, Britain's West Point, is no stranger to alcohol and has decreed that it may legally be consumed in his country, although tourism is somewhat discouraged.

There is no shortage of references to alcohol down through the ages. The Babylonians had strict regulations. Ancient Roman poet Pliny gave us the often quoted line *In vino veritas*—"In wine there is truth."

Few philosophers have bothered to point out that there's a lot of nonsense, too, perhaps because this is so self-evident. In ancient Greece Socrates warned that "If we pour ourselves immense draughts, it will not be long before both our minds and bodies reel." The ancient Greeks were very insistent that wine should be diluted with water. It was considered bad form to drink it straight.

In the 12th century Omar Khayyám had plenty to say on the subject of wine:

> Yesterday this day's madness did prepare;
> Tomorrow's silence, Triumph, or despair:
> Drink! for you know not whence you came, nor why:
> Drink! for you know not why you go, or where.

Writers from Chaucer to Dylan Thomas have leaned heavily on the world of alcohol, and Shakespeare's famous dictum that "It provokes the desire, but it takes away the performance" is a homily confirmed by many. So rich and well-thumbed is the lexicon of bibulous quotations that it's hard to find anything that does not have the dull ring of cliché.

King Charles the Second of England complained of an acquaintance that he "had tried him drunk, and tried him sober, and there's nothing in the man." An apocryphal story about Abraham Lincoln concerns General Grant, after whom a fine whiskey is named. Certain officers complained that General Grant was drinking too much. Lincoln's reply was, "Please find out what it is he drinks—and send a case of it to each of my generals!"

Bars from Pompeii to Prohibition

Excavations of the near-pristine ruins of Pompeii, the ancient Roman town covered with ash when Mount Vesuvius erupted in A.D. 79, reveal a thriving alcohol industry. A population of approximately 20,000 supported 20 inns and 118 bars. Most of these bars served wine, beer, and hot drinks (hot water added to wine or warmed beer). Tea, coffee, cocoa, and spirits were still 1,500 years down the line.

Until the discovery of the cork, wine was sweetened and boiled to steam off some of the water content. When the wine was judged ready for market it was described as "cute," and that is the origin of this adjective, so popular in American English today.

The serving of food to the ancient Roman public was discouraged by nervous emperors who thought, quite rightly, that encouraging people to sit around dinner tables might lead to sedition and revolution. Markets, held every ninth day, were also closely controlled for the same reasons. When one considers the dreadful goings-on that emerged from the unsupervised bazaars of the British Empire, one can only congratulate the caesars on their wisdom. However, they could do little about the private dining sessions where most mischief was cooked up.

At an inn, as opposed to a bar, hot food was available. Many bars frequently had all-night drinking, dancing, and singing sessions. Tradition has it that the disguised Emperor Nero was a frequent patron of such places.

In the ancient world, extensive regulations existed. A Roman 4th-century decree reads: "No wine shop shall open before 9 A.M., nobody is to heat water for the public, sellers of cooked food can operate only at fixed hours, and no respectable person is to be seen eating in public." The imperial police would have a high old time on the avenues of America today, where half the population seems to be dining on the march, pizza in one hand, soda can in the other!

At Asellina's Thermopolium in Pompeii the stone bar is still intact; its hot water container is easily identified and behind it are a number of mugs, bowls, and amphorae (the all-purpose jar containers of the ancient world). These mundane and ordinary containers, which now qualify as "artifacts," litter classical sites and waters almost as ubiquitously as the discarded soda cans of today.

Then as now location was important. The inn of Euxinus next to the Amphitheater features a street-corner bar, hot food counter, wine racks, back rooms, and an open-air courtyard. It must have been a popular place to warrant such extensive features.

The purpose and function of these establishments were the same as today's. Travelers and those temporarily cut off from the ordinary sustenance of the domestic hearth were served. But these places were also "watering holes" and gathering places where casual meetings might turn into deeper acquaintance. Alcohol loosened tongues, reality, truths, inhibitions, and morals.

Inn keepers made a good living and were prominent in society, though perhaps denied the full mantle of respectability that belonged to lawyers, accountants, and the like. Long before the age of Puritanism there were those who looked askance at inns and bars. Prostitution and gambling were associated with such establishments. Gambling was illegal in ancient Rome, but in practice it was tolerated.

A consideration of ancient places such as Pompeii, Leptis Magna, Cyrene, Appollonia, and Syracuse—more or less intact ruins of civilizations as vibrant as our own—can be almost unbearably poignant for those who choose to hear, among the crumbling stones, the echoes of ancient laughter, grumbles, wisdom, and foolishness. Reflection on the temporary nature of life itself will not be far behind.

As the centuries progressed the bar industry grew, in close association with the ever-expanding hotel and restaurant business. One wonders sometimes what Western humanity would have done without it, so much history and folklore derive from its rituals.

The development and improvement of the quality in wines and spirits owe much to the blessing of the Church and the sincere attentions of generations of monks. (It is worth remarking that Christian tradition has plenty of comments to make about the evils of alcohol abuse—drunkenness—but few about sensible and moderate drinking, which it appears to take for granted.)

By the 19th century things were getting out of control. The French poets Baudelaire and Verlaine waxed lyrical about the joys of absinthe. However, the French government was so worried about its effects on the poorer classes, which included blindness and death, that absinthe was banned except in the diluted form of what is now marketed as pastis—Pernod and Ricard.

Temperance became a crusade for many in England, where gin mills advertised their wares: "Drunk for a penny, dead drunk for tuppence"—with free straw thrown in for sleeping it off. To this day, all over the Yorkshire Dales, one will see prim "Temperance Hotels," dating almost invariably from the days of John Wesley. The one burning certainty in a "Temperance Hotel" is that, no matter how much you need it, you will not be able to get a good, stiff drink. Apparently, many derive comfort and succor from such certainty. Others may be less inspired.

Britain's recently abandoned, quaint licensing hours dated only from the First World War, when it was considered desirous that workers return to their duties promptly and reasonably sober. Yet so deeply ingrained is the old routine that many pubs still observe the old restricted hours.

Other countries have had their problems, too. Both Finland and Sweden outlawed alcohol, a move that became known as "Prohibition." Finland allowed the consumption of beer only. Eventually both countries returned to the system of legal consumption of alcohol, though with fierce punishments for violators, particularly motorists who were found to have alcohol in their blood. Sweden at one time tried a system of liquor ration books, but this was so abused that it eventually broke down. Attempts to control alcohol consumption have also been recorded in the Aztec and ancient Chinese empires, feudal Japan, Iceland, Norway, Russia, Canada, and India.

In spite of the history of failure of this measure in many countries, the United States embraced it in 1920—in all states except Connecticut and Rhode Island. Absurd as it may seem today, this legislation was a result of the collision of an American society, whose roots were founded in Puritanism, with the influx of immigrants from countries such as Germany, Italy, and Ireland, where alcohol was a part of life. Brewers were usually German. Nearly every street corner in America's cities and small towns was a bar.

As might have been foreseen, the theater of Prohibition led to an absurd glamorization of the world of alcohol. Nine years after Prohibition began, there were 32,000 "speakeasies" in New York—nearly twice as many as the pre-Prohibition number of saloons.

Fortunes were made in the smuggling and clandestine manufacture of liquor. These years gave organized crime a boost from which it has never looked back. Prohibition opened opportunities for corruption of the forces of law and order, too, as does the prohibition of gambling, prostitution, and the like. By 1933 even the "drys" had to concede that Prohibition wasn't working, and the 18th Amendment was repealed by the 21st.

The failure of Prohibition underlines the fact that alcohol consumption is a part of life for many Western people. The ever-present risk of abuse mandates certain government controls. Even the happiest and most responsible drinker cannot ignore the horrors of abuse, from accidents to violence to broken homes to early death. Indeed the specter of these extremes helps keep most responsible drinkers firmly on the straight and narrow!

The Bar's Role in Society

Alcohol consumption increased with the general affluence of the Western world. Westernization of the Orient opened up undreamed-of markets. Who, pre-World War II, would ever have dreamed that Scotch whiskey and Bordeaux wines would find markets in Japan and Korea? Who would have thought that the French with their magnificent panoply of wines, beers, spirits, and liqueurs would adopt whiskey, gin, and vodka? Or that the three-martini lunch would be replaced by designer bottled water?

Most of these changes have been brought about by clever marketing and advertising. Once you can sell upwardly mobile people the idea that what you're selling is what the smart folks are buying, you are on your way to success.

Alcohol sales worldwide peaked in the 1980s. There has since been a downturn in consumption of all alcoholic beverages—with the exception of champagne, whose sales go on and ever upward, though at a much reduced rate.

Perhaps there are still things to celebrate in these wonderful 1990s in spite of gloom in some quarters. Sales have fallen but leveled out.

The recession inevitably had some effect on this drastic market change, as did the health craze. Alcohol became a strictly forbidden no-no for health nuts, until challenged by the suggestion that a moderate intake of alcohol might inhibit the possibility of cardiovascular disease.

Except in those American families that fiercely cling to their ethnicity and the habits of their forefathers, there isn't really a tradition of drinking alcohol daily or with meals. All Latin countries embrace the proverb, "A day without wine is like a day without sun." In America nonalcoholic drinks compete head on with wines, beers, and spirits. Water, tea, milk, coffee, and above all sodas are more likely to be consumed with the average American family meal—in those houses that still feature such occasions in the age of fixing a sandwich from whatever's in the refrigerator and munching it in front of the TV set.

So powerful are the advertisements for nonalcoholic drinks that a majority of American consumers never enter what one might call "the drinking pool." There are just so many other wonderful things to drink! The United States may be the only country in the Western world where, if a man asks a woman to join him for "a drink," implying a casual meeting rather than a drunken bacchanal, he risks being brushed off with a terse "I don't drink." "How about getting together for pie and coffee some time" is a much safer line!

Though home alcohol consumption in America has increased, there is still a deep-rooted prejudice against drinking alcohol in general that bar managers will do well to bear in mind as they wrestle with the problem of keeping up, and increasing, business in ever more competitive times.

A majority of families in the United States and Anglo-Saxon countries do not routinely store alcohol at home. At Christmas they may bring home a bottle or two. In such countries two-thirds of all alcohol sales occur in the final three months of the year.

In many circles a certain stigma attaches to those who make no secret of their regular consumption of alcohol. What candidate for the presidency of the United States has ever admitted to consuming more alcohol than a tiny glass of eggnog on Christmas morning? (There was one politician who intimated to voters that the legal price ceiling on the gifts he could accept from them just encompassed the price of a bottle of his favorite bourbon—but he was brave to do so. Perhaps he was a man of independent means?)

The well-known fact that the price of two martinis in the average bar will buy a whole bottle of gin or vodka at the liquor store, if you wish to drink at home, is indicative of what the bar business is all about. Some people are appalled to hear someone confess that he or she occasionally drinks alone at home. Their thoughts instantly register an image of lonely alcoholism, which may not be the case at all. There are some people who like alcohol but abhor conviviality. There is a kaleidoscopic range of attitudes toward alcohol. The hypocrisy frequently encountered in discussion of the subject is something the bar manager will do well to understand.

Most people who want to drink go to a bar or restaurant. The industry twists and turns to make such excursions more agreeable. To combat the rivalry of television, TV sets have been installed in many bars, and this practice has been further refined to the currently popular "sports bars," where people go to watch sports on big screens, eat, and drink at the same time. Any bar that goes out of its way to allow single women to sit without any salacious overtones will attract business from the increasing number of affluent and independent females.

Just as musicians practice diligently so that the technical complexities of a piece cease to be a problem, thus freeing their attentions for artistic rendition, so good bar managers should aim to create bars that run effortlessly, like clockwork, freeing them and their staffs to concentrate on the single most important element in the whole enterprise—the customer.

CHAPTER TWO

Standard Bar Inventory

There are so many liquor brands in the world today that no bar, restaurant, or store can hope to stock them all. Nor would bar managers or owners wishing to preserve their sanity seek to do so.

The larger the inventory, the more work is generated and the more expensive space is required. For maximum efficiency and profit the inventory should be lean and mean. Many successful restaurants carry only one brand of beer. Others carry one imported and one domestic.

When the wine list in a 120-seat restaurant is allowed to grow in order to indulge the whim of every customer and the blandishments of every salesperson, keeping the inventory up to date—and having to explain every day to employees and customers alike just what is and isn't available—can cause extra work and a lot of stress. But if you have tons of space and a budget that pays a sommelier and a cellarman or two, why not, like the "Windows on the World" restaurant in New York, carry more than 5,000 varieties of wine?

And if you acquire a premises with a beer room, lines, and pumps it's foolish not to exploit the existing equipment and offer as wide a selection as possible because this can help build a regular clientele of draft beer aficionados—and there are enough of them to make these people an important consumer group. (Nor are they poor spenders—on the contrary, they're usually Yuppies!)

Local idiosyncrasies and regular customers must be catered to also. If the local steelworker's favorite tipple is a shot of Benedictine followed by a beer chaser, or if a twice-a-week diner requests Lamplighter Gin, then clearly they must be accommodated. Some inventories have quite an odd and absurdly imbalanced look, but bar owners lucky enough to sell 20 cases of Jagermeister or 12 barrels of Guinness a week must learn to cope with their good fortune. In short, while bar managers should be obsessive about keeping the inventory as small as possible, they should take care not to lose business by being inflexible.

Manufacturers know the game. They know that the only way they'll ever get a bar to carry Toodlepips Malt Beverage is either by offering special service, sales aids, and a high profit margin, or by creating such a huge customer demand by dint of heavy and expensive advertising (which of course must be recovered from customers in due course) that the bar will find itself losing business if it doesn't carry the item.

Bar managers become inured to the weary parade of salespeople who solemnly hope to sell their goods because they're nice folks and it's a great product. It's not enough. You do not have to spend many years in the business to see a few brands come and go. If there's a huge spread of national advertising, everyone's asking for the product—for a while. Often manufacturers will try to sell an item by the "Trojan Horse" method: they'll invent and advertise a fun or chic-sounding cocktail that just happens to have their product as an essential ingredient. Then the advertising stops and the item becomes a has-been, languishing in a dusty corner of the cellar and likely to be thrown out at any time. Where are the "Harvey Wallbangers" and "Pink Squirrels" of yesteryear?

It's estimated that about one in 20 new brands "take" and become retail standard items. This figure applies miraculously to everything from gin to breakfast cereals. One French company has attacked the American market in strength and force three times in recent decades with its excellent beer only to be repulsed. "God is with the big battalions," and the power of entrenched products is enormous. It's very hard to make them forfeit even the smallest percentage of their market.

Bar Supplies

The following list of bar supplies is not written in stone. A brand of scotch unheard of in one state or country may be the number one seller in another. "House selection" or "house brand" means the (often cheaper, but not necessarily) liquor or wine that is used when no specific brand is requested. They are sometimes known as "well drinks," because their home is in the well, or speed rack, (see diagram p. 11) containing the most frequently used items.

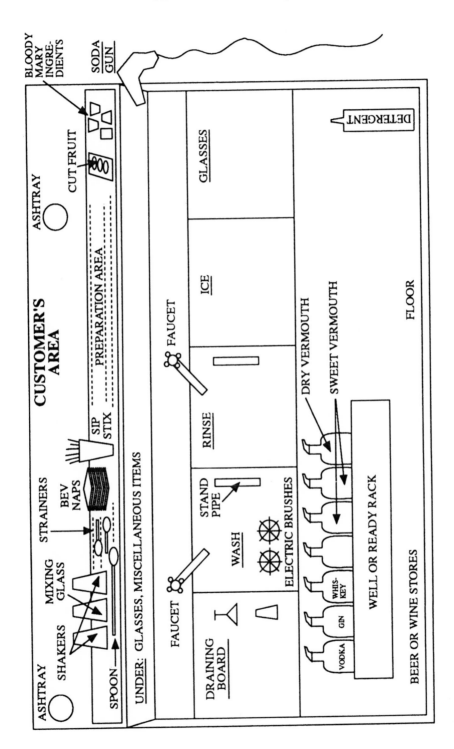

Rye or American Whiskey: Seagrams 7, VO, Crown Royal, Canadian Club, a house selection

Bourbon: Old Grandad

Tennessee Whiskey: Jack Daniels

Scotch Whiskey: Dewars, J&B, Cutty Sark, Johnny Walker (Red and Black), Chivas Regal, Teacher's, Ballantines, Black and White, Famous Grouse, a house selection

Single Malt Whiskey: Glenlivet, Glenfiddich

Irish Whiskey: Bushmills, Black Bush, Jameson's

Canadian Whiskey (Rye): Canadian Club

Rum: Bacardi (Light and Dark, Black, Gold), Myers, Mount Gay, Gosling's, Captain Morgan's Spiced, house

Gin: Beefeater, Gordon's, House of Lords, Tanqueray, Boodles, house

Vodka: Smirnoff, Gordon's, Tanqueray, Stolichnaya, Wyborowa, Finlandia, Absolut, Icy, house

Sherry: (dry, sweet, medium) Tio Pepe, La Ina, Harvey's Bristol Cream

Port: Cockburn, Taylor Fladgate, Sandeman's (various vintages)

Tequila: Cuervo, Cuervo Gold

Cognac and Brandy: Remy Martin, Courvoisier, Cordon Bleu, XO, Apricot, Blackberry, Cherry, Armagnac, Plum, Marc, Metaxa (Greek), various Spanish brandies, house

Bitters: Campari, Angosturas

Vermouth and Wine Cocktails: Lillet, Suze, Dubonnet, Cinzano, Noilly Prat, Stock, sweet red and white dry house vermouth

Cordials, Liqueurs, and Miscellaneous: Bailey's Irish Cream, Chartreuse (Green and Yellow), Chambord, Cointreau, Crème de Cacao, (cocoa, Dark and White), Crème de Casis, Crème de Menthe (White Mint, Green Mint) Crème de Noyau, Curacao, Drambuie, Frangelica, Fruit Brandies, Galliano, Grand Marnier, Kahlua, Kummel, Midori (Melon), Peppermint Brandy, Tia Maria, Jagermeister, Pernod/Ricard

Champagne: (Domestic) Korbel, Piper Sonoma, (Imported) Moet, Mumm, Krug, Dom Perignon, Piper Heidseik, Ruinart

California White Wine: Chardonnay, Puligny Montrachet, made from these varieties of grapes under many different labels, all with different character

California Red Wine: Cabernet Sauvignon, Zinfandel, Merlot, as above (Some grapes are made into both red and white wines.)

German White: Moselle, Reisling

French Red: Beaujolais, Pommard, (Burgundy wines), Margaux, Mouton Cadet, (Bordeaux wines sometimes called Claret), Côte du Rhone, etc.

French White: Chablis, Pouilly Fume or Fouissé, etc.

Italian Red: Valpolicella, Chianti, etc.

Italian White: Soave Bolla, Pino Grigio, etc.

Rosé: Tavel, Anjou, (or house white with a splash of house red!)

House Wine: Red and White (preferably in large bottles or jugs), Argentinian, Australian, Austrian, Swiss, Spanish

Beer (Bottled): Heineken, Budweiser, Amstel, Miller Lite, Guinness Stout— whatever local demand requires

Beer (Draft): Budweiser, Anchor Steam, Local Breweries, various imported options, Pilsner Urquell, Bass, Watney's, Fosters, Guinness

Nonalcoholic Beer: Buckler, Caliber

Soda: Colas, Diet Colas, 7-Up, Ginger Ale, Tonic Water (Quinine Water), Soda Water (Seltzer)

Juices and Bottled Waters: orange, grapefruit, tomato, cranberry, pineapple, lime juice (Roses and regular), lemon juice (cocktail mix); Evian, Perrier, Saratoga, local products

Perishable Supplies: milk, heavy cream, Worcestershire Sauce, Angosturas Bitters, Fernet Branca, Tabasco Sauce, salt, pepper, cherries, olives, onions, lemons, limes, oranges, cream, coconut cream, nutmeg, sugar, castor sugar, horseradish, coffee beans, Bouillon (perishable once the can is opened)

Miscellaneous: Glasses, mixing equipment, blender, corkscrews, bottle openers, sharp knife and cutting board for fruit, straws, beverage napkins or coasters or both, stirrers, straws (large and small), large dinner napkins, matches, bar mops, towels, toothpicks, pens, paper, ashtrays, cigarettes (according to local law, but always an emergency source for addicts in trauma), business cards, mop, broom, dustpan, reference book of cocktail recipes, telephone directory, dictionaries, atlas, Guiness Book of Records, TV guide, entertainment guide, daily paper, town map, first aid kit (including aspirin or alternative pain reliever), local health and hygiene requirements, "muddler" (a six-inch pestle looking like a miniature baseball bat used for crushing fruit in "old fashioned" cocktails—the bar spoon will do), watch, calendar, crazy glue, feather duster, ice buckets, tongs, electric brushes, gloves, standpipes, licenses displayed, pourers, stoppers for opened champagne, menus, cutlery, napkins (for food at the bar), ice scoops.

Each of these items is examined in a later chapter.

House Brands and Premium Labels

"Johnny Walker Black and soda" means exactly that. But when the order is simply "scotch and soda" or "a glass of white wine," the bartender pours the house brand. Often, these are cheaper brands, or even the cheapest available.

It clearly isn't the end of the world if a customer sitting at a table, not at the bar where every move the bartender makes can be monitored, orders Remy Martin and Coke and is given the house pouring brandy on the grounds that the customer can't possibly tell the difference in such a mixture. But it's a ripoff if the customer is then charged for the premium brand. Besides, why shouldn't customers get what they ask for, even if it's sometimes a bit eccentric? "The customer is (nearly) always right."

While it may be true that the majority of customers cannot tell one liquor from another, it is clearly a breach of trust to serve something other than that which is ordered. The practice is all too common—in the food area as well as beverages (pork is disguised and called veal, pollack is called crab meat, and so on). Some owners are so greedy that they will actually creep into the bar in the early morning to top up expensive brand name bottles with cheap stuff, unbeknown to the bartender!

The downside to this is that many customers judge the quality of a restaurant on the quality of its house brand drinks, especially its house wines. While gin in a gin and tonic could be anything, the brand used in a dry gin martini is easily identified by many.

Furthermore, frequent bar and restaurant customers notice details that form the fabric of the impression that creates a strong client base. Sometimes these details are assimilated unconsciously and customers leave with just the vaguest feeling—which they usually do not bother to analyze, life being short—of having had excellent value for their money, or otherwise.

You could get away with anything in a bar if most of your customers were never going to pass that way again. But if you are hoping for repeat business, as most bars and restaurants are, then it will pay to offer decent value.

The goodwill generated by delivering the genuine article will prove more important than the small profit generated by using cheaper substitute brands. One of the things that distinguishes a serious restaurant from a run-of-the-mill, forgettable joint is serving known and popular liquor brands as the normal house offering. A Gordons Gin and Tonic has a little more glamour to it than Hoboken Special, poured furtively from an undistinguished-looking bottle. And if the owner and management feel the need to add 25 cents to the base price of standard bar drinks to cover this, the average customers will consider it well worthwhile—if indeed they notice.

In recent years the quality of house white wine in many restaurants and bars became so abysmal that people really did start to notice. Restaurateurs took advantage of the fact that many customers only knew that the smart thing to ask for was "a glass of Chablis," or currently "Chardonnay," and poured cheap and often downright unpleasant wine.

A small revolution occurred as customers, once bitten and twice shy, began to frown and ask the waiter or bartender, "What wines are you pouring by the glass?" Thus, most bars and restaurants now have to offer a small selection of alternatives to the house wine, though the worst excesses of this exploitation have now been curbed by this consumer pressure.

Between the hammer of recession and the anvil of changing consumer patterns, which are partly whimsical and partly related to lifestyle changes, restaurant customers are becoming more critical all the time. Value is appreciated more.

Various Types of Liquor, Wine, and Beer

Rye and American Whiskey. Originally Rye whiskey was simply one that was made from fermented mashed rye grain. As other grains became available the mixture changed and the descriptions Rye, Blended, and American whiskey became common, and now mean more or less the same thing. If a customer asks for a "Whiskey Sour," it should be made with a domestic brand such as Seagrams 7, Four Roses, or Schenley's, or a Canadian whiskey like Canadian Club. Additions such as other grain spirits or prune or other fruit juices are what give each brand its own particular character. They are usually drunk on the rocks with ginger ale, 7-Up, or soda. If an Englishman asks for "whiskey" he usually means Scotch whiskey—so does a Frenchman. In French, *le Scotch* is scotch tape.

Bourbon Whiskey, Sometimes Just Whiskey. This is distilled from a 51 percent corn mash and aged from two to six years in charred oak barrels. In the same family but slightly different are Jack Daniels and George Dickel, which are strictly speaking "Tennessee whiskies." They are a little more refined than some Bourbons because before aging they're filtered through maple charcoal. On the whole Bourbons are sweeter than other whiskies. All Bourbons seem to command a fierce "brand loyalty." They are usually drunk on the rocks, as Bourbon Manhattans or Sours, or with soda. Some bartenders automatically make their Whiskey Sours with Bourbon because it gives the drink a deeper color that many customers find appealing.

Scotch Whiskey. This is a blend of malt and grain whiskey, characterized by a smoky flavor. "Malt" means from barley; it is the drying of sprouted barley over peat fires that creates this before the distillation process is begun. Different types of whiskey of different ages are blended in subtle and secret ways to produce individual brand name character. There are regular blends with no age given on the label, eight-year-olds, and 12-year-olds such as Chivas Regal. Again, there is strong brand loyalty. A joke in the business is that Dewar's is "everyone's second choice"—but in fairness it must be stated that it is often first choice too.

In the United States there is a preference for "light" scotch. This refers to its flavor. The popular light scotches are also somewhat lighter in color than the general run. This is entirely due to the amount of caramel coloring that is added to all scotches, and has nothing to do with their strength, which is almost invariably 86 proof.

Single Malt Scotch Whiskey. These whiskies are the ultimate distillation of the scotch experience. They are not blended but consist of one pure liquor. There are many small distilleries all over Scotland (many of which welcome visitors). Local water, peat, and subtle variations in method and ingredients produce a wide variety of tastes and aromas.

The popularity of these whiskies is increasing, but like many high-quality wines and liquors they are wasted on nonconnoisseurs. They are drunk neat, usually, or with ice and plain water. In Scotland, all scotch is usually drunk this way. Even a mild variation such as scotch and soda will define the drinker as a *Sassenach,* which means anyone who is not Scottish. The expression is quite friendly and benign, and can be used freely in conversation. It is not an ethnic slur.

It's a shame that these whiskies are so expensive, but some of them are 18 years old or more. The distiller has to recover all the outgoings involved in those years of storage and care. Some bartenders will politely warn customers, especially if they suspect that they're new to the genre, that this is an expensive drink. The aficionado will probably buy anyway. The novice may occasionally gratefully demur. Both will respect the bartenders' candid and friendly approach. Only the occasional insecure senior gangster may be affronted by the suggestion that he might prefer something cheaper.

Irish Whiskey. The companies making these whiskies are very old, and Jamesons claims to be the first whiskey on the planet, but there are several counterclaims. Irish whiskey is made rather like scotch, but is not exposed to peat smoke and is distilled three times instead of twice. This makes for great smoothness, and there are many who drink it for itself. But most Irish whiskey finds its way into Irish coffee.

The Cooley Distillery, which began production in 1989, recently launched

Ireland's only single malt, called "The Tyrconnell." The three-year-old is said to be "soft and sweet, reminiscent of an eight-year-old Scottish Lowland." Though the Irish have long resented the Scottish domination of the whiskey industry, the influence of their Celtic cousins is inescapable. Cooley's two stills are made to a Speyside design; the malt mill was once part of the Laphroaig distillery, and the distiller was brought over from Scotland. Thirty million dollars have been invested and, while 44,000 casks mature in the warehouse, there are no immediate returns. There is a chance that the distillery may lose its Irish independence by being taken over by Irish Distillers, owned by the French company Pernod Ricard. They may, however, do a deal with United Distillers, which is an offshoot of Guinness. Such are the dramas of the whiskey industry. "The Tyrconnell" was originally named after a racehorse that won the 1876 Queen Victoria Plate—the Irish Classic at the time. The horse had been rated a 100-one no-hoper.

Canadian Whiskey. Canadian whiskies are made from barley, malt, rye, corn, and wheat, and must be three years old. They tend to be light and mellow.

Rum. Clear white rum, available in various strengths from 86 to 151 proof, is the most popular rum in the United States, and is most commonly drunk with cola, ice, and a squeezed wedge of lime—a combination that packs a lot of calories. "Rum and Coke" is also called a "Cuba Libre," and in Spanish sometimes *Un Fidel.* It's also used in Daiquiris and Margaritas, and the frozen varieties of those drinks and Piña Coladas. These drinks usually elicit a groan of dismay from the bartender—inwardly one hopes. They are a bit of a nuisance to make: lots of ice in the blender, lots of noise, several minutes in the making, and general messing about. (See Mixology.) However, they are highly profitable concoctions. The extra labor, ingredients, and use of Grand Marnier (or equivalent) in Margaritas all justify a price higher than the standard bar drinks, and this price rarely meets resistance. You can build regular customers by "hitting the spot" and producing an authentic-tasting exotic cocktail, since the versions offered in so many bars do not satisfy. There's nothing wrong with having a reputation for providing the "best Margarita in town."

Most white rum is made in Puerto Rico. There are also amber and dark rums. All rum is distilled from the fermented debris of crushed sugar cane, or molasses, and must be aged at least a year. Dark rum is merely light rum to which caramel has been added in varying quantities, producing different shades of darkness that do not necessarily reflect the spirit's strength—though by tradition extrastrong rums are almost invariably densely black. Dark rums are sometimes aged five to seven years and are usually drunk with cola or in the cocktail "Planter's Punch." The recipe for this cocktail, which still occupies a place in the popular repertoire, is on the back label of the Myer's bottle. "Rum Punch" covers a multitude of delights from a fruit cup concoction to rum with hot water, sugar, and lemon, which is said to be very useful in fighting colds. The richest black or dark rums come from Jamaica or Martinique. They are often used in cooking in Spain and France instead of white wine, especially with fish. Some eccentric gourmets add rum to ketchup in the belief that this adds zing to franks and burgers.

Bermuda has its own dark rum, Goslings. It features in a local concoction called a "Dark and Stormy"—rum and ginger ale, or more correctly ginger beer. Demerara rum is made along the river of that name, in Guyana. A popular Brazilian spirit called Cana is made in much the same way as rum, though it insists on its own niche on the bar, usually at some distance from ordinary rum.

Rum has a swashbuckling image ("Yo-ho-ho and a bottle of rum" was the pirate's song in Robert Louis Stevenson's "Treasure Island") and is still issued to British soldiers and sailors. In the Royal navy it's called grog. In the Army it sits in sturdy stone jars awaiting the call to arms by the commanding officer who will authorize its issue in cold weather. Traditionally, on Christmas Day early morning tea laced with rum and called "Gunfire" is served by the officers to the men still in bed.

Rum has its very own genre of alcoholics called rummies. They are characterized by fiercely red faces, and the emaciated, malnourished look that is typical of so many victims of alcohol abuse.

Gin. "Mother's Ruin," as gin was nicknamed by Cockneys (London proletarians) in Victorian times, was once among the most popular spirits in the world. Its popularity as a cheap spirit is recalled by the expression "gin mill," meaning any bar, but usually one of low repute, and by the oft-quoted adage from a Victorian advertisement "Drunk for a penny. Dead drunk for tuppence."

Nevertheless it still has its faithful followers who drink it in Martinis, with Tonic (Quinine) Water, in "Singapore Slings," and even (rarely now), as "Pink Gins"—gin with ice, a splash of water, several drops of pink Angosturas Bitters, and a couple of onions. "Gin and Tonic" was a staple drink in the days of the Indian Empire, when Quinine, in any shape or form, was believed to stave off the threat of malaria.

The word "gin" derives from Geneva and/or *genièvre,* a French word meaning "juniper," and it is the juniper berry that gives this clear grain spirit its essential character. Invented in Holland in the 16th century it soon crossed the channel with the British Army to England where it was nicknamed "Dutch Courage." Some soldiers acquired the habit of drinking before, and during, battle. It soon became the cheapest available alcohol, and many horrific distillations were sold under its name.

A popular cocktail in England after World War I was "Gin and It," meaning "Gin and Italian Vermouth," and this was probably the origin of the fabled "Martini" cocktail. Martini is a vermouth brand name. An occasional misunderstanding occurs when an Englishman visiting the United States orders a "Martini," expecting a glass of Martini vermouth, and is given a cocktail made with gin. American imbibers, similarly, sometimes approach apoplexy when, in England, they order a Martini and are given a glass of vermouth. It may be a case of, as George Bernard Shaw observed, "Two great nations separated by language."

Though the world of gin is dominated by "London Dry" styles, America manufactures dry gin too. Dry in this context, of course, means the opposite of sweet. You will comb the shelves of your local liquor store in vain for a "sweet" alternative. It may seem quixotic to some that one of the most popular ways of drinking dry gin is to mix it with terrifically sweet tonic water, but in such a quirky business one takes it in stride.

Only one gin is actually manufactured in London today: Beefeater gin, made by the 170-year-old firm of James Burroughs, which has become, as it inevitably occurs, part of a conglomerate. Holland, or Geneva gin, however, in its distinctive stone-brown colored bottle has an intense juniper flavor that precludes mixing it with anything else. It's usually drunk as a liqueur, straight and chilled.

While the juniper berry is the dominant flavor in gin, other dried fruits and herbs are also used to enhance its character. These are quaintly called "botanicals" and include such delights as coriander, licorice, orange and lemon peel, almonds, angelica root, orris root, and cassia bark.

Beefeater and other gins are made by a process in which the prime grain spirit is heated overnight in huge copper stills along with the secret mix of botanicals. Other, cheaper gins, however, are simply laced with liquid flavorings in a simple process known as cold-compounding. In some plants you can see some of the grain spirit going down one pipe to be bottled as vodka, while the rest of the liquid is diverted to a tank into which liquid essences, or botanicals, will be mixed in order to turn it into gin.

Regular gin drinkers, especially of Martinis, can sometimes tell the difference between various brands. Once diluted with anything as strong as tonic water, however, anything goes. For better or worse, in recent years gin has been forced into a back seat in the United States by vodka. Throughout England and Europe, however, gin and tonic is probably still the most requested mixed drink.

Aquavit. This is the Scandinavian version of gin in which caraway seeds are used to impart flavor, instead of gin. It is traditionally kept in the refrigerator as it is often drunk straight and chilled, followed by a beer chaser. Occasionally, like gin, it is requested as the spirit in a "Bloody Mary."

Vodka. In consumer and business terms the story of vodka is exciting. Forty years ago it barely merited shelf space in most European and American bars and liquor stores. Now it is the best-selling spirit in the land. A clever advertising campaign featuring a new cocktail called a "Moscow Mule" (long abandoned—vodka and ginger beer with a squeeze of lime), and proposing the encouraging notion that the clear, clean spirit would leave no telltale odor on its imbiber's breath, started a roller coaster of successful marketing. "Screwdrivers" and "Bloody Mary's" soon became popular vodka-based cocktails, along with vodka on the rocks, vodka and tonic, and the vodka martini, sometimes called a "Vodkatini."

When the closing—or opening—bartender or manager writes the "Liquor List" first thing in the morning, or last thing at night, for inventory purposes and in order to know what they must bring up from the cellar or storeroom by way of replacement, they will usually find that the dominant items are white wine and vodka. Beer, of course, is a separate list, and if your bar services a serious restaurant there will be a long list (one hopes!) of the various wines sold during the day. But in the majority of bars across the country vodka is the number one selling spirit, and your bar "par" stock should reflect this. A bar that sells two bottles of scotch during the course of a day will almost undoubtedly sell four or more bottles of vodka.

The spirit, distilled usually from grain but occasionally from potatoes, originated in Russia and Poland. In these countries the spirit is almost a religion, and, unfortunately, poses a serious threat to society. Alcoholism is almost a separate medical industry; many work days are lost, families disrupted, and accidents caused by the irresponsible abuse, by many, of what is possibly the ideal alcoholic beverage.

Fortuitously, serendipitously, or perhaps by clever intent, the marketing of vodka correctly anticipated the modern obsession with health, cleanliness, lightness, low calories, and so on. "It will leave you breathless" was one of the many slogans employed. This was a clever distortion of the facts. True, most alcoholic beverages leave a telltale odor on the breath, which vodka does not. These are not particularly repulsive smells, by any means. However, they might provide evidence, back at the office, of that three-Martini lunch, and give rise to gossip. In this context it should not be forgotten that at least one major U.S. corporation expressly forbids consumption of alcohol within two miles of its premises.

Doctors' columns in the popular press often discuss the problem of bad breath, or halitosis, and they invariably explain that decomposing debris in the mouth is the culprit. But why they refuse to reveal the truth so generally known, that the worst of bad breath originates in the stomach, is something of a mystery.

Alcohol interacts with the stomach acids (especially on an "empty stomach") to produce hydrochloric acid—the smell of rotten eggs—which is one of the most unpleasant smells on the planet. Drinking on an empty stomach is a well-known recipe for disaster. Not only might it result in inebriation after only a small intake, but it can produce horrific breath.

In short, vodka itself is undoubtedly a wonderfully clean drink. It's just ethyl alcohol and water, and has the least number of "congeners" or adulterating elements, thanks to having been filtered, often several times, through charcoal. It's less likely to give you a headache than any other drink, and will, at the superficial level of mouth contact, "leave you breathless."

But overindulgence will still result in drunkenness, bad breath, and a hangover, because beyond a certain level of consumption the body just goes haywire trying to reject what is, in excess, a highly toxic substance. It should still be treated with respect.

There were at one time 4,000 brand name vodkas in Russia—the country where they have 40 different words for snow. Vodka in Russia is often so crude that it has to be heavily flavored with fruit to make it palatable. Russians sometimes sprinkle pepper on top of their vodka. There has been an attempt to popularize these fruit and pepper concoctions in the United States, with little success. But now that Absolut is advertising its lemon and blackcurrant flavored vodkas ("Citron" and "Kurant") there will probably be an improvement in these sales.

Sherry. Sherry is a fortified wine from the town of Jerez de la Frontera in the province of Andalusia, Southwest Spain, not far from Cadiz. The word "sherry" is a corruption of the word "Jerez" or "Xeres" as it was spelled centuries ago. "De la Frontera" is a qualification that accompanies many Spanish town names and means "of the frontier," meaning the one between Moorish and Catholic Spain.

A fortified wine is simply one to which extra brandy has been added. This means it packs more of an alcoholic punch than ordinary table wine, and, in some countries, attracts a higher excise tax. Originally the wine was fortified in order to protect it from opportunistic microbes that would turn it to vinegar, thus stabilizing it for travel; then it became part of the wine's style. (Port, Madeira, Muscat, and Marsala are also fortified wines.)

A unique local yeast that forms on top of the local white wine, called "flor" meaning flower (or *Saccharomyces ellipsoidius beticus* in the lab) gives sherry its special flavor. Various styles are manufactured, from sweet oloroso, through medium amontillado to the super dry fino. Some dry sherries are matured at the neighboring seaside town of Sanlucar de Barrameda where they are said to acquire a zesty, salty tang. This wine is called manzanilla. Caramel coloring is added so that the sweet sherries are very dark, and the dry a pale yellow, not unlike the color of light whiskey.

The manufacture of this distinctive wine is a fascinating process, as with champagne and other vinous products. A striking feature is the solera blending method, whereby an elaborate arrangement of connected casks allows young wine to be mixed with old, and to quickly assume its superior characteristics, thus making it ready for market quicker. In Jerez itself, vintage years are observed, but sherries are not generally marketed by vintage, only by style.

Because sherry was popular but somewhat expensive a niche opened for cheaper versions; these are produced with some success in South Africa, Australia, and Cyprus. Though these unauthentic cheaper brands sometimes attract disdain they are a good value. South African sherry in particular has a distinctive deep intensity of flavor that some prefer to the real thing.

The best known sherry in the United States is Harvey's Bristol Cream, which occupies a spot on most bar shelves. It is extremely sweet and often taken as an after-dinner drink, rather like port. A chic bar will usually carry an amontillado and a dry fino such as Tio Pepe, the best-known sherry after Harvey's Bristol Cream. The dry sherry's role is almost exclusively that of aperitif, a before-dinner drink, though some will drink it in greater quantity, especially with spicy seafood. It is best drunk chilled, while other sherries taste best at room temperature.

In Victorian times fortified wines were immensely popular. Sherry (or Madeira) was a standard middle-class tipple, often taken in the morning at eleven o'clock. It was poured, not from a vulgar, labeled bottle, but from a finely wrought cut glass decanter with a silver label round its neck, into a tulip-shaped glass called a copita. A slice of (carroway) seed cake often accompanied this morning ritual.

Sherry is used in cooking, especially of trifle. In Spain a popular first course dish or bar snack is kidneys cooked in sherry (*riñones a la Jerez*). Sometimes it's added to soup, and there is a concoction called sherry bitters, sherry mixed with peppers, which is also put in soup and represents one of the island of Bermuda's major contributions to the perpetuation of traditional world gastronomy.

Until about the late 1960s 70 percent of Spain's sherry went to England, with a further large amount going to the Netherlands. Then a terrible thing happened to sherry. It became unfashionable. To be more precise, the fierce competition from other brands, especially gimmicky brands aimed at the young market, forced it to the sidelines. Its faintly stuffy, Oscar Wilde drawingroom image, which at one time was part of its attraction, didn't work well in the age of rock 'n roll. The industry twisted and turned to maintain its sales. But advertising campaigns urging people to mix sherry with 7-up for a really trendy drink achieved only minor success.

For the American market many sherries were sweetened to a grotesque degree. (The most authentic dry sherry available now is La Ina.) Prices for leading brands remained the same. New, cheaper versions lacked the robust excellence of the traditional product. Industrial problems involving pensions and benefits have led to strikes in recent years that affected the gathering of the grape harvest.

Changing consumer habits are as inevitable as the tide and there will be casualties. However, a firm nucleus of sherry lovers will insure the continuing manufacture of this high-quality wine.

Port. Made in Oporto, Portugal, this almost invariably sweet fortified wine has become a standard American after-dinner tipple, via the English connection. Portugal is England's oldest ally and the trade has been solid for more than two centuries.

Much folklore and ritual is attached to the consumption of this powerful and complex wine, which awards dreadful hangovers to those who surrender too freely to its undoubtedly seductive blandishments. Two medium-sized glasses would be about maximum consumption for the serious and responsible drinker.

It comes in various styles: Ruby, Tawny, and Vintage. Vintage port is part of the tradition of military dining in England. At one time it was not uncommon to hear red-faced fat army majors, à la Siegfried Sassoon World War I poems, bemoaning "the night the old 44th finished off the last of the '21 Cockburn" (pronounced "Co'burn").

Most English military, air, and naval units will hold a formal dinner once a month. The silver is polished and set out on the long walnut table; everyone gets dressed up in "Mess Dress"—bow ties and hip-length red or white jackets. After the toasts have been proposed by presiding officers—to the unit, its colonel-in-chief, guests of honor, and Her Majesty—the port is passed round the table, from right to left, in a decanter that is often mounted on a wheeled solid silver gun carriage, or other warlike vehicle. Stilton cheese and Carr's Water Biscuits, walnuts, and almonds are usually not far behind.

Today's majors tend to be slim, thirtyish, and are required to jog five miles a day, but the tradition of port lives on. Regiments were able to buy liquor in bulk at bargain prices, and could also "lay down" wines and ports, in casks, to mature. Colleges, universities, schools, and monasteries did the same thing. A fashionable present to a son or nephew, at birth, was once a "pipe" (cask) of port, which remained in the wine merchant's cellar until the beneficiary reached majority—21 years of age.

Vintage port can be quite expensive. But the port trade harbors a delicious secret, and it is this: all port wine is of such high quality, that even the cheapest variety is usually superb. A vintage port has a deeper, dryer, more intense flavor than the Ruby and the Tawny. The adjective "nutty" dominates the vocabulary of description.

Again, there are less expensive imitations, some of the them of high quality and individual character. Australia does well in this area, as in other wines; their zestful analysis and exploration produce excellent brews and the future looks bright for their burgeoning wine industry.

There is also such a thing as white port. As with white wine, this simply means that early in the fermenting process the grape skins were removed from the juice. The French, and cosmopolitan English, drink this chilled, as an aperitif, or after dinner with grapes, Bar-Le-Duc currants, cream cheese, and water biscuits.

There used to be a popular pub drink in England called "Port and Lemon." This was port wine mixed with lemonade, by which, in a pub, the English mean a 7-Up-type fizzy concoction. (Real lemonade is the full production of squeezed lemons and sugar—*Citron pressé* in a French bar). "Port and Lemon," no matter how delicious to its consumer, attracted a certain snobbish scorn as being rather unchic—like a "Lager and Lime," or, in America, "Rye and Ginger" or "7&7," or in France a tomato juice and brandy, and so on.

The joke was on the snobs. A huge glut of vintage port in Portugal, complicated by the shipping difficulties of World War II, meant that even the cheapest port wines available were often of superb vintage.

As is not uncommon (see Economics 101) the same product was marketed under different labels at different prices. If only the customers had had the sense to drink their port neat they would have been tasting Nirvana, at cut rates.

Marsala. Though mainly used in cooking, this dark fortified wine from Sicily deserves mention because the industry has decided to revive the table, drinking versions. Its style lends itself to after-dinner drinking—in Italy such wines are called "meditation wines" (*vino di meditazione*). They are high-quality wines made in the same Solera system as sherries, so that new wine rapidly assumes the characteristics of the older mature wine. Regular customers in an adventurous mood, or Italophiles will probably be the main customers for this wine once it is readily available.

Madeira and Muscat. These fortified wines—Madeira from the Canary

Isles of Portugal and Muscat from France, Spain, and Australia (where a delicious liqueur Muscat has been developed)—are outside the ordinary commercial bar spectrum, but anyone interested in wine would do well to explore them.

Tequila. Alcohol is distilled or fermented from a number of sources that are far from grape and grain. Dates, rice, elderberries, apples, and dandelion leaves are all employed in various parts of the world. All Tequila comes from the Mexican town of that name and is made from the blue agave plant, a member of the amaryllis family, often loosely and incorrectly referred to as a cactus. The plant can weigh up to 200 pounds and the copious sweet sap is fermented and then distilled.

The regular white Tequila is marketed almost immediately, but Silver is usually three years old, and Gold up to four years old, stored in oaken casks. There are some special Tequilas that are aged even more but, like vintage sherries and the best of much wine, they are hard to get hold of commercially.

Tequila is drunk straight, on the rocks, sometimes with a squeeze of lime, in Margaritas, and "Tequila Sunrises" (a shot of Tequila and orange juice in a tall, highball glass with ice, and a "float" of delicious sweet Grenadine on the top). There is a curious native ritual in which salt is sprinkled on the palm area of the thumb and licked, to be followed by the down-in-one shot consumption of Tequila, and followed by a bite of a lemon or lime wedge. In an American bar a request for such a ceremony should be met with stoic and instant compliance, and occasionally followed by applause, or at least a few wondrous and admiring shakes of the head.

Anyone fascinated by this routine should be apprised that, while it will go down well in the average bar, it might cause a raised eyebrow or two in the average Park Avenue matron's drawingroom. Such a consumer is reminiscent of those students who spend a weekend in Paris and cross their 7's forever thereafter. But it is part of a bar staff's job to indulge and even encourage their customers' fantasies. The more they enjoy themselves, the more likely they are to come back—and that's the name of the game.

Tequila's fashionably green origin seems to have led to the general belief that it is a clean drink, like vodka, and less likely to get one into trouble. Front line experience tells a different story. Because Tequila is so often drunk in innocuous, fruity, sweet, youth-oriented, fun drinks, the possibility of overindulgence is strong. Bartenders and managers will do well to keep a beady eye on the youngster who is about to order his or her fourth Margarita. Especially if they reek of the "burbs" and have a car parked outside.

Brandy and Cognac. Brandy is the general term for the distilled spirit of grapes. The distilled product of other fruits can also be called brandy but, by law, the name of the fruit must be stipulated on the label—peach, apricot, apple or applejack, plum brandy, blackberry, cherry, pineapple, and so on.

Kirsch or Kirschwasser is made in the Rhine Valley from black cherries and takes its unique flavoring from the cherry pits and skins. A sweeter variety, a liqueur, finds a happy niche when it's poured over fruit salad.

Slivovitz is made throughout Central Europe from plums. Pear brandy is made in France and Switzerland, called Pear William or Poire William. One fruit brandy actually features a pear inside the bottle. How does it get there? Clearly, ship-in-bottle techniques will not do the trick. The bottle is placed over the ear when it is no more than a bud, and tied to the branch. The result is a somewhat surrealistic image but the pear grows into the bottle, and the liquor is added.

Brandy is manufactured mainly in the United States, France, and Italy. Like other spirits it must be 80 proof to qualify. It's said that brandy was invented when a shipper devised a method of removing the water from wine, intending to ship the spirit and reconstitute it at its destination. People liked the naked spirit, so another type of drink was born. This is feasible, but it's equally possible that the drink emerged by accident as have so many, champagne being a prime example.

Most brandy is consumed as an after-dinner drink, in a glass called a snifter, which is designed so that the warmth of the hand will release some of the delicious aroma of the spirit. People swirl it around lovingly and sip it languorously. It's not unknown for some to warm the glass with a lighted match before filling it with the spirit.

The most prestigious, and thus the most expensive, brandy in the world comes from France and is called Cognac after the region in which it is manufactured. Only brandy from this region can be called cognac. The manufacturing procedures, and even the type of grapes that can be used, are strictly regulated. Farmers bring the distilled spirit to the producers who then age, color (with caramel), and flavor it to their particular house style. However, because various spirits of different ages are blended in the process, no vintage year may be quoted on the label.

Intriguing letters and stars on the label describe the cognac. The letter VS indicate a Very Superior cognac and may carry three stars, indicating that it's one and a half years old. A VSOP—Very Superior Old Pale—must have been aged in wood for at least four and a half years, and may have been aged up to 10 years. Other descriptive letters are X for extra, E for extra or especial, and F for fine. Only when the cognac is at least five and a half years old can it bear the words Extra, Vieille Réserve, or Napoléon.

There is no cognac dating from Napoleon's time, and if there were it wouldn't be drinkable. Cognac doesn't improve in bottle, only in cask, and after 50 years begins to deteriorate.

The words Grande or Fine Champagne can be a little confusing but they have nothing to do with the bubbly wine from Epernay. Champagne means field, and in this context it refers to the heart of the grape-growing area. Grande Champagne means the cognac was made totally from these grapes. Fine Champagne indicates a 50 percent content, the balance coming from a nearby area called Petite Champagne.

Another kind of French brandy, with manufacturing rules the same as cognac, is **Armagnac.** It can be made only in the restricted region of that name. **Salignac** is yet another. There are various French brandies marketed under the generic name **Marc** that have a following. This is a spirit distilled from the husks of grapes (or apple pulps) after the wine or cider has been made. They are distilled to a very high strength and take many years to become reasonably palatable. Clearly, a cousin of Italian *grappa*!

Apple brandy, called **Calvados,** is made in France, mainly in the Normandy area, and (legally) in private stills. Some are extremely refined and can be up to 40 years old.

In France there is a "traveling still" industry. The still is mounted on a truck and taken from village to village. The good housewives then bring out their hoarded fruit—often semirotten and beginning to ferment already—and juice is extracted and distilled before their very eyes. It's an old tradition that may endure because having a still in the house imparts an unpleasant odor that can permeate everything. Maybe it's better to keep the equipment farther away.

Spanish brandy—called *coñac* in Spanish—is made like any other brandy, but not as strictly as real cognac. It has a character of its own, and a considerable following in Spain and South America.

Metaxa, the Greek version of brandy, is heavily flavored with licorice, and is really a liqueur. Italian *grappa,* the generic name for grape spirit of often dubious origin, covers a multitude of sins and only barely deserves to be included in the family of brandy. Its many devotees lose no sleep over this.

Brandy in general, blackberry brandy, and brandy mixed with port wine ("Fox's Blood" in England, where it often finds its way into a huntsman's flask) are reputed to be great stomach settlers, and few would argue. Perhaps the fillip to morale engendered by the spirit helps, too.

An old adage has it that "claret is the drink for boys, port for men, but he who would be a hero, must drink brandy."

Brandy can be mixed very happily with plain soda or ginger ale—sometimes called a "Horse's Neck"—but these drinks belong to an older generation and are rarely requested. When they are, it's obviously a shame to use the most expensive variety of brandy, since its essential qualities are sure to be overwhelmed by the power of the mixer. But "Remy and Coke" is not an unusual request, and though bar staff and Remy Martin shareholders alike may raise their eyebrows at this, they should not disdain the profits. "Chaque un à son gout," "De gustibus non est disputando," "Cada uno a su gusto"—every language has its own phrase for "Each to his own."

Some of the best bar customers in the world demand the strangest drinks. The more cheerfully their requests are accommodated, the more likely they are to come back, and bring friends.

Bitters. Campari is the best known in this group. It's an Italian standard, made from spirit that is flavored with various herbs, fruit, bark, and roots and artificially colored. Sometimes it's called a beverage bitters because it's drunk in various cocktails in its own right—Campari and Soda, Campari and Orange Juice, and Negronis or Vodka Negronis.

Other bitters are more concentrated, and of these the best known in America is Angosturas. It comes in a seven-inch bottle wrapped in a stalwart label not unlike Lea and Perrins Worcestershire Sauce. Sometimes one is mistaken for the other, with interesting results in the mix. Angosturas, like all bitters, is supposed to be a good stomach settler (it calls itself a "stomachic" on the label) and many swear by it. Drunk neat or with plain soda water it can be very helpful. Many use it as an aperitif, or as a drink to have when they don't really feel like drinking alcohol but do not wish to appear unconvivial. (The various Campari concoctions serve well in this respect, too.) Just once in a while there'll be a request for an "Old Fashioned" cocktail, which takes Angosturas, or a Manhattan, with a drop or two of bitters. Older English folks, especially ex-Navy types, will sometimes call for a Pink Gin: Gin and Bitters in a snifter with a splash of water, pearl onions optional.

Another Italian bitters, Ferne Branca, is also supposed to be a hangover cure. The French make all the above claims for Amer Picon, and the Germans for Underberg and St. Vitus.

Vermouth and Wine Cocktails. Vermouth comes in two versions, sweet red and dry white, generally from Italy or France. In each case they consist of wine that has been "vermuté" or flavored with an herb that is called "Wormwood" in English.

They are usually used in Manhattans, Martinis, and Vermouth Cassis. "Gin and It" was a popular cocktail in the 1920s in England and reference to it may puzzle playgoers sometimes. The "It" refers to Italian vermouth.

But vermouth also has a life of its own. It's not uncommon for someone to order either color straight, on the rocks, or perhaps with soda, and a squeeze or twist of lemon. The house vermouths should always be ready at hand in the well or speed rack. Although they go out slowly—a drop or two at a time in the case of the dry white vermouth that goes into Martinis—they are regularly used.

The various patented wine-based cocktails all have a steady clientele. **Dubonnet** is the best known in the United States, in the red version, though there is a white one, too. It is usually kept in the refrigerator so that it can be served chilled without ice. There's a Dubonnet Cocktail, too, made with gin as standard, or vodka by request.

Lillet is a straw-colored French wine cocktail usually served chilled, or on the rocks, with a slice of orange. **Suze,** though popular in France, is a rare item in the United States.

The recipes for this group are closely guarded secrets, passed from father to son on the deathbed.

Liqueurs

Cordials and liqueurs are the same thing. They are mostly made from neutral grain spirits, but sometimes from grape spirit, and flavored with herbs, fruits, barks, roots, and so on.

The French sometimes call them "digestifs," in the belief that they are an aid to digestion, as indeed most would agree they are. Served in tiny liqueur glasses, often at a hefty price, their purpose is to provide an intense taste of chocolate, coffee, or whatever mysterious concoction of herbs, roots, and fruits the good Abbé whispered to his successor as he prepared to expire.

Many liqueur recipes are secret. This secrecy is neither gimmicky nor whimsical: it has a serious purpose. Any brand name alcoholic beverage that has established a niche on the bar, in the liquor store, and in the popular repertoire of drinks commands a certain price and is thus open to unscrupulous imitation.

It is easy to imagine how successful accurate imitations might be. In practice imitations do occur, but they are marketed at lower prices and under different names. For instance, Tia Maria is the supreme coffee liqueur. Kahlua is also a coffee liqueur, but it's in a different style bottle and has become an indispensable bar item in its own right, through the popularity of cocktails ("Black or White Russians") whose recipe specifies Kahlua.

There are a small number of available imitations that are much cheaper and are used as house brands, or even, in unscrupulously managed establishments, offered instead of the real thing. Grand Marnier, the famous orange liqueur, has attracted two strong, cheaper competitors, Cointreau and Triple Sec. Most liqueurs are available in "ersatz" form, and find a ready home in cocktails served to clients whose powers of discernment are perhaps not all they might be.

The best liqueurs are made from a distillation of the fruits upon which they're based. Lesser quality products are simply grain or grape spirits flavored with artificial essences.

Imitation of famous products can be determined and elaborate. A quick glance along any bar in Spain may be rewarded by reassuring sightings of such well-known brands as Johnny Walker Red Scotch and Gordon's Gin. In fact the bottles may contain cheap local products, bottled under a label that, though very similar in appearance to that of a famous brand, just sneaks inside the law. It might be libelous to name a particular example, but the flagrant imitator of Gordon's Gin referred to is a horrific concoction reminiscent of cheap eau de cologne. Few would buy twice.

Japanese "scotch" is not seen as much of a threat, so faithful are scotch drinkers to the real thing. In Japan, where a scotch and soda can be bought on the street from a dispensing machine, it clearly has a role.

The liqueurs described here are the famous ones that most bars will carry, if only for decorative purposes. Some of them will evaporate (if the lease on the joint is long enough!) before they're sold.

Most liqueurs are extremely sweet. In England they're often rudely but affectionately referred to as "stickies." Any bartender who has triumphantly reached for the bottle of "Old Monk's Hooch" and found that the cork is totally jammed because the sugar has hardened like Super Glue will understand why.

Bailey's Irish Cream. This waistline-challenging but delicious brand name drink is made of Irish Whiskey and cream. One wonders how such a mixture can be made to survive in a bottle, but the secret recipe insures that it does. Drunk chilled and neat, or on the rocks, or sometimes with a splash of milk, it is a firm favorite, especially with the ladies.

B&B. This stands for the mixture of the neutral spirits liqueur Benedictine with brandy—actually cognac is used. It is flavored with secret herbs and spices and is a dark golden color.

Benedictine. This is the pure version of the famous liqueur, also a dark golden color. The little barrels traditionally tied round the necks of the St. Bernard mountain rescue dogs were said to contain Benedictine.

Chambord. This raspberry liqueur, in its distinctive orb-shaped bottle that always finds a home even after its contents have been dispensed, can be mixed with champagne to make "Kir Royale."

Chartreuse. This brand name mixture of brandy, neutral spirits (spirits made from grain at such high proof that they are nearly pure alcohol and thus have little taste of anything) comes in two versions, yellow and green. In both versions it has an intriguing aroma and flavor of herbs and spices.

Cointreau. An orange-based brand name neutral spirits liqueur that finds a home in Margaritas and Sidecars. Any cocktail or mixed drink that involves lemon juice can be given an extra zing by the addition of a drop or two of Cointreau (or Grand Marnier, or Triple Sec). It would be unusual for a customer not to notice and joyfully comment, so striking is the effect. The customer goodwill generated by this kind of gesture is so rewarding that many bar managers may be tempted not to charge extra.

Crème de Cacao. This is cheerfully referred to as "Cream o' Cocoa" and comes in two versions, dark and clear white. The dark finds its home mainly in the "Brandy Alexander" cocktail, and white in the now rarely requested "Grasshopper." It tastes like chocolate.

Crème de Cassis. Cassis is French for blackberry. This intense liqueur is added, in varying quantities according to taste, to white wine in order to make a "Kir" cocktail. It is named after a former mayor who devised this way of making local, and not always superb, white wines more palatable. A "Kir Royale" is champagne sweetened with this cordial. Blackberry juice is also often added to red wine in Burgundy.

A nonalcoholic drink to look out for when in France is "Pomme Cassis"—a fizzy soda-pop drink made of apple and blackberry juice. It comes in large inexpensive bottles and is delicious.

Crème de Menthe. This is a mint liqueur that comes in two versions, green and white. It is a "generic" item, as opposed to a "brand" name, such as Tia Maria or Drambuie. In other words, any manufacturer can put the words "Crème de Menthe" on a bottle.

Hell hath no fury like that of a company whose brand names are lightly used or taken in vain. The reason is simply the years of work and, more to the point, huge amounts of advertising money that go into the establishment of brand names.

There are several brands available at various prices. Green mint finds a niche occasionally in "Grasshoppers." The French sometimes drink "Menthe à l'eau," a refreshing combination of green crème de menthe, ice, and water. A small amount of white mint added to brandy produces a cocktail called a "Stinger." There is also a selection of similarly flavored products under various names such as Peppermint Schnapps, Peppermint Cordial, and so on.

Crème de Noyau. This almond liqueur enjoyed brief fame as an essential ingredient in a cocktail called a "Pink Squirrel," but is now rarely ordered.

Drambuie. This sweet brand name liqueur is Scotch whiskey plus a secret combination of herbs. When added to ordinary scotch it produces a cocktail called a "Rusty Nail."

Framboise. A dark, neutral spirits liqueur made from raspberries. When mixed with champagne it makes a "Kir Royale" cocktail.

Frangelica. A clear, hazelnut brand name liqueur, sometimes put in coffee in the same way as Irish whiskey goes into "Irish coffee."

Fruit Brandies. These are available generically in the following flavors: blackberry (which is suitably dark), apricot, peach, banana, pineapple, plum, cherry, apple, pear, and strawberry. They are actually made from grain spirits, not grapes as is the case with "brandy" or cognac. It is a loose usage of the term, which of course enhances the allure of the beverage.

Galliano. This yellow, Italian brand name vanilla, anise, and licorice liqueur is contained in a bottle whose shape is reminiscent of the Eiffel Tower, and easily the tallest on the bar. Thus it's the easiest to find on the rare occasions when it is requested, in now obscure cocktails.

Grand Marnier. The senior, and most expensive amber-colored brand name orange liqueur, made from cognac, neutral spirits, and orange peel.

Jagermeister. This amber, sweet liqueur is served on the rocks, or chilled and straight, often chased by a beer. It has a strong following among younger drinkers, probably because of its innocuous taste. When the call for Jagermeister comes, orders for "Kamikazis," "Piña Coladas," and "Sex on the Beach" will probably not be far behind.

Until recently, in England, there was a sweet, clear, generic, drugstore, product called "Gripe Water." This was given to babies who cried continuously because of stomach upsets. It was eventually banned when someone at the Ministry suddenly discovered it contained alcohol. Anyone who wishes to taste the forbidden past can do so by tasting Jagermeister.

Kahlua. A dark, brand name coffee liqueur that, far from skulking in the shadow of the image of Tia Maria, the best-known coffee liqueur, has become an indispensable bar item in its own right, through the popularity of cocktails

("Black or White Russians") whose recipes specify Kahlua. Helpfully, the recipes are written on the back label.

Kummel. This clear liqueur is flavored with caraway seeds. It is a generic name and is bottled by several manufacturers.

Midori. This brand name, green, Japanese liqueur is based on the melon fruit. Its tall bottle stands usually in a central position on the top shelf of the bar, rivaling the aforementioned Galliano. Its main claim to fame is as the base ingredient for the cocktail "Melon Ball." There are one or two other possible concoctions too—all usefully placed on the back label.

Ouzo. This is a Greek version of the French Pernod, described below. It is clear, and when mixed with water turns milky-cloudy, not yellow.

Pernod/Ricard. Based on a diluted version of absinthe, the wormwood distilled potent liquor that was the 19th-century alcoholic demon of France, and an inspiration of poets such as Verlaine and Baudelaire. These French brand name liqueurs command a steady following among French and francophile Americans. Green-yellow in appearance, they become bright yellow when mixed with water and ice, which is how they are usually drunk. The French call this cocktail "Pastis." The flavor is of anise and licorice. There is no need to incur the guilt of discrimination or value judgment when deciding between these two brands. They are both owned by the same company.

Sambuca. This generic Italian licorice-flavored liqueur is usually drunk after dinner in a snifter glass. By tradition, three coffee beans, representing the Holy Trinity, are floated on top. They are not consumed; they're just for decoration.

Sloe Gin. This dark plum-flavored neutral spirit liqueur is featured mainly in a cocktail known as the "Sloe Gin Fizz." It is still requested once in a while at Golden Anniversary celebrations and the like. A sloe is a small fruit from the plum family, more like a damson, with a deep, intriguing taste.

Southern Comfort. Usually drunk straight or on the rocks, this is a brand name gold-colored Bourbon with a mild peach flavor. It still has its faithful followers.

Tia Maria. A brand name coffee liqueur, rarely drunk straight but occasionally used in now obscure cocktails. Like other liqueurs it can be poured over vanilla ice cream with great effect, and for the truly wicked, a teaspoonful or more on top of chocolate mousse imparts extra taste.

CHAPTER THREE

Wine and Champagne

Wine

Volumes have been written about this fascinating subject. Some colleges now award degrees in wine studies; in England there is even a lofty qualification called "Master of Wine."

A luxury restaurant with a huge wine list will undoubtedly employ a special staff: a buyer, cellar-men, and probably a "sommelier." This grand figure wears, by tradition, a silver tasting cup on a chain round his neck. His job is to advise diners on the best wines to accompany their food. For this service he receives a salary and tips from the diners.

Bar managers don't need to be wine experts, but they do need a general understanding of what it's all about. In the end they will probably become experts, simply from being involved in the subject over a period of time. Most important, they will develop a fine sense for what sells, and what doesn't.

Wine is fermented grape juice. It comes in three colors: red, white (often more like a pale yellow, but still called "white"), and rosé, which means varying shades of rose pink. Three things determine the quality of wine.

First is the grape: Cabernet Sauvignon (currently the world's favorite and best known grape), Chardonnay, Pinot Noir, Muscat, Shiraz, Gamay, Grenache or Grenacha, Tempranillo, Montepulciano, Semillon, and the uniquely American Zinfandel are some of the best known. Increasingly, people ask for wine by the name of the grape. "Do you have a Chardonnay?" or "What kind of Cabernet do you carry?"

Second is the climate and, to an extent, the soil. Endless sunshine such as one sees in Spain and California helps produce good wines of excellent quality, but few star wines emerge from these areas. There is general agreement that the greater wines have to struggle harder to emerge. The weather in Burgundy, for instance, is often bad, yet this is the area where some of the greatest wines are created.

Grapes from clayey soil will yield a flavor distinguishable from those grown in gravelly areas such as Bordeaux—Graves being the best known example of this soil's wines.

Just to keep winemakers on their toes, different grapes fare better in different kinds of weather. Thus, the Semillon grape—from which the sweet, white Sauterne wine is made in Bordeaux—flourishes in warm, humid weather. The Cabernet Sauvignon from which many reds are made does not, so that in Bordeaux a vintage year for whites can be a ho-hum year for reds.

Finally there is that most mysterious of factors, the human touch. Styles vary enormously. Sometimes a winemaker has in mind the local cuisine. Italian red is aimed at tables groaning with herbs, strong cheese, and plenty of olive oil. Hence the winemaker aims for a robust style, rich in tannin—the component wine shares with tea—which derives from the skins and gives wine its muscle. (White wines contain little or no tannin, because the grape skins are removed early in the manufacturing process.) Spaniards prefer a more mellow wine. Rioja wines are good examples. At their best they can be easygoing and all things to all. At worst they are so bland as to be boring. Australians find the inexpensive California Chardonnays too sweet. Californians find Australian Cabernet Sauvignons a bit too macho.

Even neighbors will produce wines of different character. One will leave the wine longer in new oak casks. Another will blend in wine made from another grape, and so on. As to what a winemaker chooses to add to the wine in the small hours of the night is often a closely guarded secret.

In general, the longer the grapes are left on the vine, the better the wine. This principle reaches its apogee in Burgundy, France, home of some of the best, most famous, and most expensive wines. Mortars are fired to break up threatening clouds that might produce damaging hail as summer turns to fall. In September, the grape harvest (the *vendange*) is delayed until the last possible moment in order to allow a maximum of *pourriture noble* ("noble rottenness") to develop. This is a mold (called *Botrytis cinerea,* which forms on the skin of the grape, concentrating the sugar content as the grape dries.

In chemical terms, what the winemaker, or "vintner," is looking for is grapes with maximum sugar content that will convert to a characterful product. When the grapes are crushed, yeast from the skins starts the chemical reaction that eventually produces wine, which normally has an alcoholic content of between 10 and 13 percent. If the skins are left in with the grape juice, or "must" as it's called, once it begins fermenting, then the resultant wine will be red. If they are removed the wine will be white. And if the skin is left just long enough to impart a pinkish tinge, then the result will be rosé.

In general these wines are known as "table wines" or "dinner wines." But it is very common now for wine of all kinds to be drunk for and by itself. In many bars across the world white wine is far and away the biggest selling beverage next to beer. Always served chilled, it is now immensely popular as an aperitif.

Red wine is usually served at room temperature, what the French call *chambré.* Special, "vintage" wine (to be explained shortly) should be decanted (a decanter is an ornamental sort of glass container from which drinks are served) and exposed to the air so that it can "breathe" for an hour before serving, and indeed most red wine will improve when exposed.

It is not unknown in private dining at home for a host in a hurry to discreetly pour a bottle of red wine into a wide basin and stir it, in order to air the wine before serving. Even a humble house red wine will often get an extra nod of approval because, having been opened some time before, its flavor has developed.

An exception to this rule is the French red wine Beaujolais, which even the French themselves drink chilled. Skeptics might comment that in recent years some of the vintages have been so undistinguished that it's just as well.

Other red wines commonly drunk chilled by the French include the Cabernet Francs from the Loire Valley, such as Chinon, Bourgueil, and Saumur Champigny. Chilling does cover a multitude of sins, as anyone who cares to drink white wine that has become "flabby" after sitting around exposed to the warm air will testify. Some people simply prefer red wine chilled, though if they are drinking a wine of any distinction, they're missing part of the delight.

In recent years a huge public relations event has been built up around the latest vintage of Beaujolais. Teams race, by plane, helicopter, speedboat, and parachute, to be the first to deliver it to London and other European cities. A similar ritual attends the delivery of the first grouse to London when the shooting season starts on August 12.

A cautionary note must be sounded here. Once opened, wine begins to deteriorate. Prompt recorking may give it 48 hours to live. But even this precaution may not prevent the wine from deteriorating to a point where it is undrinkable. Wines vary in this respect. The light and flowery little number will not be long lived, while a more robust wine with plenty of tannin may last several days. So a precautionary discreet sniff (preferably out of sight of the customer) is not a bad idea when serving from an already opened bottle—especially if you pour your house wine from large liter, or one and a half liter jugs or bottles that clearly may not all be consumed in the course of a day. (Naturally, longevity is one of the factors to be considered when selecting a house wine, be it red, white, or rosé.) Most agree that an opened bottle should be finished off. Spirits do not deteriorate after opening, as long as the bottle cap or pourer fits snugly between pourings.

Wines vary from "dry" to "sweet." Dry in the context of alcohol means the opposite of sweet. Most red wines are dry, most rosé is sweet, and white wines can vary from very dry—a Chablis or a Graves—to a Sauterne, which is a sweet dessert wine. These French names refer to the areas from which certain types of wine originate. They are controlled names of origin (*Appellation Controlée*). Only wines from these areas may carry this name.

But there are different houses, or chateaus, within these areas. Thus there are dozens of Sauternes, but only one Chateau Yquem, which is acknowledged as the supreme Sauterne wine. It is expensive, but there is a less expensive version called Chateau Y, which will at least give an idea of what Sauterne wine is all about. The same system applies in all European wine-producing countries: France, Italy, Spain, and Portugal. There are several German "Moselles," for instance, but only one Bernkasteler Doktor—an unforgettable experience for those fortunate enough to taste it.

Wines vary in yet another way: by vintage. After bottling, some wines, not all, will mature and develop more satisfying quality and character if they are laid on their sides in cool constant temperature. Wine left standing up so that the bottle cork dries out, or stored in too hot or in varying temperatures, will simply turn to vinegar.

The vintage phenomenon is made possible by the humble cork, which actually "breathes" and thus allows the wine enough access to the air to allow it to develop slowly; complete exposure to the air would kill the wine fairly soon. To achieve this effect, the wine must be in contact with the cork. That's why wine that is not earmarked for consumption in the near future should always be laid on its side. Occasionally a bad cork will ruin a wine—a very disappointing experience for the would-be drinker. The restaurateur will obviously not charge a customer for such a disaster. However, although one should be wary if a revealed cork is less than a nice clean specimen, there is no need to fear the worst. The smell and taste are what matters. Even if a cork breaks, it isn't the end of the world. Once the debris is removed you may find a perfectly acceptable wine.

Grapes are an annual crop. Wine made from the grapes harvested in 1990 is the 1990 vintage, and so on. When a wine is considered likely to improve with age after bottling the vintage is proclaimed on the main label, or sometimes a separate label around the bottle's neck. A nonvintage wine may well be a blend of all sorts of things, sometimes disastrous, sometimes triumphant. Winners of red "vin ordinaire" (regular, ordinary nonvintage table wine) competitions in recent years have included wines made from brands as apparently disparate as Portuguese and Austrian. By common assent of a region's winemakers, certain years are proclaimed "vintage years," and the prices of the wines produced in such years can be astronomical. A long dry summer is the most common feature of such a year. The declaration of a vintage in Burgundy does not mean it's a vintage year worldwide.

Most regions of Spain and Italy never declare a vintage. This is because they are so far south that the weather does not vary greatly. You will wait a long time for a cold July day in Seville, where, by some quirk of meteorology, the summers are often hotter than the Sahara. The advantage of this is wonderful consistency of quality, so that with the inexpensive wines from Spain and southern Italy, you always know what you're getting.

As to how long a wine should be stored in the cellar before consumption is a matter of considerable discussion. Of course, the most pleasant solution is to buy so much of the wine that you can open a bottle every year to see how it's coming along, then enjoy a binge, or sell your stock, in the year when you judge it to have reached its zenith. Many companies and some private individuals do this.

This is as deep into the technicalities of wine making as one can conveniently go in this book. Even the humble cork is a separate study in itself. People who find themselves hooked on the subject will find endless libraries of books to inform them. Most companies allow visitors, given notice. There are wine-tasting courses in schools and also held by wine merchants. In France there are schools that teach nothing but wine.

Here, however, some broad wine descriptions may be useful to the bar manager.

French Wines. There are three broad groups of French wine: Burgundy, Bordeaux, and Cotes du Rhone. Burgundy is a large region of northern France, with Rheims, Epernay, Beaune, and Beaujolais being some of the towns there that give their names to famous wines. Bordeaux is both a region and a city. Cotes du Rhone means the banks of the Rhone River, which flows into the Mediterranean in a delta northwest of Marseilles, and down whose broad valley blows the Mistral, a wind that causes bad weather as far away as the coast of Spain.

Famous Burgundy red wines include Beaujolais, Beaune, Pommard, and many others. These are *appellations controllée,* and within these groups various houses or shippers will bottle under different labels.

Burgundy whites include Chablis, and Pouilly Fuissé. The sensitive bar manager or bartender may, quite rightly, have a twinge of conscience when serving the house white wine to a customer who asked for a glass of Chablis. Of course, in some cases the house white really is a chablis, but often it isn't. Usually the customer wants a glass of dry white wine, and as long as this request is fulfilled no harm will be done. The term chablis has now become as generic and nonspecific as, say, "burgundy" or "claret," as the British often refer to Bordeaux red wines.

Bordeaux reds are St. Emilion, Medoc, and so on. Again, these are *appellations controllée,* and within these groups various houses or shippers will bottle under different labels. The Bordeaux wine world is dominated by the famous chateaux such as Lafite Rothschilde, Chateau Haut Brion, and others.

Given the large number of people of Irish descent in the United States, it's worth noting that Bordeaux, like Burgundy, was an English possession for many years in the Middle Ages. The name "Haut Brion" is a corruption of the name "O'Brian," as the founder of the estate was called. These famous wines are sublime, but so expensive that they are wasted on inexperienced wine drinkers—unless they have a genuine curiosity to explore them. Of course, if they are ordered by a doting papa for the delectation of his daughter, family, and friends at her 21st birthday party, then you have no choice but to serve them and make sure you reserve a glass or two for yourself. Any twinge of conscience can be written off under "quality supervision and control."

Burgundy whites are Chablis, Blanc de Blanc, Macon, and more. They are almost invariably dry in character—or should be.

Bordeaux whites include Graves, which are generally dry, and Sauternes, which are dessert wines—meaning you drink them with dessert after dinner.

Bottle shapes have become varied and gimmicky in recent years, but if you take a look around a wine store you will see that most Burgundy bottles are distinguishable from those of Bordeaux by a narrower, longer neck.

German Wines. Germany has a thriving wine industry, although (as in France) much more beer is drunk. Currently German wines, the majority of which are white, are rather overshadowed in quality by those other nations produce. It is important to become aware of which shippers deliver the goods, and which to avoid.

The German system of viticulture, or viniculture, is rather different from the

French. It is closely supervised by the government. Three levels of quality are recognized: *Tafelwein* (table wine), *Qualitatswein* (quality wine), and *Qualitatswein mit Predikat* (special quality wine). *Tafelwein* is rarely exported. *Qualitatswein*'s labels show the vintage year, grape type, village and/or vineyard of origin, and the name of the bottler. Where the wine is bottled by the vintner it assumes a dignity the equivalent of French chateau or estate bottling. Because most German wines are best drunk young, less fuss is made about the vintage year, though the principles are observed.

German wines can be conveniently grouped into those from the Rhine Valley—Rhine wines—and those from the Moselle Valley—Moselles. Both come in the same tall, tapered bottle. They can easily be distinguished, however, because Rhine wines come in brown glass bottles, while the Moselle come in green. (The easy way to remember this fact is to register the fact that the words Moselle and green each contain two e's.)

The most famous German wine is Liebfraumilch, and this can be produced in any of four designated regions of the Rhine Valley. Another familiar Rhine wine is Schloss Johannisberg—expensive and unforgettable in quality—a *Qualitatswein mit Pradikat* indeed. Piesporter Goldtropfchen is probably the most familiar Moselle wine, but the jewel in the Moselle crown is Bernkasteler Doktor, a firm rival to Schloss Johannisberg. Anyone able to discern between tea and coffee would immediately be aware of tasting something very special indeed on drinking either of these wines. By tradition, Bernkasteler Doktor, which comes from an alarmingly small vineyard, got its name because it revived a patient who was at death's door. There are many lesser Bernkasteler wines, of course, which at least intimate the glories of the good Doktor.

German wine making distinguishes between different qualities, or "selections" (-*lese* means selection) of grapes: *Spatlese, Auslese, Beerenauslese,* and *Trockenbeerenauslese.* The latter is of most interest because it refers to the sort of grapes that are left on the vine until the last possible moment, and thus blessed with noble rot—*Edelfaule* is the German word. When you see the word *Trockenbeerenauslese* you should prepare your palate for an engaging experience, and your wallet for a beating.

Italian Wines. Italian wines vary from the sublime to the revoltingly ridiculous. More crimes are wrought in the name of Soave Bolla than this world dreams of. Ghastly, cheap Italian concoctions are often selected by greedy restaurateurs as their house white wine, in an age in which the single most requested alcoholic drink in the United States, after beer, is a glass of white wine. Many get away with it, while some are left wondering why they have so little repeat business. Unscrupulous restaurateurs, faced with endless complaints about a consignment of white wine they've bought cheaply and foisted on their customers, will give instructions that the wine is to be used only in "spritzers" and "kirs"—drinks in which, they hope, the added ingredients will disguise the horrors of the basic wine.

Of Italian red wines, Chianti, under various labels, is the best known. Nowadays it's most often seen, like most Italian wines, in a prosaic Bordeaux-type bottle, the traditional wicker basket wrapping having been largely abandoned. As with other consumer items, the packaging is an increasingly expensive overhead.

Italian wine at its unpretentious best is a marvelous accompaniment to the more robust Italian foods. Other well-known Italian wines are Barolo, Gatinara, Bardolino, and Valpolicella, all of which are styles of wine produced by many different authorized vintners.

Italian white wines, other than the dreaded Soave (though if you can find a good shipper it can be an excellent value), are Orvieto, Frascati, and many others. Some Italian whites are marketed by different manufacturers with the predominating type of grape on the label: Pino Grigio, Verdicchio, and Pino Bianco.

Though Italian wines are mainly thought of as being "cheap and cheerful," they do have an upscale area, too. Production of premium wines is small so, although they are exported, they take some tracking down.

The industry has its myths and famous families, too. The Frescobaldis own thousands of acres in Tuscany devoted to wine production, mainly Chianti. But they also produce the rare Montesodi wine, which is only bottled in exceptional years.

Spanish Wines. Though most famous for its sherries, Spain has a robust table wine industry too. Names like Marques de Riscal command great respect. However, Spanish wine cannot pretend to the glories of Chateau Lafite Rothschilde or Bernkasteler Doktor. Its weather simply does not enhance wine quality, and there is little talk of vintage wine in the Iberian Peninsula. Its fruity, robust wines are nevertheless of consistent quality; the sun beats down year after year and there are few variables in the cycle.

It is an accepted generalization in the wine industry, with few exceptions, that the best and most interesting wines tend to come from what winemakers call "marginal" areas. This explains the drive to plant vines in Tasmania and Oregon, where the weather is as unpredictable as in Northern Europe. However— just to show that nothing in the world of wine is written in stone—England, which is notorious for its undependable weather, now has several flourishing wineries. They have revived an industry brought over by the Normans in the

12th century. Pleasant though many of the wines are, none has yet made the earth move.

Spain produces the strongest wine in the world, at Tarragona, which is in Catalunia. Red, as one would expect, it's called Priorato. Made mainly from the Garnacha (Grenache) grape, it achieves a strength of 18 percent alcohol by volume. This is not a fortified wine. For complicated reasons of chemistry this is probably as strong a wine as can possibly be produced (at a certain point of development other reactions kick in and the substance ceases to be recognizable as wine). Much eucharistic wine comes from this area. It's rumored that Priorato is the Vatican wine of choice, but this would be hard to confirm.

Portuguese Wines. Through Portugal is most famous for its port, it also produces some light and fruity white wines called *vinho verde,* literally "green wine," which alludes more to its youth than its color. Mateus Rosé is a popular wine in the United States.

American Wines. Until recently this meant mainly California wines, and sparkling wines made in the same way as champagnes (*methode champenoise*), but now several regions, notably New York, are producing fine wines. The climate of California is tailor made for grape production, while the North Shore of New York's Long Island somewhat resembles areas of Burgundy, with a type of soil that lends itself to characterful grapes.

An interesting feature of American wines is that great emphasis is laid on the type of grape used, which is reasonable since this largely determines the character of the wine. Thus wine drinkers will ask for a Chardonnay, a Cabernet Sauvignon, a Pino Noir, a Merlot, and so on. The grape variety is prominently displayed on the bottle.

Bartenders no longer need to bother their heads with "French 75's" or "Blue Blazers," but the space should be filled with some knowledge of what wine is all about. Specifically, they should know something about the wines they feature, and be able to describe them in appropriate wine lore terms.

Customers now regularly ask "What kind of Chardonnay do you have?" or "Have you got a nice Cabernet?" The fact that they will often know more about the subject than the bartender is perfectly all right. They'll enjoy a flattering feeling of superiority, which is, on the whole, to be encouraged.

Wines from Other Countries. It is tremendous fun, keeping an open mind and exploring new products as they appear on the market. Good bargains are to be had, too, and these can be passed on to grateful customers. Chile and Argentina both have thriving wine industries, and will occasionally surprise and delight with their quality.

No country or manufacturer of wines or spirits finds success overnight. Whenever you look at a Standard Item bottle you are almost certainly looking at not less than 20 years of hard work. New wine-producing countries must fight through the gimmick phase before they assume the status of serious producers. The most aggressive, successful, and interesting new wine producer may be Australia. Though they have chosen, like others, to lead with their robust, complex, but on the whole a bit too strong wines made from the Cabernet Sauvignon grape, they make it clear that their hat is in the ring with serious purpose. They are starting from scratch, and they clearly intend to exploit this advantage.

Many wine lovers, as they grow older and their liver functions slow along with all the others, complain that they can no longer enjoy red wine with their meals because it gives them a headache. Though medical experiments have so far failed to identify the culprits in this sad state of affairs, the Australian winemakers suspect that the problem ingredients are histamine and tyramine. They are developing wines that contain minimum levels of these chemicals.

It is easy to imagine the vast fortunes that await the producer of a headache-free wine. "Oh, I simply adore Wogga-Wogga Wine—it's the only one that doesn't give me a headache!" One hears this sentiment ascribed to various liquors, especially certain brand names of vodka. There may, of course, be an element of personal reaction involved.

Sparkling Wines and Champagne

Sparkling Wines. These are in a different category from champagne. The only thing they have in common is bubbles, and the fact that they are served cold. In Italy, sparkling wines are called *spumante,* and in Germany *Sekt.* They are usually sweet and are not aimed at the connoisseur market.

When the chairman of a German bank in New York invited colleagues to celebrate the reunification of Germany he offered them cheap chemical *Sekt.* It was considered an ill omen—and so it has proved. Restaurateurs and bar managers should be careful which sparkling wines they select, as those at the bottom end of the spectrum often border on the undrinkable. They are perhaps best reserved for that currently commonplace ceremony in which the winners of car races spray each other with "champagne" by way of celebration. Distributors will try to unload them—at what appear to be bargain prices—to restaurants that offer the fashionable weekend brunch with a complimentary cocktail, which might be a Bloody Mary or a Mimosa: champagne and orange juice. Unless you are running the kind of bar or restaurant where people will come whatever the prices, or however dreadful the goods and services—and many such places exist—it simply does not pay to serve low-quality wines.

Champagne. Champagne shippers are notoriously sensitive to anyone attaching the word "champagne" to anything other than those wines produced and registered in Epernay. They have fought, won, and lost some spectacular battles. A huge headline battle was fought to prevent a London shipper from calling his sparkling Spanish wine champagne. The court eventually ruled that the word "champagne" could be used, but it had to be preceded by the qualification "Spanish." This was not considered a very satisfactory outcome, but it was the best deal available. In the United States, champagne-type wines have been made by the champagne method, (*mèthode champenoise*), but the area of origin must be clearly stated on the label.

Champagne—"Bubbly," or "The Boy"—requires its own slot because it is very special. It is the traditional wine of celebration, and so far as dining is concerned, many consider it an all-purpose accompaniment, though this would be stretching the point if one were eating lamb or beef. European countries are all agreed that the only wine that can be described as "champagne" is that which originates in the French district of Champagne in Burgundy, with the town of Epernay as its focal point. The oldest champagne is said to be Dom Perignon, and the monk of that name who discovered it is said to have exclaimed, "I am drinking stars!" when he tasted it.

Real champagne is generally expensive, even in the nonvintage version. Vintage champagnes can cost as much as 100 dollars in the liquor store, so that the typical restaurant markup will often bring it comfortably into the 200 dollar range. Luxury bars and restaurants will, of course, offer a range of champagnes, secure in the knowledge that their illustrious patrons will demand them from time to time and not bat an eye at the price. More middle-of-the-road establishments will do well to carry a small selection: at least a reasonably priced domestic brand, and a real nonvintage choice. You never know when someone will suddenly want to celebrate. At Christmas, chances of selling champagne quadruple.

A current fashion is to offer a weekend brunch for an all-in-one price that includes either a Bloody Mary or a Mimosa (known in England as a "Buck's Fizz"). In such a concoction vintage champagne would clearly be wasted. This is where the domestic brands find a useful niche.

Even if champagne does not prove to be the most profitable item in the spectrum of your bar or restaurant, the goodwill promoted by happily providing this libation may pay dividends. Good bar managers do not limit their considerations to the money their patrons have just spent. They look forward to the green pastures of what customers are going to spend in their many future visits to the establishment.

The famous champagne names cascade deliciously. Dom Perignon, Taittinger, Veuve Cliquot, Ruinart, Moet Chandon ("Moet" rhymes with "No wet" by the way), Piper Heidseik, Mumms, Krug. American brands such as Piper Sonoma (owned by the French company Piper Heidseik) and Korbel hold their heads high, too.

Some people like to sweeten their champagne with Crème de Cassis, or Chambord, the raspberry liqueur, calling this a Kir Royale. It has been suggested that many champagnes taste a lot better when the first refrigerator chill has worn off a little. People who find Bubbly too fizzy can purchase a device known as a "swizzle stick," a sort of cocktail stirrer with three prongs, each with a little ball at the end. They are made by people like Cartier, often in nonrusting gold. The sight of someone busily taking out bubbles that were quite hard to install may seem strange to some.

Champagne was discovered accidentally (according to legend) when a bottle of white wine started a second fermentation in its bottle and became effervescent. Occasionally this phenomenon can be observed in any white wine, but the result is not usually spectacular; the fermented wine is either used in cooking or thrown out.

In Epernay the wine is stored, in bottles, in special racks. At a certain point in its maturation sugar is added to initiate the "secondary fermentation." In French this is called *dosage*. At intervals the bottles must be turned delicately in order to continue the creation. This process is called *remuage*.

Champagne, like all wine, should always be stored on its side if it's going to be left more than a few days, in order to maintain the magic synergy of air with wine through a damp cork, and served chilled. If you should accidentally open a bottle of warm champagne, it will almost invariably spew forth. At the table, it should sit in an ice bucket with a small towel so that the pourer can wipe the bottle to stop it from dripping over everything and everybody. The towel also has a serious safety use. When opening champagne, the wire that restrains the cork must first be uncoiled and discarded. While this is going on it's important to hold the cork in place with one hand that is protected by a towel.

In the best circles the loud "pop" as the cork is extracted is disdained, but in restaurants there may be a case for making festive sounds so that everyone gets the message. If the wine is warm and has been agitated, perhaps by being rushed up from the cellar at short notice, the chances of it spurting out forcefully are high. It's a waste of champagne and messy. The emergency procedure when champagne spurts is to pour it into a handy glass. You'll inevitably lose some, but the bulk should settle down promptly.

An even more important consideration is the cork. This can be a dangerous projectile, especially if it hits someone in the eye as—Murphy's Law being as implacable as it is—it occasionally will. An often-quoted average annual figure for the number of champagne cork inflicted eye injuries in the United States is 400.

In the 18th century in England a bottle of "The Boy," as it was sometimes called, cost the equivalent of a maid servant's wages for a year. It's a bit cheaper now, to every "Champagne Charlie's" relief.

Many confess to disliking champagne because it's too "acidy." This is a personal issue, but it must be said that such complaints are unlikely if the champagne being drunk is of vintage quality. The difference is unmistakeable.

Serving Wine

Champagne, white, and rosé wine should be served chilled. While it's always a good idea to be well stocked up with chilled wines, your usual par stock, and perhaps more in the beer room or other refrigerated space, should be plenty.

A bottle of wine plunged deep into ice is ready to be served in 10 minutes. However, this should be done with care and attention. If the bottle is left in ice too long the label will come off and the wine will have to be used up as house wine at the service end of the bar.

At the bar, a bottle of wine can be kept in the refrigerator between pourings, or even on the ice in the sink. Strictly speaking this is wrong and even illegal, because the ice may be served in drinks, and debris from a dirty bottle might contaminate it. If a hygiene inspector sees this being done he or she will undoubtedly mention it. In practice, however, bottles are clean, contact is not heavy, and the bartender usually reserves one corner of the ice supply for keeping things chilled, dredging ice for drinks from another area of the sink or container. Since ice, once exposed to the air, immediately starts to melt it is in a sense self-cleansing, provided that the container in which it resides—usually a sink—has a drain. It's all right to recycle the ice used to make a "Martini Straight Up," too, but ice used to make mixed drinks must be discarded in the slop sink or garbage.

At a restaurant table an ice bucket filled with ice (and some water to soften it a little, so that the wine bottle can be plunged deep into it) should be provided to keep the wine chilled between pourings. Solid ice cubes in the bucket can be impenetrable. A clean napkin must be on hand to dry the wet bottle before passing it around the table, and to wrap around the cork during the opening of champagne.

Strictly speaking, each type of wine has its own special glass, but this refinement is now only observed in a few surviving top-scale restaurants. Most establishments nowadays have a standard wine glass for all wines, including champagne. One less thing to have to bother about in a busy bar or restaurant!

If owners or management insist on killing valuable space and creating opportunity for mistakes by having the strictly correct type of glass for each beverage, then their suppliers will advise them as to what they need. In some establishments, especially "theme restaurants," the number of glasses is very restricted because they have to fit the decor. As to whether a "Famous Grouse and Soda" tastes better in a heavy Waterford cut glass or a pink plastic mug shaped like Donald Duck is of course a matter of personal opinion.

Red wines should be served at room temperature, *chambré* as the French say. Once the choice has been made, the sooner the wine is opened the better, because its character and flavor will immediately start to improve upon exposure to the air. In a luxury restaurant vintage wines will often be selected by the customer before dinner, opened some time before the appointed hour, and even decanted (i.e., transferred, minus any sediment, into a decorative clear glass pouring container) if they merit the "full treatment."

In all cases, when the wine is brought to the table, it should be shown to the person who ordered it, so that the label can be checked. By tradition the wine should be opened at the table in the presence of the consumers. But many younger servers have not had, and do not get, much practice at opening wine. Furthermore, the quality of corks has declined with the wine boom. So accidents will happen from time to time. Pomposity is unfashionable these days, and most diners and drinkers will view opening difficulties with humor.

The best opener is the "server's corkscrew," which is rather like a jackknife. It consists of a small blade, a corkscrew, and a useful lever that, poised on the neck of the bottle once the corkscrew has been inserted, usually allows easy withdrawal. These are often handed out by wine salespeople, but can be bought, too.

The first thing to be done once the buyer has nodded approval of the label on a red, white, or rosé wine is to cut away that part of the foil or plastic protecting the cork—or all of it: it matters little. Sometimes there's a thread or a little hinge of plastic, which, when pulled, exposes the top of the cork. The rest of the foil or plastic can be left on. Then comes the most important stage—likened by some to the final thrust of the matador's sword—the insertion of the "worm" into the cork. This should be done slightly off-center and screwed all the way down to give maximum grip on the cork. Then, holding the bottle firmly upright on the table, the lever should be placed on the rim of the bottle opening, and the cork withdrawn in one smooth stroke.

As discussed earlier, champagne requires a little more care. Once you start unwinding the wire the cork must be held in place, covered with a towel, and aimed at the ceiling as it is gently and slowly extracted by a combination of screwing and pulling. Again, if the champagne is not chilled, or has been agitated, the chances of it frothing wildly are high. If this happens the best thing to do is to pour some of the liquid into the nearest available glass, at which point the deluge should stop. Customers may not take kindly to their precious, and not inexpensive, champagne being squirted around, so a little care is in order.

If a cork is stiff or broken, then you can ask your customers if they'd mind you opening it at the bar—"off-stage" as it were—in order to avoid the risk of sudden extraction, possible spillage, or a black eye from a flailing elbow. People will usually go along with it.

After satisfactory extraction wipe the cork and the inside of the bottle with the towel. Put the cork on the table for the buyer to smell and examine, or, more likely, ignore. Then pour a small amount into the buyer's—or a designated guest's—glass, so that they can taste it in order to be assured that it's fit to drink. They (usually) savor it, and nod, which means "go ahead and pour." Many customers these days just wave an airy hand and say, "Pour it, pour it . . ."

In the event of a rejection for some reason—a defective cork may have ruined the wine, it may have been improperly stored, or moved around a lot— fetch another bottle. If the whole consignment is "off" it's back to the wine list for a new selection. The defective bottles should be kept to show to the wine salesperson when next he or she appears. You will get a refund, and the supplier will be grateful for the information, which could save embarrassment with other customers.

A lot of the occasional stiffness and awkwardness in restaurants is generated by nervous staff, intimidated by the staring customer on the one hand, and a glowering insecure maitre d' or manager on the other, so it pays to try for a pleasant atmosphere.

Once the wine is opened and approved all you have to do is fill each diner's glass halfway, and put the wine on the table, if it's red, or back in its bucket if it's white, rosé, or champagne.

An overturned glass on the table means the person doesn't want to drink wine. This could mean he or she simply doesn't drink or is the "designated driver" for the evening.

When the bottle is empty it should be removed. This may act as a prompt to order another bottle—which is what you're there for. Empty white wine bottles are sometimes placed upside down in the bucket. Again, this may be a cue for a polite inquiry about ordering another.

If four people share a bottle of wine near the bar it's hardly worth setting up an ice bucket, particularly if space is cramped. There's only a glass and a bit for each person. It's perfectly in order to ask the customer if you may store the bottle at the bar. If the ice bucket sits for a long time, remember that it will only contain water when you dismantle the setup, and if it was too full there's a good chance of spillage.

While bartenders are soon comfortable with handling wine, the floor staff can sometimes be a little nervous about it. When the bartender is opening up a bottle or two of house wine at the beginning of a shift it's a good idea to have the servers (if they're not too harried) practice opening wine without the distraction of customers. Practice makes perfect. And when the maitre d' or an experienced server wait on a party, it's a good idea to have the rookies watch discreetly and observe, not only to learn how things are done, but also perhaps to learn a little style and the patter that goes with the job.

The Wine List

In a fully staffed luxury restaurant or hotel with plenty of storage space wine lists aren't a problem. They're designed, reviewed, and renewed regularly. The wine steward notices from the computer inventory that a certain wine is selling very well, and orders more in good time before running out. If the wine is listed it's available—probably in large quantities in the cavernous cellar of the establishment.

In the much more common smaller type of operation it's a different story. Even when a wine list is kept to a minimum of less than 20 wines, there are endless irritations—of which the main one is a customer ordering a wine that's out of stock, so that the server or bartender has to start turning somersaults to find out what *is* in stock. Often, once this chain of events is set in motion, Murphy's Law will become fully operational and the customer will order three wines in a row—all of which are out of stock.

The solution is simple. Somebody has to be in charge, and if it isn't the bar manager, or bartender, then an assistant manager should take responsibility. Inventory should be updated every day. If a wine runs out then it should be deleted from the wine list, and/or from the blackboard, or however the availability of wines is intimated to the customers. This is an area that should be tackled head-on. Wine is very popular now, and even the least pretentious establishment must carry a small selection of wines—which, by the way, are an excellent profit item.

Even in the most informal, busy kind of place it really makes life less stressful if you know what you've got available. If efficient inventory keeping and updating of wine lists are maintained, then the only other thing you need to insure smooth operation is a general awareness. Bartenders and servers should be encouraged to "poke around" and ask questions—without becoming boring busybodies, of course—and acquire easy familiarity with the inventory.

Restaurateurs who are deeply insecure—and the breed is not uncommon—often resent what is really a healthy interest on the part of their staff. "Don't let the servers behind the bar," they'll growl. Why not? Why not let them become familiar with where things are kept and how things are done? And if the bar manager or bartender is having a bite to eat and reading the newspaper in the quiet afternoon, is there any reason why a server shouldn't put together a simple drink order?

The marvels of word processing and copying machines now enable restaurants to easily produce a brand new menu and wine list every day. The manager recalls the menu on the word processor or computer. He deletes, say, the Pouilly Fuissé, which has just run out and which he forgot to reorder, being human, and adds the new Australian Cabernet Sauvignon he just bought because he thinks many of the regulars will go for it. He prints it, and strolls around to the copy shop, or sends the busboy who will be delighted at the opportunity for a quick tour of the neighborhood. Shortly thereafter he returns with several copies of a wine list that is true and accurate in every respect—one more potential headache nipped in the bud.

In assembling a wine list it must be recognized that many people find Piesporter Goldtropchen Trockenbeerenauslesen a bit of a mouthful. How much simpler to call it "Number four!" Numbered wine lists work wonderfully as long as whoever is in charge can read, and really does put the Beaujolais in its correctly numbered slot, rack, or cupboard.

Whether a wine list is a grandly designed and decorated cardboard as big as a tabloid newspaper, or whether it's a leather bound book with several sections, or simply a daily list run off the house computer, it must show the same information.

A small list need only separate the reds, whites, rosés, sparkling wines, and champagnes. A fuller list should distinguish between Burgundies—red, white, and rosé; Bordeaux—red, white, and rosé; American—red, white, and rosé; Spanish wines; Italian wines; German wines—Moselle and Rhine; and so on. The wines can be numbered, if this system is adopted, as is likely in the case of an extensive list. Availability of half bottles, carafe wines, and wines by the glass should be shown and, of course, the price. A brief description of the wine and what foods it complements best can be very helpful.

Often a shipper or wholesaler will design and provide a wine list for your establishment. Of course there'll be a small quid pro quo in that their wines must predominate, but that's okay.

It must be remembered that the wine list is a *sales tool*, as well as an inventory of wines. Therefore it must be clear and simple. It's a good idea to have some very reasonably priced selections for customers on a budget, and for the prices to be sensibly spaced. Offered the choice between a 40 dollar bottle of wine and a 10 dollar bottle, a majority of customers—even in the most chic and expensive restaurants—are going to select the cheaper alternative. If there are no reasonably priced wines then the customer is likely to settle for a beer, or nothing, and become rather nervous about what sort of a final bill he or she is going to receive. But they might have happily paid 20 dollars—you'll never know.

Good bar managers must put themselves in the customers' place and see things from their point of view. If you're 22 and on your first date with a smart young lady, and when you ask for the wine list a huge leather bound tome of expensive wines is put before you, you won't be too happy. Good servers and bartenders will rapidly assess customer situations and know how to handle them—and how to sell.

What's wrong with a server saying, "You're having the steak—if you're thinking of having wine with that we have a nice Chateau So-and-So, really popular, 10 dollars a bottle, or by the glass if you like."?

On one occasion at an unbearably stuffy New York restaurant the Duchess of Windsor was being dined. The Crown Prince of Sweden sat with his party at a nearby table, and Charles Bronson was also there with a Hollywood crowd—that kind of place. The Duchess's host, meaning well, said, "Living in Paris you must know your wines. Perhaps you'd like to choose?" Promptly the huge leather bound wine list was set in front of her. The Duchess at this time was well in her 70s and somewhat frail. She gazed at the wine list with some trepidation and said plaintively, "Oh, I'd just like some red wine with my dinner, like we do in France." At this point the gentlemen seated at her side, who happened to know his stuff, did the right thing. He picked up the list and briskly ordered on behalf of the whole party. This is yet another example of the way in which the "pomp and circumstance" of wine can work against it—and importantly, against its sales.

It's worth remarking that almost all the "smartest" deluxe restaurants in New York offer reasonable all-in-one deals these days—a prix fixe lunch or dinner—and these are often bargains, as restaurant prices go. If it's possible to have some wine alongside without stretching the price absurdly then you may see some very happy customers.

There are many reasons for the recent downturn in restaurant business and one of them must be the aggressive pricing policy so many establishments pursue. Often they're forced into a higher pricing policy than they really would like, but are in a bind because of high overheads—which usually means the rent. But this isn't the customers' problem. They are free to "shop around," and they do.

Restaurant journalism is now a field in its own right, and a good write-up from a local correspondent can make a restaurant or bar. However, by some quirk or convention, it's unusual for them to extol the virtues of a restaurant from the value point of view, on the lines of "Excellent food and a marvelous bottle of wine, and the bill for two was less than 40 dollars." Perhaps this would be dangerously judgmental in an age when political correctness is the journalists' mantra.

A curious psychology attends the business of cost and price in the United States. People are actually sometimes a bit ashamed to have to ask how much things are. On the other hand, many people who are spending "plastic" don't care what they pay. "A credit card feels no pain" is one of the war cries of a famous New York bar owner, notorious for inflating her bills. But there may be a "silent majority" who are quietly doing their sums in their heads and assessing which bar delivers the biggest beer for the buck. In neighborhoods harboring large numbers of students or retired people, restaurateurs will very soon see which way the wind blows.

Selling Wine

Some wisdom is forever, and some wisdom has its time and fashion. In the Middle Ages, a vintner would erect a bush on top of his house to tell the world that the new vintage was available. This gave rise to the proverb "Good wine needs no bush." It may have been true then, but it isn't true now.

There is so much competition in the modern consumer society that even the most sublime products have to be advertised. The first line sales aid for wine in a bar restaurant or hotel is the wine list. This should name its wines, describe them briefly, and, perhaps mention which foods they will complement best. A general awareness on the part of the staff will help here too.

"I'm having steak and my wife's having scrod. Which wine should we have?"

"We have a light claret . . . number 14 . . . which should be ideal for you both."

"Red wine with fish?"

"Maybe not with a delicate fish like sole, but a lot of people enjoy red wine with a fish like scrod, especially with a robust sauce."

Sold.

But if not sold, why not a half bottle of red, and a half of white, or wine by the glass?

This counsel is admittedly a bit glib, because outside "serious," expensive restaurants, the help may be seriously intimidated by having to immerse themselves in wine, especially if they are not restaurant professionals, which—whether you like it or not—will often be the case. But they can be coaxed, led, and even (with luck) really interested in the subject and derive pleasure from it for themselves, as well as bumping up your sales.

Many restaurants have a bottle of wine sitting on the table as part of the standard setup. This is often the bargain special of the week. Sometimes they have two wines, a red and a white. Many customers are happy to have their minds made up for them. This isn't necessarily because they are weak-minded or out of their depth. They may have romance or business on their minds and not wish heavy digressions from the routine and simple question of what to eat and drink. It's a good idea and good business to prompt diners in a friendly and knowledgeable way. Customers who trust the establishments in which they regularly wine and dine are the easiest of all, and often the most fun.

Here is a guide to what sort of wine goes with what sort of food.

Appetizers	Champagne, dry white, medium or dry sherry
Beef	Hearty red
Lamb	Hearty red
Veal	Dry or medium white or rosé
Chicken	Dry or medium white or rosé
Fish, or seafood	Dry or medium white or rosé
Dessert	Sweet wine, port, madeira

The ground rule is simply red wine with red meat, and white with white meat, fish, or seafood. National wines often complement national cuisine, so that a good choice with spaghetti Bolgnaise, for instance, would be a red Chianti or Bardolino. Greek wine really only comes into its own alongside Greek food, and serious wine will be wasted alongside highly spiced food. With Indian curry, for instance, beer is by far the best accompaniment.

These rules are based on long experience of what goes best, but there's plenty of room for personal preference, scrod with red wine being a good example. It's fun experimenting. The customer who regularly sits at the bar and orders a plate of clams on the half shell and a glass of Cointreau may cause a raised eyebrow or two, but it's a free country.

Some restaurants keep track of which server sells the most wine, and pay a small bonus, say a dollar a bottle. This is harmless enough, and the regular winners will have something to brag about.

Occasionally, diners will wish to bring their own wine. If they do so they can legally be charged "corkage"—an amount of money to cover the profit the restaurateur is losing. This need not be too punitive. It doesn't happen often enough to pose a threat or a problem. Some very successful restaurants are called "BYOs"—"Bring Your Own Wine," or perhaps buy it from the liquor store across the street. Such restaurants don't have an alcohol or wine license, usually through some tedious technicality of the law having to do with location or the building. In this case, no corkage may be charged.

Some General Comments on Wine

The remarks on wine made here provide ample knowledge for the average bar manager. In a restaurant or bar where greater than average emphasis is placed on wine, more knowledge of the vast range of wines might be required. Fortunately, such knowledge is easily acquired. There are hundreds of books on wine, courses and classes available in most major cities, and there is even a video available now, by international wine pundit Charles Johnson, devoted to the art of wine tasting.

Everyone working in service industries will from time to time have to put up with the lectures of self-styled experts. The wine expert often wears argyle socks, a tweed jacket, a funny hat, and smokes a pipe. His or her tip basically consists of change, including pennies. The best way to deal with them is to switch off one's mind and nod gratefully, secure in the knowledge that whatever these pundits may have read, it is unlikely that they have ever entered the sacred inner sanctum at the winery where the grave faced men in white coats do the final, secret blending, which is then sent to market.

Such a customer will occasionally reject a wine because it is "corked." This means that the cork has rotted and spoiled the wine. It does happen occasionally, but many such complaints are frivolous. As is often the case, the real purpose of the exercise is to indulge a theatrical urge. While customers are complaining they hold center stage and everyone savors their comments. Might they be right? Are members of the long-suffering public being ripped off yet again by the grim forces of Mammon?

It might be opined that in some ways the huge mystique that surrounds the world of wine does the industry a disservice. Wine lore does provide a useful arena in which people doing a Dale Carnegie course in self-assertion can practice on hapless young servers. But many potential wine customers are put off, or become impatient with what they perceive as a lot of precious humbug involved.

Many non-Europeans are embarrassed and even intimidated by the whole subject. What sort of wine goes with what kind of food is often a burning area of doubt and misgiving for the upwardly mobile, aspiring hostess.

Some fall into the trap of thinking that if they buy the most expensive option these are more likely to give satisfaction. In fact, well-known brands are sometimes poor value because a large percentage of the retail price is necessitated by the cost of the advertising that made the customer buy it. Smarter folks take the time to learn a bit about the subject of wines and spirits and save lots of money by spotting bargains.

Bar managers can make excellent opportunity profits by keeping their eyes open for bargains. Most suppliers have monthly "post-offs," or "specials." When the liquor storage area is suddenly dominated by 20 cases of one item, eyes may widen, but chances are that a considerable profit is about to be reaped. Regular customers in midprice neighborhoods will be delighted when the benefits of good buys are passed on to them.

The glories of wine can be a tedious quagmire for that large segment of the population that has no interest in alcohol in any shape or form whatsoever, but which has—usually for business reasons—to accommodate people who consider alcohol an everyday part of life. Bar managers must help bridge the gap.

Europeans go to another extreme. They are often seriously "underwhelmed" by the mysteries of wine, and treat it as an everyday consumer item. Wine in France is often bought in six-packs or in cardboard containers at the supermarket, and served without fuss at lunch and dinner. In all the wine-producing countries of Europe it is perfectly normal to add water to ordinary table wines at lunch or dinner—though not of course to the 1951 Chateau Lafite. (Some might see such an urbane gesture as "super cool," others would faint.) Wine is issued to the French army as part of its rations. And inevitably stories are told about it being doctored to reduce libido. It is almost invariably watered at the table.

The French even go so far as to cheerfully describe some wines as ordinary— *vins ordinaires*. Searching for the best value in ordinary daily table wine is a universal European hobby. In England an annual competition is held to decide which nonvintage wines are currently best value. Such is the excellent publicity that the winner can expect to be a best-seller beyond the year of its victory, even if it has to yield the number one spot to a competing wine, because its brand name will be instantly established in the consumer vocabulary.

It is worth mentioning that such winning wines are almost invariably blends of various wines, often from different countries, assembled by wholesale wine shippers. Maintaining consistent quality in a blended wine is the devil's own job because of the endless variables in the weather and grape harvests in the various contributing countries. That's why this year's winner may not be on top next year.

Attempts to popularize wine are sometimes reminiscent of the valiant efforts of a recent chairperson of the Metropolitan Opera to expand its audience to a younger group. "Of course you can wear blue jeans to the opera!" was one of her lines, as was, "Why not bring a picnic basket for the interval?"

In the 1960s twisting and turning to sell wine to consumers other than the snooty "A" and "B" consumer groups, one advertising slogan was "Wine's a winner with your Sunday dinner." Punchy, but hardly on a par with "Fly the friendly skies" or "Don't leave home without it."

There is an enormous amount of wine in the world waiting to be sold. Zimbabwe, Belgium, Czechoslovakia, Peru, Colombia, and Ireland have recently thrown their hats into the ring. In Europe it's called "the wine lake."

For better or worse one is stuck with the theater and ritual of wine. Many a hostess will serve Liebfraumilch with steak for years until one day it dawns on her that a dry red wine complements such a dish in a far more rewarding way. Fortunately, as is bound to happen in a busy consumer world, some well-defined broad brush strokes have emerged that will guide the bar manager and restaurateur through the jungle.

Wine Tasting

What should one look for in wine? The elaborate rituals of wine tasting have to do with appearance: color, body, smell or "nose," taste, and "finish" (the aftertaste).

At a formal wine tasting the experts will hold a glass of wine up to the light to assess its color, and swirl it around to observe its "legs"—the extent to which the wine trails cling to the glass. Then they'll stick their noses deep into the glass to get an idea of its "nose." Next, at last, they actually taste it—chew it, almost—rolling it around the tastebuds thoughtfully. Finally, they'll spit it out into a sawdust-filled bucket and savor the aftertaste for a moment before making their notes. Then they'll perhaps nibble some cheese or sip some water, to "cleanse the palate."

If it all sounds rather unattractive—it is. What are they looking for? What are they trying to assess? The better a wine clings to the glass when you swish it around, the more full-bodied it is. "Good legs," as the streaks of wine are called, implies a full-bodied, robust wine. However, light-bodied wines have a place in the hierarchy too; they are for casual drinking, and with lighter foods.

Smell, aroma, "bouquet," or "nose" is the next consideration. This is part of the pleasure of everything one eats or drinks. A cold white wine will have little or no "nose." Reds improve as they warm to room temperature.

As to actual taste, the first consideration is the degree of sweetness. If, as a result of the creative process, all the sugar from the grapes has been consumed, then the wine will be "dry"—in this context the opposite of sweet. But sweetness clearly will not be disdained if the wine under consideration is supposed to be a dessert wine.

Then there is the aftertaste or "finish"—the instant satisfaction, or otherwise, of having savored the wine.

Finally, there is the overall character of the wine—very nebulous and difficult to describe but, as we shall see, there is no shortage of vocabulary on the subject.

The English invented wine snobbery. A "Punch" magazine cartoon of the late 19th century featured an earnest host offering wine to a guest with the comment, "It's just a harmless little domestic burgundy of little or no breeding, but I think you'll be amused by its precocity."

The wine taster's vocabulary includes such descriptions as fat, thin, fruity, smoky, right-bankish taste of young Merlot, lively, spicy, new-turned earth, rotting leaves, good depth, well mannered, good tannin—to "hold it together," a whiff of coal tar gas, nail varnish, minty, smell of old books, smoky green leaves, cat pee, crushed nettles, and on, and on.

In Europe, huge wine tankers trundle through the night taking wine from Morocco and Spain up to France and Germany. The wine has no name and little pedigree, but somewhere it will find a home. It will be blended, and christened—possibly with an illustrious name that certainly doesn't evoke the dusty plains of La Mancha or the sandstorms of the Sahara.

In Burgundy, blackberry juice is added routinely to the "ordinary wines" to give them character. Sucrose—fruit sugar—will almost invariably "improve" the taste of wine. Many vintners use this as routinely as the food industry uses salt, sugar, and monosodium glutamate. Sulfites (wine bottle labels now carry a warning about these) are used in wine as part of the stabilization process. Pesticides and weed killers play a part and, in Germany, the ominous sounding chemical potassium ferro-cyanide is used as a fining agent for some wines.

Two major wine producers, one in Austria and the other in Italy, have recently been heavily fined for using glycol as a sweetener in their wine production processes. The beautiful daughter of one of these famous houses, on being teased about this, shrugged and commented, "It was only the cheap wine."

However, some chemicals are used with good reason. As many an amateur manufacturer of "organic wine" has discovered, fermented grape juice, plain and simple, is a very delicate concoction. Left to its own devices, especially in a warm climate, the chances of it turning to vinegar are very high. Sulphur dioxide is used as an antiseptic to protect the juice as it turns to wine.

It is just as well we have consumer associations to scrutinize the marketplace. Behind the scenes great tension exists between the wine industry and lobbying consumer groups in Washington that would like wine producers to list all the ingredients of their product on the label. It would be a long label indeed, since wine contains over 1,000 chemicals.

At the same time, the wine producers are lobbying for the right to display the words "Red wine reduces the chance of heart attacks." This cheering claim is based on some rough and loose observations in France, 25 percent of whose hospital beds are occupied by patients suffering from alcohol related complaints, most of whose citizens are genetically ectomorphic (i.e., inclined to be thin), and whose diet embraces lavish amounts of salad and olive oil.

At "blind" wine tastings, where the wine is not identified until it has been tasted, described, and valued, a standing joke is the regularity with which cheap and unadvertised wines score heavily over famous, expensive name brands and vintages. But the bottom line was recently demonstrated in a champagne tasting involving five champagnes or sparkling wines. Four of these wines were ho-hum cheap offerings. The tasters were occasional champagne drinkers, not professional wine experts. There was much disagreement about the four inferior products. But all tasters were unanimous in describing the vintage Mumm champagne as being distinctly delicious.

A European TV program on wine, in which experts are asked to identify and price wines chosen at random from store shelves, produces the most uncannily consistent correct results. It's not all flim-flam.

Class and quality win out. They only need to whisper; they don't need to shout. The problem is the bemused wine consumer. Just like the young man who takes a girl out to dinner and spends 60 dollars (if he's lucky) for the privilege of discovering that he and his date have nothing whatsoever in common, wine buyers often spend money on wine they find disappointing.

Good bar managers mediate between the two worlds of the seller and the buyer. Sales can be improved by demystifying the subject of wine and concentrating on its convivial and gastronomic role, rather than on its snooty up-scale aura. By doing a good job they'll earn respect, job satisfaction, and a good living.

CHAPTER FOUR

Beer, Nonalcoholic Beer, Sodas, and Bottled Waters

Beer is the biggest selling alcoholic beverage in the world. It outsells all other alcoholic drinks in France and Germany; more than twice as much beer as wine is consumed in these countries. Despite its light and innocent air, beer can be abused like any other alcoholic beverage. More than half of Britain's alcoholics are "beeroholics."

The beer companies all over the world are enormously powerful both as economic units and as political influences. Firms like Guinness and Heineken are really worldwide empires and often diversify into other related businesses. In Britain the powerful beer families are known as the "Beerage," a play on the word "Peerage," which is the name given to the members of the House of Lords, where of course many brewery barons sit.

Until recently the British brewery conglomerates enjoyed vertical monopolies. They owned the fields where the "hops" from which beer is made are grown; they owned the brewery, the bottling plants, wholesale depots, and the pubs and liquor stores (called "off-licenses") themselves. By buying wine chateaux in France they did the same thing in the wine area. In other words, they neatly sewed up production, distribution, and retail sale in the same highly profitable package.

Recent legislation means that each company in Britain can own a maximum of 2,000 pubs. This has provided both crisis and opportunity for many entrepreneurs as the breweries have swiftly moved to sell off their less profitable pubs, spelling desolation in some cases, but prosperity where an enterprising operator has breathed new life into an ailing pub, helped by the fact that he is now free to stock just whatever he wants, and start a restaurant operation, too.

In addition individual pub managers or landlords, who sometimes lease the pub from the brewery or are sometimes straightforward employees or tenants, must now be permitted to stock items other than those produced by the parent brewery. Thus, if a pub manager finds his regulars asking for Whitbread, though the pub belongs to Bass, he can stock both.

A down side to this has been an unpleasant pressure brought to bear on pubs by some area managers who can be studiously uncooperative if a pub owner insists on stocking rival products. Clearly brewers are reluctant to surrender their product exclusivity.

A landlord will complain that he needs more refrigerated space. Head office will come and have a look, and agree to install more. Then they discover the landlord is stocking a rival product and suddenly the eagerly awaited improvements are not forthcoming. This smacks of cutting off one's nose to spite one's face, but it happens. Of course, the landlord's income is directly tied to the volume of sales.

Beers and Other Brews

So poor did the quality of popular beers become in England 20 years ago that a society was formed to protect it. CAMRA, the Campaign for Real Ale, gives its seal of approval only to those beers it considers deserving, and has influenced quality control by the big brewery groups considerably. Some pubs proudly display its sign of approval.

This background will be of interest to those bars and restaurants that stock British and Irish beers, ales, and stouts. When you sip a beer it's interesting to contemplate that there's a whole world of industry and intrigue behind it! Such happenings are unlikely in the United States where antitrust laws are fiercely applied (remember Standard Oil?). But the beer companies will fall over themselves to give good service if you agree to plug their wares by using their coasters, or even, as is seen quite commonly, putting a neon sign bearing the name of the beer in the window.

In the industry, all over the world, companies struggle to establish exclusivity, but it's a losing battle. There are too many products. Most bars *must* offer a selection of beers if they are going to do the repeat business that is essential to the success of most operations. Only a very few up-scale restaurants can get away with stocking only one or two beers, and these are almost invariably the sort of places that wouldn't expect to sell much beer anyway.

It is just as well that the profit on beer is so healthy because, in many ways, the product is a pain in the neck. The first thing about beer is the amount of space it consumes—including expensive refrigerated space. True, the bartender is not greatly taxed by having to open a bottle, or "pull a pint" of draft beer. But customers, whose brand loyalty is just as fierce if not more so than that of scotch and gin drinkers, are obsessed with frigidity, effervescence, and appearance. Beer must be very cold, lively, and look right—with a proper head on it, too, in the case of draft. (Not an enormous "Coney Island" head either!)

It is worth noting that a glass used for beer must be absolutely clean and rinsed, with no build-up of powder detergent. If it isn't 100 percent clean, the beer will not look right. It will not sparkle or foam correctly.

Bartenders who congratulate themselves on receiving a simple order when a customer orders a bottle of beer, as opposed to a Brandy Alexander with its trip to the kitchen, may forget the humping of beer crates and the installing of endless bottles into the refrigerators or ice buckets. This is understandable if it isn't their responsibility, of course.

Once you're set up and organized, serving beer is child's play, but there is a lot of preparation involved. The empties too are a problem. In a busy bar the garbage cans have to be emptied at regular intervals and the bottles taken out to an ever-growing pile. In some states returned empties earn five or 10 cents each, and although it seems wasteful to disdain this, the effort involved outweighs the rewards. Even medium-sized supermarkets in some areas must employ two or three people solely to accommodate bottle and container collection.

Keg or draft beer is less of a problem because the trusty beer delivery men, in their weight lifter's belts, will roll the kegs down to the cellar and into the refrigerated beer room, and often connect it, too.

The word "beer," one of the earliest foods devised by humankind, comprises a large family. At the strong and dark end of the spectrum there are "malt liquors" sold under various brand names. Alcoholic strength is what defines a malt liquor, and in the United States this can be as high as six percent by volume. Colt 45 and Champale are examples. Britain boasts a powerful concoction known as "Barley Wine," which is really a very strong malt liquor. Malt liquor is not a standard bar item—except in those areas where consumer demand mandates its presence. "Bock beers" are in the same group.

San Francisco is the home of Anchor Steam beer, a uniquely American style. Many "boutique breweries" have sprung up in recent years, and their product is often excellent. New Amsterdam, for instance, is popular in the New York area.

Ale is beer of a certain style, usually with a coppery color. Occasionally one will come across a specially brewed beer or ale called "Porter." Then there is stout, of which the most famous examples are Guinness and Murphy's, both from Ireland. Germany produces lager and pilsner. Last but not least comes American domestic beer, often referred to colloquially as "suds," and not without reason as, chemically speaking, it is a first cousin of those splendid detergents that work so well in washing machines, restoring tired socks to pristine freshness.

Some beers come in barrels or kegs and are served as draft. Others come in bottles. Many are available as bottle or draft, but distribution varies and while, for instance, draft Guinness and Pilsner Urquell are widely available in America, they sometimes take a bit of finding. Draft beer has a certain mystique that also commands a faithful following.

There are hundreds of different kinds of beer. The Pioneer supermarket at West 74th Street in New York carries more than 130 different beers, and each week one or another of them is on sale—a sort of beer Mecca.

So profuse are the types and styles of beer that bar managers need to be quite ruthless in choosing those that they will regularly stock. The requirement will vary regionally. But the installation of almost any famous beer on draft will draw aficionados from far and wide.

Once a clientele is established, draft beer is a marvelous profit maker. Nor, despite what one's first thought might be, is it a "down market" item. On the contrary, the customers who will go out of their way for their favorite draft beer are more often distinctly middle class—if not downright yuppies.

All beer-type beverages are produced by variations of a basic method. Barley is wetted and spread on the floor. It then turns into malt. (Yes, it's reminiscent of whiskey making.) The malt is then ground in a mill, at which point it is called "grist" (hence "grist for the mill").

"Hops"—or whatever secret chemical equivalent may have been selected—are then added. This is what gives beer its distinctive taste. Hops are small green flowers, unique in appearance but a bit like catkins. In England hops are mainly gathered in the county of Kent, which adjoins London. Until recent years many poorer Cockney families would go hop-picking by way of a paid holiday, and much folklore attaches thereto. The hops are stored in distinctive conical shaped buildings called "oast houses."

The next critical step is the addition of yeast, which causes the mix to ferment and produce both alcohol and carbon dioxide bubbles. At this point the beer is either bottled or "racked" into kegs or barrels. The more malt, and less water, the stronger the brew. Of course, there is much, much more to it than this brief exposé. Each manufacturer has secrets and methods of imparting unique character to the product. However, the quality of beer is determined mainly by the water used. When manufacturers, such as Coors, make a fuss about their Colorado spring water, or whatever, they are serious.

Some of the big names in this huge industry are Pilsner Urquell—a Czech beer, the oldest pilsner in the world, and in a class of its own (all other pilsner-type beers derive from this)—Grolsch, Heineken, Amstel, Bass, Whitbread, Watney, Lowenbrau, and on to the King of Beers itself: Budweiser.

Most breweries welcome tours so that people can see just what they do. Years ago at Lowenbrau the "pièce de resistance" of the grand tour was to see the Master Brewer tasting a vat at the final stage of production that was about to be bottled. He would taste it stagily, sniff it suspiciously, then, with a dandified gesture, select from a trolley laden with dishes of various herbs and substances, a mere pinch of powder. This he would flick grandly into a vat almost as big as a small house. Then he would nod and pass on. The beer was ready to be bottled and sold.

Serving Beer

Beer in America is served ice cold. The obsession with frigidity can be irritating, as customers taste cold beer, shake their heads sadly and ask plaintively if you could please put a couple of bottles deep in the ice. For some customers it's never cold enough.

This consumer taste has its farcical side where imported British draft beers are served. Such beers—Whitbread, Bass, Watney, Charringtons, and Guinness being popular examples—are not supposed to be chilled, and indeed their character is somewhat altered when they are. But you may need to serve them cold anyway.

Sometimes a complaint that the beer isn't cold enough will alert you to the fact that the refrigeration has gone down and needs to be fixed. Occasionally the temperature setting may have been accidentally changed. Many old-fashioned beer rooms—the walk-in refrigerated space where the draft beer kegs, and other beers and wines, are kept—work on a simple principle. When you walk in, you switch on the light to see what you're doing. This also turns off the refrigeration and removes the uncomfortable icy blast of air that, if you're going to be spending a few minutes inside working, you can definitely do without. On leaving, the light is switched off and the refrigeration is turned back on. But despite notices and pleas, once in a while someone will forget to turn off the light. It may be three hours before anyone discovers what's happened, and it will take another hour or two to cool the space down. Routine vigilance and awareness are required to avoid mishaps.

The first member of the bar staff to arrive in the morning should make sure all refrigeration and ice-making equipment is working so that if it isn't it can be fixed immediately. A plumber or electrician may have to be called. Ice may have to be bought from an ice company, which may or may not be able to comply promptly with your order. If the bar manager and bartenders are thoroughly familiar with the ice machines, as they should be, no time will be wasted on calling expensive electricians or plumbers to replace an accidentally disconnected plug. When hiring new personnel it's a good idea to show them your equipment, and make sure they can take care of routine requirements such as tapping a keg of beer or soda.

Sometimes many different people have access to a central ice machine, and less experienced workers may commit the cardinal sin of leaving the plastic ice scoop on top of the ice inside the machine when they've filled up their bucket. Thus, the next person who needs ice cannot find the scoop that now lies buried beneath a mound of fresh ice cubes. This turns a two-minute job into a ten-minute job, which is not a good thing at peak periods of business. A chain attached to the scoop handle is one solution. Common sense is another, and particularly, new or temporary personnel should be warned about this trivial but irritating problem.

Many restaurants in friendly neighborhoods will supply ice free to locals when they are entertaining. Think twice about this if the shoe store wants two big buckets on the night you have a large party booked, especially if it's a hot humid day and the ice machine is struggling to produce.

A bottle of beer should be served as follows. The coaster, or bev-nap, is placed on the bar or table in front of the customer, or a little off-center if a plate is there or likely to arrive there shortly. The empty glass is put on top of that. Then the server or bartender pours an inch of beer into the glass and sets the bottle down. There's no need to open the bottle at the table; the server will save time by opening the bottle at the service bar. You don't wait for the customer to taste and approve; you are just making service gestures. In many bars today this gesture has been abandoned, and customers under 40 who see it may be slightly bemused, as they might be if requested to take their baseball hats off at the table!

When a bottle of beer is opened by mistake, it can still be served with a clear conscience for up to an hour, provided it's kept chilled. It's a mistake to replace the cap, because you can't replace it firmly enough for it to fulfill its sealing function. If it gets mixed up with other bottles, when you grab it and serve it, it will almost certainly be flat. (Think about what happens to a bottle of soda at home. No matter how tightly you replace the cap, the soda may stay lively for a day, but not for two.)

Such mistakes often find a happy home among the staff, if it's the kind of restaurant where they're allowed a beer. Some servers are prone to invent mistakes on behalf of their innocent customers in order to liberate a spare beer for their personal consumption, but as long as it doesn't happen several times a shift it's hardly worth getting paranoid about—unless, of course, this constitutes one more item on the offending employee's list of shortcomings!

Inevitably there are a few variations in the business of serving bottled beer. The customer will sometimes say, "Don't pour it." Many customers nowadays like to drink their beer straight from the bottle, even people in up-scale restaurants. Where this lugubrious custom sprang from is unclear. Is it perhaps reverse chic? In Europe, until recently, a child caught drinking from a bottle would be reproved sternly. It almost certainly comes from television and is part of the whole range of body language—the exhalation of smoke, the gripping of a filter cigarette between the teeth, the sticking out of a twig of chewing gum, the grimacing, the gritting of teeth, and the odd hand gestures—which indifferent actors use to convey bravado, insouciance, or coolness.

So, cries of alarm will sometimes be heard when a well-trained server or bartender ritualistically pours beer into the glass, as though a privilege had been denied. "I didn't want a glass," they'll whine, before reluctantly sipping, or sometimes totally disdaining the beer you've poured and grabbing the bottle. "Down market" bars don't even offer glasses anymore. The customers neither want nor expect them. Well, it saves washing up.

In hotels and large restaurants, glasses are often sent to the dishwashing area to be washed. This should mean that they are well and truly clean and sterilized—at least they are immersed in really hot water. But in practice, as many lipstick-stained glasses (especially wine glasses, because white wine is the lady's number one tipple) return from the dishwashing area, having been overlooked by bartenders who wash up as they go along.

A bar should have three sinks for washing glasses, on the principle of "wash, rinse, cold rinse." The first sink should have hot water, detergent of a non-streaky kind, and ideally motorized brushes. The second should contain clear luke-warm water, and the third fresh cold water. In the second and third sinks a dripping faucet can maintain a cleansing flow.

But most bars only have two sinks per station. If other sinks exist, one may be full of ice, and the other may be the "slop" sink, into which dregs and squashed fruit from empty glasses are thrown. So, unless the bartender is prepared to put on protective gloves every few minutes and wash up a batch of dirty glasses with the motor brushes in really hot water (the minimum temperature specified by law would be scalding, by the way), the glasses will not be satisfactorily washed. They'll be "more or less" clean, and the rinse in the second sink will help, but invisible residue actually builds on the glass and in a short time anything you pour into it will be spoiled.

The only answer to this problem is an obsessive thoroughness at all stages, a sort of military drill by which each glass is held up to the light and checked for grease and lipstick stains, and given a final rinse under cold flowing water to give it a sparkle as it drains dry on the draining board.

You can remove potential irritation and stress by knowing that available glasses at the bar are clean. If you are taking over a bar the morning after a very busy night, there's all the more reason to be careful. If the closing bartender was working alone and got busy, he or she may well have gotten a bit sloppy, being, like everyone else in the restaurant industry, only human.

It sounds like a bore, but it's comforting to check, when you start a bar shift, to see that the first six glasses of all types are spotless and sparkling. Some bartenders work with a small pool of glasses that they wash themselves carefully, thus avoiding any mistakes an earlier shift's workers may have overlooked. This works fine at a steady-paced front bar, but breaks down when it gets busy—especially at the service end—when all available glasses, including the ones gathering dust at the very back of the shelves, or wherever, need to be deployed.

Hell hath no self-righteousness like a customer given a dirty glass, and quite rightly, too. It's a lousy advertisement for the bar, and doesn't say much for the bartender. In a neighborhood bar with regular customers you can probably wriggle around it; a drink "on the house" is a general cure-all for such small mishaps.

Glasses should never be dried with a cloth. Sometimes stubborn stains require a cloth, but once the glass is cleaned it should be washed again and rinsed. By wiping a glass with a cloth—still done religiously in many bars—you actually make the glass dirty again because the cloth soon starts sprouting bacteria once it is used.

Bars in which draft beers predominate will sometimes chill their glasses. This can be a real space killer, but it is a nice "classy" gesture that will not go unnoticed by the faithful. If you have an ice-crushing machine you can even have a tub of crushed ice right up on the bar as a sort of display piece, with beer, and perhaps martini glasses, stuck in it temptingly. A bar manager should consider such gestures very carefully. Someone has to do the work, and even in recessional times overworked people will move on just as soon as they can, leaving you to recruit and train the next sucker.

"Pulling" or "drawing" draft beer requires a little bit of practice to get it right. In fact, those splendid traditional looking pump handles are phony. When they're pulled they turn on the CO_2 gas that propels the beer upwards from the cellar or storage space. The days of hand induced air pressure are long gone, thank goodness. Pulling pints in the old days could be quite tiring.

As discussed, the glass must be "beer clean." There's no reason, if you have a fresh water faucet next to the beer pumps, why you shouldn't give the glass a quick rinse in flowing water. The trick is to let the first squirt of beer that emerges when you pull the pump go into the drainage, not into the glass. It's usually just foam anyway. Then you stick the glass under the flowing beer, but hold the glass at an angle so that the beer gently hits the side and forms a liquid body, as opposed to a mass of undrinkable foam. About half an inch from the top, you let the beer flow directly, vertically, and this will give you the requisite "head" that beer drinkers find so attractive. Remember, you won't create a head in a greasy glass or one that has an invisible film of detergent.

If you have a selection of drafts you'll find that they vary in liveliness, and this is something you just have to get used to. If you've poured one pint, you can usually go straight on to the next from the same pump, taking advantage of the established flow.

Guinness, as its devotees will agree, is in a world of its own. It comes out slowly, and invariably creates a foam that takes time to settle. So if you get an order for three drinks, one of which is a pint of Guinness, the first thing you do is pour the Guinness, letting the creamy foam reach about three quarters of the way up the glass; then make your other drinks. By the time you get back to your Guinness, that which you have already poured will have settled. Then you just have to top it up, leaving the inch or so of foam head on top, which is the Guinness trademark.

An order for six pints of Guinness is a bit of a show-stopper, but then, so would be an order for six Piña Coladas, a Brandy Alexander, and a Long Island Iced Tea. Bartenders must learn to take this sort of thing in stride, reminding themselves that one can only do a day's work in a day, that it doesn't happen all that often, and that the profit is healthy. Guinness drinkers are familiar with the ritual, so there's no need to apologize for the delay. But if you're busy, don't forget the pint of Guinness awaiting topping-up. Some bartenders will draw a little shamrock in the foam on St. Patrick's day, but in a busy bar this should not be mandatory. If you have a highly Hibernian clientele, you can even get green beer for this august celebration.

The beer pipes have to be cleaned regularly. This is a service you should have done on a routine basis. From time to time you'll get a "wild" barrel, or there'll be a gas problem that will give you such a furious flow that you can't pull a glass of drinkable beer—all you get is foam. The beer company will send a troubleshooter at short notice, usually. They want you to sell their beer—as fast as you can.

A certain folklore attaches to the first draft pint of the day. It's believed by some, correctly, that part of the contents thereof will consist of beer that has sat in the pipes all night. So this should be drained off at the start of a new day's business, or when you pull the first pint.

Some beer drinkers will frown after they've sipped their beer, and ask if perhaps it's getting near the bottom of the barrel. It very often is, as will be demonstrated by the fact that when you next pull from that pump, all you'll get is air. There shouldn't really be any discrepancy between the first and last glasses drawn from a keg of beer, but these complaints are often justified, and are usually made by habitual beer drinkers who, unfortunately, seem to have a case. So healthy is the profit on draft beer, however, that the small loss incurred by having to replace a man's bottom-of-the-barrel drink with the first from the new keg is negligible—and you'll have another satisfied customer.

Although the beer delivery people will often connect the kegs they're delivering, in their absence, if a keg runs out, the bar manager or one of the staff will have to tap the replacement. It is now many years since the freak accident in which a bartender tapping a beer was killed by the spiggot exploding and penetrating his jaw. The current system is very user friendly and easy to fix. You turn off the gas to reduce the amount of hissing and spluttering that makes the task a bit intimidating until you get used to it. Then you disconnect the empty cask, by twisting and removing the metal screw connection. This is light, because empty, and you roll it to wherever the empties are assembled. With studiously bent knees, because beer kegs are very heavy, you roll the full replacement into position near the connecting pipe. If the delivery people know their stuff they will have lined up the barrels for their appropriate connecting pipes, which means you shouldn't have too much rolling to do. Then you take out your trusty Swiss Army knife, or use the blade from your server's corkscrew, and remove the plastic label covering the entrance point in the center of the top of the barrel. There's sometimes a little plastic tag that invites you to try and pull it off with your bare fingers, but if you get it wrong you may have a painful broken fingernail to add to your woes. Then you simply insert the connecting tap on the end of the line, twist it, and you're back in business. As long as you remember to switch the gas back on, that is. If you forget, you'll be doing double travel back down to the cellar.

Once a week the beer room should be swept, because loose labels accumulate damply on the floor. If you store bottled beer in cartons in the beer room, and very sensibly in order to make sure you have a reserve of cold beer, these should be taken out and moved up to the bar at least once a week. The beer room is inevitably damp, and once the carton is soaked it will disintegrate when you lift it, and bottles will spill all over the place. If there are any spare "bus trays," the cartons can be placed in them to prevent accidents.

Don't forget that you get 10 dollars or more back on empty kegs, so you must update your inventory after every delivery. Guinness requires a separate gas pressure system of its own, but having it installed is painless.

Suppliers of draft beer will be happy to fix you up with very nice looking beer tankards, or distinctive glasses, smartly decked out in their brewery logo. Because they are so decorative, they are very attractive to souvenir hunters, and there is always a steady attrition—as with decorative ashtrays and towels in hotels. Therefore, it's always a good idea to have a backup supply of undecorated mugs for the draft beer. When it gets really busy, servers must be warned to recover empty tankards—and indeed all glasses—from the tables as soon as they are empty, so that they can be swiftly washed and recycled.

Light Beer

Beer is quite high in calories. In former times it was quite nutritious. Today's occasional boast that there's "a steak in every glass" is pushing it a bit, but there is a general awareness that ordinary beer might be fattening. The expression "beer belly" clearly brings no pleasure to brewery copywriters.

Thus, the invention of light beer, with much fewer calories, was a considerable breakthrough. James Coburn, for a mere (it was rumored) half million dollars, went on TV and said two words—Miller Lite—and the rest is history. Amstel Light is another great favorite, as is Coors, which also exists in draft form. Some beer drinkers, much as they care about their waistlines, find the thinner taste of light beer unsatisfying, and won't buy it.

The only thing you can take out of beer, if it's to retain any resemblance to the real thing, is alcohol. So the amount of alcohol by volume is reduced. This puts the brew into a lower tax bracket, so far as the brewery is concerned. Unfortunately, the extra production steps involved in removing some of the alcohol make it impossible for the breweries to pass on this savings to the public.

Nonalcoholic Beer

Though some consider this a rather pointless exercise, sales of nonalcoholic beer are significant, and many bars carry at least one brand. It finds a home with drivers, or people who simply love a beer with their meal, but, for one reason or another do not want the alcohol. Buckler is popular, as is Kaliber. Other breweries are gradually bringing out their own versions.

A tiny, negligible amount of alcohol is retained in the brew. Drivers who are worried about being tested for alcohol should remember that there is a small amount of alcohol naturally present in the blood anyway, so it's perfectly safe to drink from this point of view.

There is definitely a place on earth reserved for "the drink that isn't a drink"—in other words a drink that satisfies the alcoholic urge, but doesn't impair the faculties or put one at risk from traffic cops. It is unlikely that such a drink will ever be discovered, but in the meantime people can make do with innocuous concoctions such as Campari and Soda, Bitters and Soda, and other variations, including nonalcoholic beer.

Sodas

Colas, ginger ale, tonic or quinine water, 7-Up or Sprite, soda water or seltzer, and their low-calorie sisters, are here to stay. The power of the soft drink manufacturers exceeds even that of the breweries.

Indeed, for subtle marketing reasons, they are a powerful rival to the alcohol industry, despite the fact that they are to an extent intertwined: rum and coke, scotch and soda, 7 and 7, gin and tonic being as popular as they are. Their advertising is massive. So hooked on sodas are Americans—and from earliest childhood in some cases—that many people never even flirt with alcohol.

Soda is to many Americans what *vin ordinaire* is to the French. There is a solid body of consumers to whom not one drop of alcohol will ever be sold, except perhaps at Christmas, or their weddings.

Sharp-eyed bar managers will notice, as they stroll around the town, ever on the lookout for better ways of doing things, that in the sort of smart restaurant bar, or luxury hotel bar, where a Dewars and Soda is 7 dollars (but served in a carpeted, nicely decorated, flower and picture adorned room, along with a couple of dishes of nuts or hors d'oeuvres) soda comes in a little bottle.

Clearly, this is the "proper" way to serve a drink. But soda bottles are expensive space killers. Inevitably, the "soda gun" was invented to get around these problems. Nowadays, in a majority of establishments, every bartender's "station" on the bar, including the service station, has its own soda gun from which colas, ginger ale, and others are squirted.

You press a little button marked L (for lemon) to get 7-Up, G for Ginger Ale, Q for quinine or tonic water, T for Tab, S for soda water or seltzer, and sometimes W for plain water. Sometimes there will be variations on this theme, and when working on a new bar it's one of the things you must be careful to check, or the bartenders may find themselves serving gin and cola, instead of gin and tonic.

The gun is connected to pipes that descend to the cellar, very often in the area of the beer room, where they are connected to three-foot-high containers of syrups of the various flavors. When a container has run out, clearly it weighs less. If you can lift it easily it's probably empty. If you *can't* lift it, just make sure that it really *is* full, and not merely stuck to the floor by accumulated drips of syrup, which when dry have almost the tenacity of Super Glue. (This can happen with beer kegs, too.)

Two pipes are connected to the top of the container, in most cases by what is called a "bayonet connection"—push down, twist, and the connection locks. One line's metal plug will have three apertures, the other two, to be lined up with the appropriate lugs on the container so that you can't mix up the lines. Make sure there's enough light to visually check what you're doing; it can be a frustrating task, as you struggle to achieve that which has been carefully designed to be impossible. The other common kind of connection involves a screw, and this must be regularly cleaned with hot water to remove the accumulated syrup.

Because of the huge amounts of syrupy fluid involved, it's easy for the works to get jammed up. Regular dousing with hot water at the connection points will prevent this. Above all, the containers and their pipes should be easily accessible.

At the bar, when the button is pressed, syrup and plain, fizzy soda water combine to produce the required product. The system never seems to yield the same quality as freshly opened bottle sodas, but it has been accepted by the industry and public alike. Complaints about gun soda being flat, or not sweet enough, or too sweet, are occasional. They are not frequent enough to jeopardize the acceptability of the equipment. The dismal truth is that one of the things that allows the hospitality industry's world to keep turning is the fact that most customers are undemanding and uncomplaining. Imagine what extra hell the business would be if every customer demanded the best, and knew what the best was all about!

Murphy's Law being what it is, these containers will always give out at the least propitious moment, and someone—usually the busboy or manager—will have to go down, disconnect the empty, and connect the new, full container. There is plenty of room for things to go wrong. Nobody likes the job of changing these tanks. They are not user friendly. All the more reason why attention should be paid to making sure that several people know how to change them and get a bit of practice in doing so. They are here to stay.

At the bar, connoisseur drinkers will sometimes look a little pained at the prospect of the soda gun. There's something truly horrific about some ace, hero bartender sticking the whiskey bottle and the gun at the same time into a nasty looking glass jammed to the rim with rapid melting *small* ice cubes, though such an operator may well be the apple of the boss's eye because of his mean, highly profitable drinks, and the speed with which he dispenses them. There's no reason why a small reserve of bottled sodas shouldn't be kept to one side for such customers. They probably won't object to being charged 50 cents extra— serious drinkers are more interested in getting a decent drink than in bargain hunting.

If you carry a selection of bottled waters, they are often more acceptable, especially with scotch, than the soda gun.

Bottled Waters

Anyone old enough to remember the old three martini lunch days knows that the suggestion, in say 1965, that one day people would solemnly be drinking water at 5 dollars a bottle would have been greeted with mirth. A more careful observer might have noted, as some clearly did, that in fact, bottled water existed and thrived in a small but significant market.

Queen Elizabeth used to drink only Malvern Water, a not too effervescent water from England. This was sent ahead of her on her many travels to obviate the risk of upsets from local water. In French restaurants and homes bottled waters like Vitel were normal and common enough. Their place in life was assured by the fact that, until recently, you couldn't always drink the tap water. Either it wasn't pure enough from the germ point of view, or it just didn't taste good. It should be remembered that one of the original reasons for the creation of alcoholic beverages was the unpleasant nature of so much fresh water. Even if it started out drinkable, it became unpleasant after much storage on the backs of camels or at sea.

In some areas, even of rich countries, the water, though harmless, is not good to drink because of its unfortunate taste. It is often recycled, with all the unappetizing prospects that this suggests. (In Sussex, England, a local belief is that the average glass of water has passed four times through human kidneys.)

Fierce marketing, heavy advertising, and the growing obsession with either pursuing good health, or at least wishing to be perceived as being in pursuit of fashionable fitness, all came together to create a whole new market. What lycra-clad, sweater-wrapped, aerobics aficionado would be seen dead without a bottle of Evian, carried at the correct angle, just like the beautiful girl in the ads—

especially after Evian water became the official water of the Gulf War army? Evian is a still water—no bubbles.

Consumer resistance to this charismatic product is minimal. Two bartenders recently had a competition to see how much they could charge for bottled water on a busy Sunday afternoon. The listed price was $3.50. They had hiked it to 5 dollars a bottle at the bar without the faintest raising of a consumer eyebrow before the boss, trying to keep a straight face, told them to behave. The true price ceiling therefore remained a mystery.

Perrier (an effervescent water—usually referred to as "with bubbles") took a bit of a beating after benzine was discovered in a shipment, and the product had to be withdrawn from the market temporarily. You had to read the small print on the label to find out that the bubbles were added after the water had been dredged from its subterranean depths. The breathless revelation in some of its advertising that Perrier water had originally been rain must have impressed many.

Bottled waters are here to stay. (It is rumored that there's a bar in Paris that only sells different kinds of designer water). The ancient Chinese made almost as much fuss about water as modern wine lovers, distinguishing between 40 different styles. This isn't necessarily so ridiculous. The water in New York is excellent, as it is in Madrid. In Paris and London it's rather ho-hum. In some parts of the world it's fit only for washing—you don't dare even to make tea with it, and many kitchens have elaborate extra purifying systems installed.

Bottled waters present yet another threat to valuable refrigerated space, because many customers order them cold, without ice. Others like them with ice and a wedge of lime or lemon. They are a good profit item, and help to create a chic image, if that is part of your objective.

Serious drinkers, on spying the dreaded soda gun, will now often order a Perrier or other carbonated bottled water to accompany their scotch. The bar manager must decide a compromise price for this request. It seems a bit punitive to charge such a customer for two drinks separately, the scotch and the water, but many establishments get away with it.

CHAPTER FIVE

Bar Supplies and Equipment

Perishable Supplies

Certain perishable supplies need to be checked and frequently replaced on a day-to-day basis. These are the nonalcoholic items on the bar that tend to deteriorate fairly quickly even when refrigerated.

Milk, Half-and-Half, Whipped Cream, and Heavy Cream. These are needed for various cocktails, to be drunk alone occasionally in the case of milk, and to accompany coffee or tea at the bar. In practice, so unfashionable are the cocktails that require it (Brandy Alexander, Grasshopper, etc.) that most bars can safely leave the heavy cream in the kitchen. Milk is required for a White Russian, an occasional request, and, especially in winter, whipped cream will be regularly in demand for Irish coffee. And when a delicious looking Irish coffee is taken through the restaurant, usually further orders will swiftly follow, so, if the whipped cream is running low after one serving, wise bartenders will make sure they have a backup handy.

The only practical whipped cream for bar use is that which comes in a pressurized container and is somewhat reminiscent of hair mousse or shaving cream. Perfectionistic bar managers will insist on the real thing. Let us hope they have the staff with the time to whip it. The important thing is that consumers have accepted the product, and in practical terms why should bar managers and their staffs be martyrs to a perfection that is unlikely to be appreciated anyway? There's a case for real whipped cream to be served with desserts, but it's a pointless and thankless stretch at the bar.

Worcestershire Sauce, Tabasco, Horseradish, Salt, Pepper. All these items are needed to build the Bloody Mary cocktail, which is a perennial favorite and an excellent profit item. Its first cousin, the Bullshot, has a small following too. Horseradish is an optional ingredient for the Bloody Mary; some bars use it automatically. In other places it's a "by request" item. Apart from horseradish, which tends to dry up when exposed to fresh air, the other items have a long shelf life when refrigerated—but not an indefinite one.

Salt is used to rim the glasses for Margaritas. Usually a saucer full of salt is prepared so that the glass, swiftly rimmed with a wedge of lime or lemon so that the salt will cling to the moisture, can be dipped into it. This saucer should be changed every day, since the salt soon starts to harden and look rather unappetizing.

Coffee Beans. Three beans go into a glass of Sambucca, representing the Holy Trinity. Many bars don't bother any more, because the Sambucca clientele don't know they're supposed to get beans. But in some places, especially Italian restaurants, failure to provide them may be considered a Federal Offense, especially if their omission robs a host who's a little short on conversation of the opportunity to explain what they're all about.

Cherries. Red maraschino cherries should accompany Manhattans, Sweet Rob Roys, Sours, Collins concoctions, Roy Rogers, and Shirley Temples (kids' cocktails). They are also squashed into the Old Fashioned cocktail. Once displayed for easy access at the bar they start to rot quickly and will usually need to be replaced every day.

Olives. These are for Martinis and vodka Martinis. Somewhere along the line an olive became pluralized and many people now ask for olives, with a heavy accent on the s. A brilliant breakthrough for the Olive Marketing Board! But olives die fast; they need to be replaced daily.

Onions. Little white pearl onions have one function only: to turn Martinis into Gibsons. Thus, they are still an essential item.

Lemons, Limes, Oranges. The lemon peels, wedges, and slices, the lime wedges, and the orange slices must be freshly cut to be appetizing and to do their work. Cutting fruit is dealt with elsewhere. Apart from orange slices, all the other items here will do a better job if they're thoroughly squeezed into the drink by the bartender's immaculately clean fingers, and this includes lemon peels. When serving Martinis with a twist of lemon a nice touch is to squeeze the peel and rub it once round the rim of the chilled glass. Anyone who doubts the wisdom of this should try the following experiment. Take a fresh lemon peel between your finger and thumb. With your other hand strike a match. Squeeze the peel into the flame. You will see a brief (and harmless) firework display as the juice burns in the air. You can flavor a glass this way if you like, especially if you are going to serve neat Grand Marnier.

The French expression for a lemon peel tells the whole story of the joy of citrus fruits' happy marriage with alcoholic drinks: "un zeste de citron."

Mean owners may insist that the fruit be cut thin and lean. Customers will simply respond by asking for "extra lime." Are you going to charge them extra? Using good fresh chunky fruit really enhances drinks. All cut fruit deteriorates quickly once exposed, though, so the cutting of fruit is a daily job on a bar. This is a "show-stopper" of a job, and can take half an hour or more in a big busy bar, so the sooner it's done and the backup containers filled and refrigerated, the better.

Most places don't serve orange slices with Whiskey and other Sours anymore. Also, as the cocktail fell into disuse too many oranges were being cut, only to find a pointless grave in the garbage at the end of the bartender's shift—if they had not been nibbled to death by idle servers hours before.

Juices. Sweetened lemon, orange, grapefruit, tomato, pineapple, and cranberry juices are standard requirements at the bar. Unsweetened lemon and lime juices are optional. Many places like to put a dash of one or the other of these in their Bloody Marys.

It is a good idea to read the labels on the carton, can, or bottle to determine the temperature at which they must be refrigerated. Juices in cartons must be refrigerated even before they're opened. But cranberry and tomato juices can be stored in any cool space until they're opened, at which point they must be stored in the refrigerator.

Bartenders should not be tempted to store cardboard cartons on the ice that is used to make drinks. Not only is this illegal, but at a certain point the carton will become so wet that it will disintegrate and leak, possibly ruining a batch of ice that must then be replaced, and wasting the contents too, which also need to be replaced—more trips for someone at the height of the rush hour. Juices for immediate pouring should be transferred to glass bottle containers.

Years ago many bars conspicuously featured a sturdy Victorian looking juice squeezer. But squeezing enough lemon juice for a day in a busy bar, at a time when all those strange sounding cocktails were still popular, was a real chore.

When a Sour, Collins, or Daiquiri-type drink was requested, the first thing the bartender had to do was put a teaspoonfull of castor sugar (that's the fine fast-melting kind) from a dish suspended underneath the bar into the mixing glass, and then add the other ingredients. You will occasionally see these dishes on old installations, most probably decorated with long-hardened sugar. In order to make sure that the sugar was well and truly dissolved there was a whole lot of shaking going on. It could be very boring on a summer Sunday afternoon when all the ladies sallied forth in search of Daiquiris and Tom Collins.

You will get an occasional request for "extra sweet" drinks when castor sugar would be useful. But ordinary sugar will do as long as you give it a good stir. An alternative is to offer the customer a shot of Grenadine, which is supersweet.

Fortunately, the quality of carton juices improved to the point where it really wasn't much to choose between them and the freshly squeezed variety when mixed with other ingredients. Now the only places that serve freshly squeezed juices are luxury hotels and those family owned neighborhood coffee shops, which used to abound, but which are now rare, thanks to the changes in the real estate situation. Even where "freshly squeezed" orange juice is advertised, it is often mixed with the carton variety. Remember, words like "fresh" have one meaning in the dictionary, but another in law. Fish pulled from the ocean can legally be described as "fresh" five days after their demise, provided they've been frozen.

The grapefruit, orange, lemon, and lime juices that once were squeezed are now generally replaced by bottled sweetened products such as Tropicana, Lemon X, and Real Lime Juice. The public finds them generally very acceptable, and they are certainly a boon for the bartender.

Everyone takes products like Lemon X for granted when making Daiquiris, Sours, and Collins drinks. But they have made life easier. In the not-so-distant days when the juice had to be squeezed you also had to add Frothee—a kind of detergent that put a small head on shaken cocktails. Now the froth-creating agent, sugar, and preservatives are all blended in the same bottle.

A bar manager was recently approached by a vendor who offered freshly squeezed orange juice on a daily delivery basis. The manager thought this would be a nice touch, especially for the Mimosas that were served at the very popular weekend brunch. However, there was no feedback or comment from the regular clientele. The gesture had not registered with them and so was, arguably, wasted.

But the bartenders complained bitterly that washing glasses in which the fresh juice had been used was the devil's own job. The tiny polyps that contain the juice in all citrus fruits were clinging to the glasses quite tenaciously, especially if they'd had a chance to dry, causing extra work. The fresh juice was discontinued.

Pious gestures that really have more to do with managers congratulating themselves on being alert and concerned should always be taken with huge pinches of salt and examined to see if they are really worth making. American corporations can be quite masochistic in their pursuit of change for the sake of change that involves no improvements whatsoever, but merely makes it look as if someone's doing a job. If it ain't broke, don't fix it! And don't invent work.

Grenadine. This red sweet juice is the only begotten product of the multipitted pomegranate fruit. It is used to color and flavor certain drinks, including the Tequila Sunrise and kids' cocktails such as Roy Rogers or Shirley Temple (7-Up or ginger ale, ice, big straw, cherry, dash of grenadine). It does not need to be refrigerated once opened and usually languishes next to the sweet and dry vermouths in the well.

Nutmeg. This powder can be sprinkled on top of Brandy Alexanders, or, sometimes, on Irish coffee, or the several variations on that theme that use other liquors such as Kahlua or Grand Marnier.

Coconut Cream. This is an essential item in the making of a Piña Colada. Once the can is opened, you might as well mix it with the pineapple juice in a batch that can be stored and refrigerated in a juice bottle. It is well to be set up for this drink as, otherwise, it becomes a lengthy process—and inevitably at the busiest time.

Beef Broth or Bouillon. This canned soup is used to make Bullshots: a Bloody Mary with beef juice instead of tomato juice. There's another concoction called a Bloody Bull, which is a mixture of the two. Once opened "promptly refrigerate in a separate container."

Equipment

There are many indispensable items needed on a bar that do not fit neatly into a group—though one tries to list them rationally—and therefore they must be consigned to the world of the miscellaneous.

Ash Trays. A rough guide to the number of ash trays you need to set out on the bar is one to two stools. But a large percentage of people who enjoy sitting at bars also smoke and often chain smoke. So it's always a good idea to have a reserve supply. Ash trays disappear mysteriously, especially when they are decorated with the bar's logo. The old Stork Club's ash trays had a little inscription on the bottom: "Stolen from the Stork Club."

Bar Spoon. This is the 10-inch long spoon used for stirring cocktails, specifically Martinis, Manhattans, and Rob Roys, when they are served "up"— without ice.

Beverage Napkins. Often called "bev-naps" these 4-inch-square napkins are what you place the drink on. They soon get wet and disheveled-looking and need to be replaced if the customer is having more than one drink, so it's a good idea to have a reserve handy. They can be decorative, especially if they carry the bar's logo, and help in the instant clean up process that the bartender does as soon as a customer has left. An alternative is little cork mats called "coasters" that many breweries supply. Either item does the job. Some managers prefer one, some the other, and some use both.

If you serve food or even hors d'oeuvres at the bar then you'll need large paper or linen napkins, according to your house style.

Each bartender's station should have a bar mop, a foot square of absorbent polyester or cotton, normally kept in a little wire cage suspended from the underside of the bar. They are used for cleaning the surface of the bar between customers, though spillage and accidents can often mean they have to be used more than once while the same customer is present. There should also be a towel clipped to the bar for the purpose of drying the bartender's hands.

Some arrangement must be made for the wiping of ash trays. Either a special bar mop or a dampened bev nap can be employed.

Blender. You will certainly need one, and possibly more, electric blenders somewhere on the bar if there is any demand for drinks such as Frozen Daiquiris or Piña Coladas.

Books and Papers. It is useful to have a calendar handy, and an atlas can be fun, too—especially when customers start telling each other about their exotic travels. The current newspaper, a town guide, and a TV guide will all be called for regularly, as will telephone directories. The *Guiness Book of Records* is also an old standby.

Let us not forget the Bible, and the book of cocktail recipes that the bartender will need to look at once in a while when someone asks for an ancient and obscure cocktail for which the useful excuse, "Sorry, I haven't got the ingredients," won't wash.

Whether or not you serve food at the bar, it's always a good idea to have a couple of up-to-date menus and wine lists handy for potential diners to peruse. Some states require a large print menu for people whose sight is impaired.

By the side of the register there should be a supply of bar checks, a place for the used checks to be collected, and perhaps a box for signed checks where you have "house charges." You'll also need slips for all the credit cards you accept. Also in this area you can keep a stapler, or paper clips, and rubber bands. For less than 30 dollars you can buy a forged bill detector that lights up when a forgery is passed through it. An alternative is a special pencil that writes gold on genuine bills, but black on forgeries. These devices should always be used on fifties and hundreds, and there is an occasional epidemic of forged twenties too.

A good supply of disposable pens should be available (the kind you buy by the packet that will cause no grief if they get lost or taken as souvenirs). Customers often ask for pen and paper to make notes. Often the reverse side of a kitchen dupe will be adequate, but if you don't use such documents, then scrap paper should be available. Bartenders should get into the habit of dispensing the disposable pens and refrain from lending out "serious" pens.

People often use bars as temporary offices. This is good for business generally, though people who monopolize the telephone and never buy a drink can be irritating, even if the bar does obtain a small revenue from the telephone company.

Customers often request business cards to remind themselves of where they've been. They are not expensive and form part of the whole "word of mouth" advertising area that is so good for business. If you run out, match books with your logo, name, telephone number, and address will do just as well.

Bottle Openers. At intervals underneath the bar, or mounted elsewhere, you should have fixed bottle openers—the kind where you stick the neck of a beer bottle in and ease off the cap; it falls into a container that might be the garbage can or the sink, and from which caps will have to be removed as they accumulate. Some bartenders get into the habit of catching the cap in their hands and throwing it into the garbage.

You also need portable openers, sometimes known as "church keys." The most popular design has a beer bottle opener at one end and a sharp point for making a hole in a can of juice. The beer suppliers often hand these out free.

Brushes. Each washing up sink should have a set of brushes, preferably electric motor brushes, to facilitate washing glasses. The brushes wear out over time, so a spare set should be held in reserve. The machine also needs servicing once in a while.

Cleaning Equipment. This also includes clean up equipment for those occasional accidents involving breakage and spilling. Somewhere near the bar, just offstage, there should be a dust pan and a mop so that accidents can be cleared up instantly without disrupting service.

For the cleaning of the bar you may need polish, mirror cleaning fluid, and detergent for washing glasses. A reserve supply of detergent should be kept in the cupboard.

Clock. If there's a big clock on the bar, make sure it tells the right time or someone will blame you for a missed appointment. If it's electric, make sure it isn't switched off accidentally. If it's off all night someone will realize it fairly swiftly. Being switched off for an hour or so can cause much frowning. And don't forget the spring and fall time adjustments: "Spring forward, fall back."

Corkscrews. Several of these essential tools should be deployed, at least one at each station, a spare in the drawer, and one that the servers may borrow. They should all have an allotted space to which they are returned after every use. This applies to all bar equipment. A good place for the server's corkscrew is the bartender's back pocket, but, because of all the bending and reaching, many bartenders like to work with their pockets empty. You will often see a little pile of personal effects alongside the cash register.

Cigarettes. Many states now prohibit cigarette machines in bars. The reason is that these machines are considered to be a temptation for underage smokers. Cigarettes can sometimes be sold from behind the bar, and if you have the space there's no reason why you shouldn't sell them. In practice, there's never enough space to offer a full selection. Also, you will be tempted to charge a price that exceeds that in the store, and for some reason cigarette smokers can be incensed at even a small addition to the price they are used to paying. A small cache of cigarettes can be kept for "emergencies." This can be replenished regularly from the not quite empty packs often left at the bar by departing customers. Matches are always in demand by smokers. They are a useful advertising tool, and should be available on each bartender's station.

Cutlery. If you serve food at the bar you'll need a handy supply of knives, forks, and spoons. Occasionally, on busy nights, irate waiters will complain that they are running out of cutlery because the bartenders insist on maintaining such a huge supply. If this is the case, the sin must be confessed and the cutlery handed over.

Feather Duster. A minute's whisk around the bar every day with this formidable tool will keep the bottles sparkling and avoid the tedious task of picking up and wiping each individual bottle. It's best to do this before opening time in order to avoid wisecracks! If you use a duster then you'll only need to remove the bottles for a thorough dusting once a week.

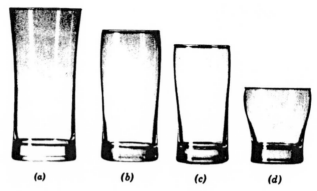

(a)   **(b)**   **(c)**   **(d)**

Figure 5.1 (a) Tumbler glass of 12–16 oz. (b) Highball glass of 10–12 oz. (c) Highball glass of 8–10 oz. (d) Rocks glass of 6–8 oz.

First Aid Kit. This is often mandated by state law, but whether it is or not every bar should have one because there are often small mishaps that need patching up. Some states require protective masks and gloves to be provided to eliminate the risk of catching AIDS when handling casualties.

Aspirin or other pain relievers are useful. Some states forbid dispensing aspirin to customers, but unless paid informers have infiltrated your operation this shouldn't be a problem. The bar has a whole range of remedies for upset stomachs. Bitters and Soda is an old stand-by, and port and brandy, sometimes known as Fox's Blood because the mixture often finds itself in a huntsman's flask, works wonders.

Fruit Cutting Equipment. This consists of a sharp knife and a cutting board. The kitchen will usually have a knife sharpener, which will make life easier.

Glasses. The fewer types of glasses you have the easier life is. More types of glasses means more inventory work, more checking, more space, and, if your regular glass supplier cannot provide all you require, another account to be opened, talked to, and paid. You can work efficiently with six or seven types of glasses.

You'll need a large 12-ounce tumbler for nonalcoholic iced tea or coffee, Pinā Coladas, and so on. (See Figure 5.1a.)

You'll need a "highball" glass of 10 to 12 ounces (Figure 5.1b) that can be used for sodas, Collins drinks, and—since 90 percent of cocktails are now ordered on the rocks—even Daiquiris, Sours, Slings, and Margaritas. Such a mixed drink served in a rocks glass is small and feels wrong.

A slightly smaller highball glass of eight to 10 ounces (Figure 5.1c) comes next, and this can be used, naturally, for "highballs"—a slightly dated term for

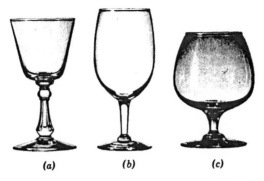

(a)   *(b)*   *(c)*

Figure 5.2 (a) Cocktail glass of 4 oz. (b) All purpose wine glass of 5 oz. (c) Brandy snifter 12 oz.

scotch and soda, gin and tonic, and so on. It can also be your house water glass. When people ask for a "tall glass," as opposed to a rocks glass, this is generally what they mean.

A rocks glass of six to eight ounces comes next. (See Figure 5.1d.) This is for Martinis, Manhattans, scotch on the rocks, and so on.

For Martinis, Manhattans, and Rob Roys served without ice—"up" or "straight up"—you'll need a stemmed four-ounce cocktail glass (Figure 5.2a). Some restaurants, even to this day, still offer a Jumbo Martini in a much larger glass, but they are a dwindling band.

All wine, sherry, and port can be served in the popular stemmed five-ounce wine glass. (See Figure 5.2b.)

For brandy and cognac you can use balloon shaped glasses of anywhere from a tiny four-ounce size to a highly expensive and fragile twelve-ounce glass that will "sing" when its rim is rubbed by a moistened finger. This glass will double very adequately for liqueurs. (See Figure 5.2c.) Finally there are the beer glasses. Bottled beer is served in the smaller highball glass, unless otherwise requested. If you serve British draft beers you'll probably have a supply of pebbled tankards with handles, of pint or half-pint size. Other brands such as Guinness offer their own special-shaped glasses. These often get stolen with such relentless efficiency that you must have a suitable alternative in mind to cover the period between running out of them and the brewery sending you a new batch.

The amount of beer dispensed is entirely at the bar owner's whim. But most people have a pretty good expectation of what they should get for their money, so no bar owner is likely to get rich by selling short beer.

Some bartenders serve pints when the customer doesn't specify size, weathering the complaints when it becomes clear that a smaller, half-pint version had been in mind. Pints and half pints are entirely a British conceit that can often confuse American beer drinkers. An American pint is smaller than an Imperial pint. The first time you ask customers if they'd prefer a pint or a half pint and they plaintively ask, "Which is smaller?" you may secretly smile, but after a while you'll get used to it.

Conspicuously absent from this discussion of indispensable glasses are "copitas" for sherry, liqueur stem glasses, sour glasses, and the traditional glasses in which claret, Burgundy, Rhine, and Moselle wines are served.

Clearly if your bar restaurant is called "Granada," "Andalusian Patio," "Stein Way," or "British Bulldog" you may wish to pursue your theme by featuring the appropriate glasses, but nowadays standardization is the name of the game. It makes life easier. It comforts people.

It should be noted that "serious" glassware has become extraordinarily expensive (check it out next time you go shopping). It is thus impractical for all but the most expensive restaurants and bars.

It is important to lay down house rules as to which drinks go in which glasses. In most cases this is self-evident, but where it isn't the bar manager must specify. This is partly for neatness and standardization, but also for portion control. With young and inexperienced bartenders who still have a trick or two to learn, it's a good idea to make sure they know that when a glass of 20-year-old port is poured, it is not the same as a glass of red house wine. And you don't want your hefty Bloody Marys being served in stingy rocks glasses.

Gloves. Rubber gloves are rarely used by bartenders when washing glasses because they are fussy and look funny. This is a shame because they can protect hands that can be seriously damaged by neglect. They should at least be offered as an option. Many a bartender has had to stay home because of hand problems, which can be both painful and unsightly, and offend customers.

The ordinary rubber washing up or surgical gloves are not suitable for this task. They take too much time to put on and are so thin that they do not protect against the very hot water you should be using. The best-known product at this time is "Bluettes"—less than 5 dollars a pair—a little more "heavy duty" and "easy on-off" as all the best catalogues put it.

Ice Buckets and Scoops. Ice buckets, together with their stands (which are not always used), are usually stored at the bar. The plastic kind, though less decorative than the shiny steel ones, are more practical because they can be quickly washed. The metal variety soon start looking worse for wear.

Ice scoops are for putting ice into glasses. You could use your hands, but by the end of the day they'll be sore. Besides, using the scoop looks better. They must be removed from the ice sink before the ice is put in, otherwise you won't see them again until either the ice melts or is used. Amateurs often scoop the ice directly into the glass. If a glass breaks, then *all* the ice has to be removed or melted to make sure there are no glass splinters lurking—a great waste of time and ice.

Ketchup and Other Condiments. Where food is served at the bar, each station should have ketchup, mustard, salt and pepper, Worcestershire Sauce, vinegar, steak sauce, and so on. The Bloody Mary set of ingredients can be raided too, and frequently are, mainly for the Tabasco sauce.

Mixing Glass. This is the 12-ounce glass in which cocktails and mixed drinks are prepared. Its companion is the 14-ounce metal shaker.

A common and very useful tool now available is the smaller 10 to 12-ounce metal shaker that can be used to shake a cocktail right in the very glass in which it is to be served. This is a significant time saver at the service end of the bar, especially at Bloody Mary time.

Muddler. Another name for this quaint instrument is "pestle," which chemistry buffs will recognize as the instrument that accompanies a mortar in a laboratory. It's a 6-inch long tool shaped like a baseball bat and its purpose is to "muddle," or crush, cherries, slices of orange and lemon, sugar, and several drops of Angosturas in the bottom of a rocks glass as the basis of the Old-Fashioned cocktail, which you may be asked for once a month or so by some old timer. If you haven't got a muddler, use the bar spoon, or any spoon.

Pourers. These are the little spouts, sometimes metal tubes stuck in a cork or plastic stopper, and sometimes one piece of plastic. They help insure consistent measure by giving the bartender better control over how much liquor is being dispensed. When you open a liquor bottle you should immediately replace the cork or cap with a pourer. If you were to pour straight from the opened bottle, you would almost invariably find yourself pouring too much, and if the bar is to make a profit there must be standard portions. With very little practice a bartender can pour an ounce-and-a-half (or whatever your bar rules stipulate) every time, with uncanny precision. The metal spout and cork pourers soon rust and deteriorate, and need to be replaced. Nevertheless, most bartenders prefer them to the washable plastic kind—perhaps they pour better.

Most bars today have "free pouring," that is to say the bartender pours the liquor straight into the glass without measuring it in an old-fashioned jigger or shot glass. You may find one or two of those lurking somewhere on an old bar.

This is still carried out in some states, and in foreign countries such as England where the law doesn't allow free pouring. In such places a gin and tonic is served in two glasses: the tall glass containing the tonic water and a wedge of lime, and a miserably tiny shot glass on the side containing the gin. The server or bartender ceremoniously tips the liquor into the soda. This baroque ritual is supposed to demonstrate to customers that they are getting a correct measure. But this is a rather redundant gesture when you consider that, when it comes to mixed drinks, unless customers watch the bartender preparing them, they are totally at the mercy of the bartender's generosity, or otherwise. Besides, supposing the liquor is watered down anyway? The whole thing works on trust. This breaks down once in a while, but any establishment that wishes to continue in business will do well to serve fair and consistent portions.

Stoppers. After a bottle of wine or champagne is opened, the remaining wine must be resealed as well as is possible. In the case of ordinary still wine, just putting the cork back is as good a device as any because the chances are the whole bottle will be poured in the course of a shift. Ideally, however, a special kind of cork should be used. This is inserted into the neck of the bottle with a little gadget, and the whole effect is to remove air from the bottle.

This is a useful device for those bars that offer a selection of wines and ports, some of which may be quite expensive and not sell very quickly. They are obtainable at most serious wine or liquor stores.

The champagne stopper is simply a regular cork fitted with metal wings that fit under the lips of the bottle neck. This keeps the cork in place despite the pressure from the bubbles. Using these, an opened bottle of champagne can be used for up to two days (more in the case of some brands) and still be fizzy enough to qualify as "fresh."

Strainers. There are two types: a smaller one for use when pouring from the mixing glass, and a larger one that has a coil spring attached, for use when pouring from the metal shaker. You use them when serving drinks "up," without ice. Having shaken or stirred the mixture in the mixing glass or metal shaker, you put the strainer over the top before pouring the drink into the glass and this holds back the ice.

Standpipes. These are metal or plastic pipes 10 inches or less in length and about one-half inch wide that stand in the drain hole of the sink. They allow a flow from the full sink when the faucet is allowed to drip, particularly in the rinse sink. This constant flow insures the cleanliness of the water.

On quiet afternoons the drip may be intrusive, and frowning customers may ask if something's dripping. You can either insist that it continues to drip for hygienic reasons, or turn it off, depending on the status of the customer!

Stirrers. These can be decorative cocktail stirrers or plain plastic. Most drinks require one, so a large supply will be needed.

Straws. The smaller variety, "sipstix," can double as stirrers. The larger kind are needed for sodas and tall drinks.

Tongs. Some bar managers insist that fruit and olives should be put in drinks with tongs, not bare fingers. Few customers object to the bartender's fingers because they are supposed to be well-scrubbed. If you think about it, all food in the kitchen is handled at some point in its preparation—though where food, especially salads, is prepared in front of the customer tongs should always be used. These things are a matter of convention.

All the above items are listed on a separate page for your convenience and can be used as a routine checklist when setting up the bar at the beginning of the day. You will almost certainly wish to add and delete one or two items in accordance with the particular nature of your bar operation.

Checklist of Perishables

Milk, half-and-half, heavy cream. Worcestershire Sauce, horseradish, Tabasco Sauce, salt, pepper, ketchup, steak sauce, mustard, vinegar. Cherries, olives, onions, lemons, limes, oranges. Beef bouillon. Juices: orange, grapefruit, cranberry, pineapple, tomato, Lemon X or equivalent. Coconut cream, nutmeg, sugar, castor sugar, coffee beans.

Checklist of Equipment

Glasses, mixing equipment, blender, corkscrews, bottle openers, sharp knife and cutting board for fruit, stirrers, small straws ("sipstix") and large, paper, pens, pourers, checks, credit card slips, stapler, forged bill detector, rubber bands, licenses displayed, menus and wine lists, reference book of cocktail recipes, telephone directory, calendar, dictionaries, atlas, *Guiness Book of Records*, TV guide, entertainment guide, daily paper, town map, kitchen dupes, cutlery (knives, steak knives, forks, teaspoons, soup spoons), ash trays, cigarettes, matches, business cards, cleaning materials (polish, dusters, mirror cleaner, detergent, mop, broom, dustpan), first aid kit (including aspirin or alternative pain reliever), local health and hygiene requirements, muddler, watch, crazy glue, feather duster, ice, ice scoops, ice buckets, tongs, electric brushes, rubber gloves, standpipes.

CHAPTER SIX

The Bar Manager's Guide to Opening

Most bars run more or less the same way. If you've worked in one place, you can work anywhere.

Naturally each place will have a certain stamp of individuality dictated by owner's and manager's whims, the tastes of the regular clientele, and local brand loyalties. Another variable is the degree of paranoia that owners bring to bear in the form of insistence on doing things that add nothing to the efficiency of the operation, but which satisfy some deep insecurity—such as a feeling that their authority is challenged.

Then there is the question of who does what. Responsibilities vary from place to place. In one bar the bartenders will have keys and replenish the bar as required, unsupervised. In another only one person will have keys to the liquor room, will require seeing an empty bottle before issuing a full one, and will be prepared to make a fuss if the bottle has been broken. Here the busboy loads the bar with ice and the porter brings up the bottled beer (sometimes tipped by the bar staff for this service, and sometimes not, according to precedent and custom); there the bartender has to do it himself, and so on.

Routine Tasks

Words with which no bar manager should put up are ones all too commonly heard: "It's not my job." If you hear that phrase once you can be sure of one thing: you may have a crew, you may have a staff, but you do not have a *team*.

However, it is the bar manager's job to allocate tasks, and there must be no gray areas. If Suzie volunteers to go to the cellar to tap a keg of beer because she knows the bartender is a bit under the weather, that's fine. But the task remains the responsibility of the bartender and one must be careful of creating precedents that one day rebound, inevitably at the worst possible moment.

It is a good idea to have a written list of routine duties that must be carried out every day, and this applies to all employees. It may sound persnickety, but it can be most helpful on those foggy Monday mornings when the brain just won't get into gear. You can coast along on automatic.

On arrival at work a bar manager should check those items that, if not in good order, are going to take time to sort out. The main potential trouble spots in this area are electricity, water supply, and refrigeration.

The first member of the bar staff to arrive in the morning should make sure all refrigeration and ice-making equipment is working so that if it isn't someone can get on the case immediately. A plumber or electrician may have to be brought in. With a deadline for opening time, it can be very frustrating to ring the 24-hour plumber or electrician and get an answering machine.

Ice may have to be ordered from an ice company, which may or may not be able to comply promptly. If the bar manager and bartenders are thoroughly familiar with the ice machines, as they should be, no time will be wasted on calling expensive electricians or plumbers to replace an accidentally disconnected plug. Most servicemen charge by the hour, regardless of whether they replace a plug or strip equipment to the bone.

Financial Transactions

In most establishments money is counted and the book work done in the early morning before opening for business. Because this ritual is so well known to criminals it is always a good idea to make sure that you are safe behind locked doors while you count the cash.

On arriving at work the bar manager will normally find that the closing cashier or bartender from the previous evening has put the money from the registers either in the safe or an arranged hiding place that, for security reasons, may be routinely changed. The opening manager combines the cash, previous day's checks, credit card slips, receipts, and invoices, and goes to work.

From the cash must be subtracted the "bank" or "float": the amount of money put in the registers at the start of business to make change for the customers. It is usually a standard amount—say 300 dollars in mixed bills and change. The remaining cash is what was taken in.

Then the total amount taken in by way of credit card and house charges must be added to the cash figure. This amount should appear on the register tape, but naturally it will not be visible in the form of cash.

If your business is only marginally successful you may have a day-to-day cash flow problem, that is, not enough money to pay for essential deliveries. Of course, if you've arranged credit facilities with a purveyor, you can probably pay on a weekly basis, but it's amazing how many apparently well-established companies want to be paid cash-on-the-nail. So you're always hoping that the bulk of your business will be cash. However, with new computer systems, credit card transactions can be paid into your account almost instantaneously. House charges are usually settled monthly. There will inevitably be a small number of unpaid bills in this area, but every business has to allow for "bad debts."

Sometimes the closing cashier or bartender will "ring out" the register, that is, ring the final totals of cash or charges taken in—usually broken down into food, liquor, and tax, and totaled on the "cash" key. If not, or if after a busy night it is forgotten, the bar manager can ring out in the morning.

Some big establishments, especially hotel chains, now have elaborate computerized registers on which every imaginable item has a key of its own, and the cash drawer can only be opened when a transaction has been correctly rung up. These machines are popular because they automatically take inventory as the business rolls along.

Nevertheless, they are almost universally hated by their operators. For no explicable reason the drawer will fail to open, or a nonsensical transaction will be recorded. While the customers go thirsty and wonder whether or not to take their business elsewhere, the manager who knows how to operate the machine will have to be found. With many heavy sighs, but perhaps enjoying his moment of glory, and unable to resist a few patronizing remarks at the expense of the helpless, hand-wringing bartender, things will be laboriously put right and the show will go on.

More employee hours and sales opportunities are lost by lazy managers failing to take the time to fully instruct their staff in the correct operation of computerized equipment than this world dreams of. Yet the basic fact is that until its operators are absolutely conversant with it, expensive computer equipment is likely to be a millstone around the neck. The investment of 10 minutes of uninterrupted instruction time, and the provision of written instructions for quick and easy reference, will pay enormous dividends.

Sales taxes vary from state to state. It is important to know when you should add it to a check, and when not. In New York, for instance, the stated price of a drink at the bar must include tax. If a customer orders a sandwich at the bar, then the whole amount, including the drinks, must be taxed. If people sit at a table but have only drinks, they pay tax.

The credit card slips need to be checked, especially if you have a computer system by which the transaction can instantly be transmitted to the credit card company for immediate payment into your account. Have they been processed, or are there some that need to be attended to? House charges need to be identified and recorded—those scrawled signatures may have defeated the new cashier or bartender. There will often be personal and traveler's checks to be counted and deposited along with the cash. Then the bank, or banks, to make change for the day's business, must be set up. In most registers the drawers are removable. You can take them right to your desk or table, load them with cash, and reinsert them.

The system for issuing banks varies according to the whim and pattern of business of the bar. Some managers put the money in the drawer and require the bartender to count it. Others do *not* require the bartender to count it. Obviously, if this results in a series of errors for odd sums of money that do not immediately and clearly represent a transaction or adjustment, then the system needs to be reviewed. Odd amounts are the hardest to account for; a neat error of, say 100 dollars, is usually explained after everyone has taken time to think.

A busy bar restaurant with 100 seats and 15 bar stools would usually put 300 dollars in change in the center bar register and the same amount at the service end of the bar, or in the cashier's register, where the money from the restaurant floor is handled.

Some owners or managers keep a huge wad of money in their back pocket for paying vendors as they make their deliveries—a constant process throughout every day. Others pay religiously by check, though this can be a nuisance for the small businessperson such as the neighborhood window cleaner.

Others pay their bills from the register, so, on the day that the main meat delivery is expected, it must contain enough money to pay the butcher and still have enough money to make change at the bar. Where this system applies, the bartender must make sure to get an invoice or receipt for all transactions. One excellent way of controlling odd pay outs from the register is to keep a stenographer's pad alongside it and jot down the details of every transaction.

Both personal and traveler's checks can be signed over as part of the payment to vendors and purveyors, thus saving you the trouble of depositing them. Sometimes the vendors grumble; sometimes they're glad to be paid promptly even if there is a slight delay involved. If you endorse and pass on a personal check that bounces you may incur double charges at the bank, so caution is in order.

In many states liquor may not be paid for COD; it must be paid for by check in accordance with the liquor laws. If a check to a liquor company bounces, the supplier will risk losing its own operating license if it does not report the matter to the local Liquor Authority, who will then investigate. Until the matter is resolved liquor deliveries *must* be paid COD—a curious twist. Much of this legislation seems to have been invented with no greater purpose than to keep us all on our toes. It varies from state to state and bar managers must be aware of its quirks.

It is vital to have enough change available. The problem, often, is that if the business is running on a shoestring, or business is down, or hungry partners are demanding cash regularly, there just isn't a lot of liquid cash available. It can be dispiriting and time-wasting to have to dispatch an employee on a change safari around the neighborhood.

When possible there should be a reserve of cash of all bill denominations and coins, in addition to the money put in the registers as the bank. Singles, tens, and fives are the critical amounts because the single most common currency offered in a bar these days is a 20-dollar bill. If a series of customers each has only one drink and pays with a twenty, the depredations on your change supply will soon be apparent!

If you have a cigarette machine, a juke box, a public telephone, and parking meters on the sidewalk, then there will be a constant demand for quarters. The bank should allow for this.

The clear, quiet morning light will often reveal errors made in haste on the previous day. It may reveal forged bills too! These can be detected quite easily at the bar by one of two devices already mentioned.

The unique quality of the paper used for currency is the basic defense against the forger. Bars are favorite places in which to pass forged bills, especially at busy times. It is not suggested that every 20-dollar bill should be examined, unless word goes out that a load of forgeries has just been marketed. But with fifties and hundreds it is an excellent idea.

There is no need to panic if a credit card slip is unsigned. Just write on it "signature on file." If an American Express card has been used on a Master Card slip, it won't matter as long as the information is clearly displayed. The first four digits of a credit card number identify its type, the remainder identify the account.

The "hard copies"—the stiffer of the two credit card copy slips that the establishment retains—should be collected and put in the preaddressed envelopes provided by the various credit card companies. If the copy is missing, then send the flimsy version, having made a note of the details of the transaction.

Many owners who have no training in the restaurant business don't know these details and will panic at the thought of losing even small amounts of money, as though it threatens their whole being. A good bar manager can help to maintain perspective in such situations.

If, as happens once in a while, the card has been put in the machine upside down and no imprint has been made, then, unless the person signing it is known to you, you've lost the transaction. Should the careless bartender or server who made this mistake pay for it? Most often the answer is no. Failure to collect 50 dollars does not mean the bar has "lost" 50 dollars, though rigorous graduates of Economics 101 may cite the principle of "opportunity loss." In some cases on the bar, the sale of one drink pays for the whole bottle, in which a further 30 drinks await sale. The manager's decision in such cases will depend on house policy, or the general performance of the employee.

If the incident represents an unusual lapse on the part of someone who generally does a good job, then let it ride. If it's yet another oversight in the increasingly depressing career of someone you regret having hired in the first place, then insisting that the amount be paid will either bring that person into line or encourage resignation. Such incidents also offer opportunities for the display of managerial largesse and magnanimity, which may improve staff morale. Let us hope that such gestures do not fall on stony ground.

Many owners and managers resent the commission that the credit card companies charge for their facility. Some even offer reductions for cash payment. But in general the credit card system pays off. Like it or not, you will serve several customers a day who would not be in your bar if they couldn't pay with plastic.

There was a point at which criminals were ransacking garbage to locate the carbon copies from credit cards, then using the number to order merchandise to be shipped to them. Since then a slightly absurd convention at the bar insists that the carbons from the credit card slip be torn up before the very eyes of the customer.

In a busy place open for lunch and dinner there clearly must be a change of shift at some point. This inevitably happens at a busy time, usually at 6 or 7 in the evening. There is no reason why the outgoing bartender shouldn't simply ring up the totals so that management has an idea of how much day business they've done; then simply carry on working from the register.

Some bartenders may wish to insist on counting the money they've earned, even at this most inconvenient time, causing disruption of service throughout the establishment.

Brilliant! If the thirsty, impatient customers spy another bar across the street where they think their chances of getting served faster are better, they may take their business there. Philosophical bar managers and their staffs may sometimes wonder what all the urgency is about, but it's a case of "their's is not to reason why." Service is the name of the game. This is the age of instant gratification or forget it.

One method that allows smooth transition, and indulges paranoia too, is to have the relieving bartender come in a few minutes early and count a separate bank in its own register drawer (you can get spares), which simply replaces the outgoing bartender's drawer. You take out the "used" drawer and replace it with the new one. It is an excellent idea for the evening staff to come in a little earlier anyway, in case they need to bring up more supplies or set up for a special party. A good way to make this an attractive proposition is to allow staff a wide choice of food if they eat before going on duty.

Why, restaurant tyros may wonder, must the "changing of the guard" take place at a busy time? The answer brings you into the area of the hard reality of the bar business.

Day bartenders will make a certain amount of money in tips during the lunch period. There may well be a trickle of business through the afternoon. But unless they are allowed a couple of hours of the early evening cocktail hour trade, they will simply not make enough money to make the job worthwhile. The nettle has to be grasped, but with streamlining, practice, and simplification, it need not be too traumatic.

Once the money has been resolved, the surplus after allowing for the day's change requirements should be deposited in the bank, together with any checks. The checks and the relevant register tapes should be bundled together and stored somewhere in case there are future queries.

Invoices should be put in the relevant folder—butcher, baker, candlestick maker—and the credit card envelopes mailed, except in those cases where the company actually sends someone to collect them.

The bank's deposit receipt should be filed in its own folder, and an entry made in the ledger that refers to that account. This amount is crucial information to neurotic owners, though the success or failure of a business cannot be deduced from daily receipts. A weekly and monthly review will give a good indication of just where the business is going.

Neither managers nor owners should panic just because they have a slow day for which there is no apparent reason, just as they should not rejoice at a bumper weekend. Nothing smaller than a monthly picture really counts, and even then there may be a need for calm nerves if July and August are summer doldrums.

Also, if two years in a row a certain month yields excellent business, but in the third year proves to be rather slow, then an investigation is required. A regular convention or trade show changed its venue? The new bar in the neighborhood has bartenders who look like Mel Gibson or Melanie Griffith, or is beating you on price and service? Can anything be done? A little philosophical detachment is handy here. There won't always be an explanation.

Restaurateurs are notorious for their short attention spans, and an inability to see "the bigger picture." An attentive bar manager soon gets a feel for the pattern of business and can soothe frayed nerves.

Scheduling

Diligently kept records of day-to-day business have a further use: they enable you to plan ahead and regulate your staff schedule. If, for instance, Sunday nights are a bit slow six weeks in succession at a time of year when there is no specific reason for it, then you might put on only one bartender instead of two for that shift. The bartender working alone may have to work a little harder, but will make more tips. The house will save a salary. With luck the bartender who loses the shift will pick up another.

Greedy bartenders will sometimes volunteer to work shifts alone in order to avoid sharing the tips. Greedy owners may sometimes think this is a good idea, as it reduces the payroll. But a sensible bar manager must assess very carefully the implications. If the solo bartender is too "stretched," then service, particularly to the restaurant tables, may suffer to a degree that is unacceptable to a serious and established business. Furthermore, work quality may degenerate— lipstick smeared glasses, incorrectly prepared cocktails, and so on. Again, a bar manager must make firm decisions in this area. Saving a bartender's half shift pay may not justify loss of customer goodwill.

The morning is the time to review any schedule changes and post them on the notice board. Remember, any task requiring thought and some time spent in discussion or consideration should be done before the doors open for business, because after that the customer is king. If something has to be attended to during business hours, then it's best to get a relief person to cover the tasks you attend to during opening hours, find a quiet corner, and give the matter your full attention.

A feature of ailing, and ill-managed restaurants and bars is an inordinate number of meetings at which little or nothing is discussed or decided! No doubt the same observation might be made for other businesses, too.

Inventory

The other major task to be confronted is inventory. Bar inventory is simplicity itself once your bar "par" stock has been established.

"Par" is the number of bottles you have on the bar when starting from scratch. For instance, you might say that your bar par for vodka was 10 bottles.

Three might be open at any time, the others either displayed or in the cupboard, whatever. The important figure is 10 bottles.

You count the empties—or maybe last night's closing bartender, or this morning's opener has made up the "Liquor List." Four bottles poured? Then four bottles are issued to replace them. The same system applies to all spirits and wines, and even to beer if you wish. But beer is best reviewed separately, perhaps once a week. Otherwise you'll find yourself with half cases. And there's no way of assessing the contents of a keg of beer (at least not for accounting purposes) except at the two ends of its career: when it's full, and when it's empty.

Of course, inventory isn't quite this simple because your par stock will be revised from time to time. One vodka will be discontinued because it isn't selling, or two new malt scotches will be featured, so there will be changes. At a stage when you are experimenting with various wines great care must be taken. Above all you must be decisive about whether you want to reorder. When things go awry you'll find yourself with 20 wines on your computer, or in the ledger, but not much of an idea how much you actually have in house.

Whether you like it or not, bottles get broken or go astray for other reasons, and there is no point in having an inquest every time this happens. Therefore, up-to-date though your bookkeeping may be, it's essential to relate the paper to the reality of your stock regularly. The fact that you show two cases of the house vodka on your computer or in your ledger will avail you nought if, due to error or oversight, you are actually down to your last three bottles with a busy weekend coming up.

Your bartenders should feel free to nudge you, too, and you should dignify their interest with results. "That new Cabernet is selling like hotcakes; I've only got two bottles left" is a cue to reorder, unless there's a reason not to. Awareness and input from all employees can save a lot of stress.

From time to time—sadly, usually to establish whether or not someone is stealing money—you will need to take a total inventory, even down to a fifth of a bottle (or even a tenth in cases of extreme concern!); this in order to compare that which has been dispensed with the money that has apparently been taken in according to the register tape and checks.

It is simple. If your cash intake indicates that you should have sold 20 bottles of various spirits, but a detailed inventory reveals that 30 bottles have been dispensed, then something's wrong.

There are various possibilities, not all necessarily sinister. You may be able to straighten out good employees who are perhaps a little inexperienced or have gotten the wrong end of the stick somehow. Maybe they are pouring outrageous amounts of liquor in good faith, thinking they're doing the right thing.

If you allow bartenders to give customers drinks on the house at their discretion you automatically open up a gray area. Experienced bar managers can sniff a bartender a mile away who's "giving the house away" to increase tips, but it could be that an inexperienced bartender is actually being overgenerous from naivete or even goodwill. Also, your inventory keeping may be at fault.

But if none of the above proves to be the case then something's got to give. Some owners insist that bartenders keep a list of the drinks they give out "on the house" and to staff where permitted. But with experience you somehow just *know* what's going on.

An old joke in the business concerns the owner who admitted to a friend that he knew his bartender was stealing 50 dollars a day from him. "That's absurd," the friend said. "You should fire him right away."

"Not at all," the owner said. "I feel safe with this guy. At least I know what he's doing!"

A bar uses many items besides beer, wine, and spirits, and at least once a week your bartenders should check the supply of straws, beef bouillon, coconut cream, glasses, bev-naps, and so on. The time to be on guard is when you come back to work after a weekend or two days off, and see that these days have been busy.

Your part-time relief manager is probably not as diligent as you are, good worker though he or she may be. After vacation, too, half an hour spent just looking at your supplies will be well spent. If the books or the computer shows you have a good supply of an item, it doesn't always mean you really have it, and regular physical checking is essential. Goods get stolen. And if you do not get into the habit of checking every delivery as it arrives, sooner or later you will be short-changed.

Salespeople will often call you seeking orders. Though they can be irritating when you're busy, they often serve a useful purpose by reminding you to check some item, or to order something you've overlooked. Salespeople are just workers too. Life's a lot easier if you cultivate good relations with them— without being a patsy for every new product in town, of course.

Once the opening deadline has been passed and everything is rolling, the pace is less demanding. Many establishments maintain a "Day Book" in which managers, and others, write their observations throughout the working day. Some of these may require managerial action: a repair of equipment, an order for some much requested item, and so on. The other important book is the one in which you write all the telephone numbers relevant to the job. There should be one master, which you guard and keep up-to-date. But there's no reason why you shouldn't have a copy free floating, with its own little niche somewhere on the bar.

CHAPTER SEVEN

Who Are the Customers and What do They Want?

Bar Customers

The majority of bar customers are middle-aged men. But they are only a majority, say 40 percent. All other age groups of legal age and both sexes are well represented.

Some bars maintain a cheap and cheerful aspect, appealing to working men, and often offer good value—especially the old-fashioned kind that provides inexpensive hot food at 5 P.M. Sometimes such a bar will resemble a Hogarthian gallery as overweight men in working clothes suddenly descend en masse, drinking Niagaran torrents of Budweiser from the bottle and cursing the latest media-elected villain. Such customers can be intimidating. They are usually noisy, but harmless, consuming vastly and tipping generously. (Methods of dealing with unwanted customers are dealt with elsewhere.)

A large proportion of people who go to bars regularly are single, and in this respect the industry undoubtedly offers a useful service to the community. In happier neighborhoods bar-restaurants are often part of the social fabric. It cannot be denied that many "singles bars" have an unfortunate reputation that is to an extent deserved. At worst one envisages lonely young women sitting at the bar smoking morosely and hoping that Mr. Perfect will walk in any minute and say "Hi," only to be disappointed when the door opens and a group of men walk in, all slightly drunk, giggling inanely and likely to insult staff and customers alike—particularly if the bartender decides not to serve them. At best singles bars will attract people of similar background who perhaps work in related areas. They'll go to the local church, visit each other's houses, and put together softball teams. The bar will be their informal headquarters, and the staff will be "part of the crowd."

Other bars are aimed at the "ladies who lunch," offering designer glasses, chic decor, and, on the dining tables, flowers and pink linen.

There are "kids' bars": the kind that serve no food whatsoever, have no tables (except perhaps pool tables), only a small number of stools, and are dominated by a huge television screen, where anyone over 30 would feel distinctly out of place. Some establishments even have velvet ropes and door attendants to control the line of customers waiting to get in!

Often the local fire chief will send an officer to such establishments to confirm that the "maximum occupancy" figure has not been exceeded. This is the largest number of people who can be safely accommodated on a commercial premises and evacuated in case of an emergency—of which the most obvious and common one is fire. The Coconut Grove nightclub fire in Boston many years ago, in which scores of customers were killed, is a staple of recyclable tabloid newspaper stories, and is only one of many such incidents in the United States within living memory. If the place is too crowded the Fire Department has the authority to close it immediately. Usually business can be resumed the next day, though the owner will be lucky to escape a fine.

Such a closure is often flaunted—a badge of pride! "Kids'" places do bumper business as long as the heat of publicity is on. "Word of mouth" buzz and regular press blurbs referring to celebrity visits can have a dynamic effect on business. But they tend to have a high sudden death rate as—often for no reason that anyone can fathom—the crowd switches its allegiance to some other bar.

Why do ordinary, nice people sometimes turn into monsters and idiots when they enter a bar? Bar staff may sometimes be tempted to wonder why some usually nice people so often turn into petulant children or even temporary imbeciles when they enter their premises asking for the ludicrous in self-righteous tones, and expecting immediate gratification.

The answer is that, as in so many service industries, the restaurateur or bar owner has positively encouraged customers to be outrageous. "We'll give you love and groveling servitude as well as excellent food," is often the absurd message conveyed in advertising. No wonder an eccentric and demanding response is evoked in a few.

Generally bar customers are well-versed in the rituals and standard kind of goods and services offered. They know what to ask for and what they're supposed to get for the money. It isn't a good idea to depart from the norm too readily—and then only for good reasons that will benefit both the customer and the house.

An experienced bar-restaurant employee can have great fun predicting the requirements of customers by their looks. The Sloe Gin Fizz and the Remy Martin and Coke will rarely be intended for the tall, blonde man in the Brooks Brothers suit and his pony-tailed date. The single most easy order to anticipate is the Martini straight up. Bloody Marys are pretty predictable, too. Old hands will look along a bar and see, not only the guy in the gray suit, the guy with the pony tail, and the gal in the white blouse, but also the Tanqueray Martini up, extra olives, the Tequila Sunrise, and the white wine on the rocks.

Tips, too, can be forecast with amazing accuracy. Though some bartenders will never accept it, the truth is that in most bars and restaurants the daily tips average out to an almost uncannily regular amount. It would be unnatural not to bestow a slightly broader smile on the big tipper than the meanie, but snarls and curses at the sight of an inadequate tip are not in order. For every "stiff" there's a generous tipper. There is no law that says any customer has to tip at all. And the origin of the word "tip" should be borne in mind, too: "To Insure Promptness." Sensible bartenders learn to take the rough with the smooth because they know it all averages out anyway. One bartender put up a sign on occasion reading, "Customers are requested to tip before ordering in order to insure prompt service." It was a joke, of course.

Abstainers

It is instructive to get a picture of just who does *not* drink alcohol. Many teetotalers flaunt their views rather self-righteously. But is abstention necessarily such a proud virtue? It's as easy for the ungregarious who have no taste for alcohol to go without alcohol as it is for the undersexed to remain virgins.

Some are forbidden to drink by their religion. Others hate the taste of alcohol. Many of these people are eventually seduced into the alcohol habit by cleverly constructed cocktails, usually of the sweet variety. Who would ever suspect that if you drink enough Piña Coladas you'll get as drunk as though you'd been drinking "Boiler Makers" (shots of neat whiskey chased down by beer)? Some teetotalers are exalcoholics who simply dare not risk lapsing.

Others object intellectually to the principle of imbibing anything that might interfere with their normal thought processes. People from broken homes where a major factor in childhood unhappiness was alcohol abuse will often forswear it forever—though a proportion of such unfortunate people will inevitably continue the pattern.

There may be a genetic disposition that, when complimented by life's circumstances and temptations, will produce an alcoholic. Children of alcoholics are often extremely careful about their own intake, for obvious reasons.

The Bar Menu

Increasingly, food is made available at bars. Sometimes a whole menu is served. In some establishments, because serving "the works" gets too complicated, a limited bar menu is offered, and this will usually consist of appetizers and variations on the hamburger theme. This means that your bar staff must also learn the server's skills. For instance, if a customer orders a hamburger, there are two urgent questions to be resolved. What is the required "temperature" of the hamburger? Do they want it cooked rare, medium rare, medium, or well?

The second question, usually, is, do they want the "deluxe" version, which, at a small extra charge, brings in fries, lettuce, and tomato? The more conversant the bar staff are with floor and kitchen routines the better. Even if you don't serve food at the bar, bartenders should be conversant with the menu, and its daily changes, in order to advise bar customers who may be intending to move to a table.

When a group of customers order at various levels—one guy just wants an appetizer, his wife wants an appetizer and a main course, and their friends want one appetizer and two main courses—a very good idea is to send two separate dupes to the kitchen: one with the appetizers or "starters," the other with the main courses. Very often you've got to do the kitchen's thinking for them. They are only human, too, and it's easy in smaller establishments for kitchens to get out of sequence.

Your bartenders are salespeople not only of the bar, but of the whole establishment. When the manager or maitre d' is busy the bartenders are inevitably the first point of reference for the incoming customer. When the cheerful crowd arrives and asks the bartender if the lobster special is on the menu tonight, they should get a "yes," a "no," or at least a "Let me find out for you." The one thing the customer shouldn't hear is a lame and disinterested "I don't know"—which is of course the single most common response you will ever get from a bartender in this kind of situation.

Alcohol Abuse

It is sad that any discussion of alcohol must almost immediately concern itself with its abuse. But considering the dangers, it is probably just as well. When used in moderation, alcohol may be good for the health, and by depressing social inhibitions it makes for conviviality.

There is a persistent belief that alcohol stimulates artistic production, particularly that of writers and poets. Keats wrote about claret (a British term for red wine from Bordeaux) that "fills one's mouth with a gushing freshness." Oscar Wilde complained that "Work is the curse of the drinking classes." Dylan Thomas drank himself to a premature death in New York. John Berryman, the American poet who wrote "Dream Songs," was an alcoholic who eventually threw himself off a bridge over the Mississippi. The French poets Verlaine and Baudelaire both extolled the virtues of absinthe. Ogden Nash wrote, in "Reflections on Ice-Breaking": "Candy is dandy but liquor is quicker." W. H. Auden, another American poet, lauded the virtues of the perfect Martini.

Other writer-drinkers were Behan, Boswell, Faulkner, Fitzgerald, Hemingway, Johnson, Joyce, Kerouac, Maupassant, de Musset, O'Brien, O'Neil, and Dorothy Parker.

Guest at party: "If I have another drink I'll be under the table."
Dorothy Parker: "If I have another drink I'll be under the host . . . "

Poe, Rhys, Steinbeck, Stevens, Waugh, Wilde, and Williams are also on the list. Four of the seven Americans to win the Nobel Prize for Literature were alcoholics. Clearly, the relaxing effect of alcohol may stimulate more adventurous thinking, which might help some writers. Many, however, prefer to do their drinking after they've done their daily stint. Some inspirational writers have two "speeds": a swift creative flow, often stimulated by wine, when they get a lot of words on paper, and an early morning speed when they edit their product of the previous evening. Typing and word processing, like driving, are definitely not improved by alcohol.

But what *is* alcohol, and what does it actually do?

Ethyl alcohol occurs in unfermented orange and tomato juice and, as a solvent, finds a home in lacquers, varnishes, stains, and perfumes. The coloring in most drinks is just vegetable dye. The flavor is achieved by other additives that will be discussed later.

There are other sorts of alcohol such as Ethylene Glycol, used in antifreeze, and Isopropanol, which is rubbing alcohol. Methyl alcohol occasionally gets put in by mistake into a student party Christmas punch. The kids see the word alcohol and don't understand that it isn't booze. This mistake often results in blinding, because the chemical causes the optic nerve to swell, or death.

The strength of alcohol is expressed as degrees of "proof," for example, 86 proof, and this can be confusing. In the United States proof is twice the alcohol content in the bottle by volume. Thus, a bottle of spirits marked 86 proof indicates 43 percent alcohol by volume—the rest is water. There are rums at 120 proof, Bourbons such as Wild Turkey at 101 proof, and vodkas at 100 proof. The French simply give the percentage volume of alcohol in a system known as the Gay Lussac scale. In Britain yet another system is used.

So, if you look at the label on a gin bottled in England, it may very well say 86 proof. But it would only be labeled 75.25 had it been bottled under the U.S. system. Some find this lesser strength adds to the delights of certain British spirits.

American spirits are now often labeled thus: "Alcohol 40 percent by volume, 80 proof." All a bar manager needs to know is that the higher the proof indicated on the bottle, the stronger the liquor.

A whole bottle, meaning a fifth, of regular strength whiskey, vodka, or other spirit drunk as one dose will kill the average healthy young man within 24 hours. Occasionally in "rites of passage," or for drunken bets, people will drink a whole bottle. They go to sleep and don't wake up.

The danger line is narrow. When the blood alcohol content is between 0.4 percent and 0.6 percent respiratory failure can occur, followed by death from asphyxiation. To put this in perspective, in most countries where motorists are "breathalized" to check their alcohol intake, 0.05 percent BAC is the upper limit tolerated by law. In some countries the faintest trace of alcohol above the tiny amount naturally present in the blood will result in prosecution.

What gives each individual brand of liquor its essential character are the "congeners" that accompany the basic mix of alcohol and water. This might be as mystical as the yeasty taste of the enzyme *Saccharomyces ellipsoideus beticus*, which gives sherry its unique tang, or as simple as peppermint or fruit syrup, or the juniper berries and fruit flavorings that are added to vodka to turn it into gin.

Although generally reckoned to be a "clean" drink, gin has 13 other components besides water and alcohol. Vodka has the least number of congeners of any drink available. Some believe they are sparing their systems the worst ravages of alcohol by drinking only wine and beer. But wine can contain up to 1,000 separate chemicals, and many a heavy tippler's liver would welcome a dose of uncomplicated vodka as a pleasant change from nonvintage Chateau de Ooh-La-La.

So, chemically speaking, liquor is a fairly simple entity: alcohol, water, and congeners. But, different drinks have various reputations in alcohol folklore. Gin is supposed to be rather depressing, but all alcohol is. Alcohol first depresses mental inhibitions, which is relaxing and helps conversation. But it then starts depressing everything else, which is when overindulgence starts to rear its ugly head. Instant character changes can occur. The shy person becomes forward, the quiet person looks for a fight.

Scotch is thought by many to have a very comforting effect, and champagne has the reputation of swiftly inducing good cheer. This is simply because the champagne bubbles whisk the alcohol through the stomach wall and into the bloodstream efficiently so that the effects are felt in the brain almost immediately. Any liquor drunk with carbonated water ("scotch and soda," "gin/vodka and tonic") will have the same effect.

Alcohol doesn't linger long in the stomach but goes quickly to the small intestine from which it continues to enter the bloodstream. The presence of food at this point in the works can inhibit this transference and help delay inebriation—the polite word for the effects of alcohol, or drunkenness.

Everyone knows that one shouldn't drink on an empty stomach because this will accelerate the effects of alcohol. Some consume milk before drinking, or delay their drinking until after a meal. Still others have been known to drink a spoonful of olive oil before imbibing.

Eventually most alcohol is metabolized (processed out, deconstructed, or broken down) in the liver, where enzymes convert it into acetaldehyde, then acetate, carbon dioxide, and water. The entire blood supply of the human body circulates through the liver every four minutes or so. Some alcohol is excreted through urine, sweat, and, notoriously, breath. The liver processes alcohol rather slowly: three hours for an ounce of pure alcohol, which means about an hour for a Martini or a glass of wine. Volume is really the bottom line of drinking. Once the broad definition of "moderation" is exceeded, then chaos breaks loose, as anyone who has ever had a hangover can testify. But the human liver will take enormous punishment. It is the only organ that can regenerate. People can lose two-thirds of their liver and survive, albeit on a circumspect diet.

Trick question: if you drank a bottle of whiskey every day for 20 years, what would your chances of getting cirrhosis of the liver be? The answer is: only 50 percent.

This surprising statistic grimly underlines just how much you have to drink to damage your liver. Oddly enough, while almost all those who develop cirrhosis are alcoholics, two-thirds of alcoholics never develop this disease. However, this is entirely an academic consideration because long before the liver and health are threatened, the effects of alcohol on the nervous system render the drinker incapable of driving, thinking rationally, functioning sexually (in the case of the male of the species), or operating machinery. A few minutes after a pregnant woman takes a drink her fetus is drinking it, too. It is believed that even a small intake of alcohol can cause fetal alcohol syndrome, so most moms-to-be these days go on the wagon for the duration of their pregnancy.

The heart can be dangerously enlarged by excessive alcohol intake. Alcohol also affects the brain function that governs urine retention. Hence the heavy traffic to the restroom.

You will not need to spend much time in a bar before you realize that most drinkers also smoke. Thus, heavy drinkers have greater chances of getting throat cancer, not because of the liquor, but because of the cigarettes.

Many responsible drinkers worry about their habit. Are they indulging themselves in a harmful way? The only definitive way to assess alcohol damage is to have a liver biopsy, in which a needle is inserted in the lower half of the rib cage and a sliver of the organ is removed for examination. An easier but slightly less accurate method is to have a straightforward blood test called a liver function test. If the "Gamma GT" cell count is elevated, then this is suggestive of liver damage. Alcohol also increases the size of the red blood cells, and this can be detected by the same test. However, most people don't need medical tests to know whether they're overdoing it or not. Friends, family, and colleagues will usually find a way to issue a warning.

And now for the GOOD NEWS! The world's heaviest drinkers are the French. By cutting their alcohol intake by a third they have reduced their alcoholism deaths by 60 percent. At the same time it appears that the French are less prone to heart attacks than people in other nations, and the finger of suspicion as to the reason for this is pointed directly at red wine, of which much is consumed. While one cannot ignore the salad and olive oil intensive French diet, plus the fact that they are not a fat people, much credence is given to the possibility that moderate alcohol intake, especially wine, could be good for you. Some American wine producers are lobbying for permission to post a reference to this on their labels—perhaps to balance those depressing warnings about sulfites and the dangers of drinking during pregnancy that are now mandatory.

It appears that something in alcohol generally, not just red wine—though that is the established favorite in this area—increases the level of fats other than cholesterol, called HDLs, in the blood. This may protect the heart.

Modern man does not consume as much potassium as his ancestors did. This trace element is necessary for the health of the heart and nerves, and a high level of it is found in wine, where it is used as a brightening agent. Iron, calcium, and vitamins are also present. Some less welcome ingredients are histidine, histamines, and tyramine, which are suspected by some of causing the headaches that ruin the pleasure of even small wine consumption for many. Burgundy wines from the Pinot Noir grape are the least offensive in this context. Urethanes, which are carcinogens, are found in negligible quantities, and most wine is routinely filtered through sulfur to stop rotting. Wine is grape juice, so why should it be any less prone to rotting than the hapless tomato left thoughtlessly on top of the bachelor's refrigerator?

White wine gets a lot of its quintessential sparkle from potassium ferrocyanide. But these shocking revelations should be taken with a pinch of salt—after all, a commonly dispensed modern medicine that is an anticoagulant started its life as rat poison.

It remains to be seen whether red wine sales will go through the roof as a result of recent allegations about its benefits for the health of the heart. Not all doctors agree with the findings, however. The *British Medical Journal* recently asked the Health Education Authority to retract its advice that "drinking within sensible limits may provide some protection against heart attacks." In this, as in so many other things in life, we are all on our own—for the moment anyway. Research is continuous. Perhaps St. Paul should have the last word: "Use a little wine for thy stomach's sake."

Following in the footsteps of Doctor Cooper, the aerobics expert who was at last able to define physical fitness, there is now a good idea of how "moderate drinking" can be defined. Currently this is reckoned to be 21 units of alcohol a week for men, and 14 for women. A "unit" is an ounce of 86 proof alcohol. For a man this is approximately three beers a day, or one and one-half Martinis, or three glasses of wine, with rather less for women. The discrepancy does not represent some chauvinistic conspiracy, but rather a differing mechanical capacity in female physiology.

Some might consider this a rather stingy allowance. A very common daily drinking pattern among men who clearly are not alcoholics is two Martinis followed by a beer or large glass of wine with dinner. There is a wide range of individuality of appetite and response. Regular, moderate drinkers will take heart if they go to work in a bar. The prodigious amounts put away by some people who appear to remain sober can be astounding. What will become clear also is that there are various levels of alcoholism ranging from a mild dependency similar to the liking for tea and coffee, all the way to total destruction.

A doctor who accidentally nearly became an alcoholic (if that can be believed) by keeping rather too much company as a very young man with a beloved uncle, was shocked when his uncle died from cirrhosis. He made a study of alcoholism his medical hobby, asking all his patients if he could please test their blood, and would they please tell him what their drinking habits, if any, were?

Someone showed him the statistics for alcohol consumption in a mining district. The figures were enormous. Thinking that he had found a rich lode of material to explore he investigated the community. The incidence of cirrhosis was almost nil, which was perplexing.

It transpired that, although the miners would drink like fishes on Fridays, Saturdays, and Sundays, they drank hardly anything for the rest of the week. This meant everyone had time to recover. It sounds like a bit of a treadmill, but perhaps there is a case for even moderate drinkers to go on the wagon once in a while, if only to prove to themselves that they aren't hooked!

A New Image

Efforts are being made to soften the image of bars and restaurants. The W. C. Fields, Jackie Gleason, Dean Martin school of alcoholic humor doesn't get quite the same laughs these days as it once did. As people generally drink less the industry must work harder to attract women and families.

Such considerations as this do not exist in continental Europe where alcohol is simply a part of life, and the average café on the weekend is likely to contain all age groups and sexes, including children. It must be conceded that this easy acceptance of alcohol as a part of life accounts for a lot of alcoholism, for which the figures are higher in continental countries than in puritan-influenced, Anglo-Saxon countries. But in spite of this you will not see much drunken behavior in France, Spain, or Italy. There is a common pattern of drinking there that involves drinking all day in small quantities, usually of wine only. This is often seen in the restaurant industry in this country where the genial manager stays that way by maintaining a gentle buzz throughout the day. It is a dangerous habit, and one to avoid.

CHAPTER EIGHT

Hiring and Training Bartenders

Hiring Bartenders

Inexperienced bar managers are often helpless when it comes to hiring bartenders. They don't know what to ask or what to say. Their insecurities will distort their thinking. "Okay, the applicant may have worked for five years in a busy upscale bar, and have excellent references, but does that necessarily mean he knows what he's doing?"

"Let's just see if this bartender knows her stuff. Let's ask her a few tough questions. Does she know how to make a Sazerac?" The crestfallen applicant, eminently qualified for the job in most respects, will have to confess that, although she knows there is such a cocktail, she doesn't know how to make it, and has never been asked to make it.

"Don't call us, we'll call you if we need you," the inexperienced bar manager says, grateful for the freeing effect of decision. What kind of a bartender doesn't know how to make a Sazerac, he may sneer. After all, it's in all the cocktail recipe books.

The next applicant, who looks as through he needs a good bath, shave, haircut, and change of clothes, will be asked the same question.

"Sure," he'll splutter, through black and yellow teeth in a grin of triumph. "You need Peychaud's Bitters and a little Pernod . . . "

The bar manager glows. Here's the man—the very fellow. Hired!

The experienced bar manager knows that there's much more to successful bartending than knowing how to make Blue Blazers. Attitude, personality, general awareness, natural good manners, familiarity with equipment and situations—all of these count for much more than knowledge of outdated, obsolete, and largely disdained technique. There are about 5,000 extant cocktail recipes, but even the extended popular repertoire numbers no more than about 20.

It is perhaps not unreasonable to ask a job applicant how to make a Martini, or a Daiquiri, just to be on the safe side, and to give the person an opportunity to demonstrate general knowledge. But knowledge of cocktail recipes represents about 5 percent of the job. So why some managers get bogged down in it is a mystery. A possible explanation is that they themselves don't really have much of an idea of what they want in an employee—a situation as old as the flabby consumer.

Applicants claiming to know 1,000 cocktail recipes should immediately be asked if they know how to tap beer. This is discussed elsewhere in a discussion on hiring techniques: what bar managers *should* be concerning themselves with.

Bar Protocol

When a bartender opens the establishment in the morning there is time to check the whole inventory of the bar. (This is discussed in the chapter on miscellaneous bar equipment.) This should be done anyway because the opening bartender, by tradition, is also responsible for setting up the bar for the evening crew. The day person is the one responsible for bringing up the liquor, loading the sinks with ice, cutting the fruit, and so on. Sometimes a porter or "bar-back" (usually a young bartender learning the ropes) will do these jobs. But if the porter's sick, or sidetracked to emergency duties somewhere, then the day bartender will get stuck with it.

The par stock of liquor will vary from place to place, but it should be written down somewhere to allow a quick check, and to remind bartenders what sort of bottle should go into an anonymous space. Usually, the list of empties will complement the spaces where full bottles must be placed—usually.

Where an abundance of assistant managers with nothing much to do allows it, or even where it does not, every spot on the bar can be marked with an adhesive plastic tag naming the brand whose home that space is. It isn't hard to work out though, with experience. The shelves behind the bar form part of a bartender's station and there the scotches will be grouped, here the gins, the vodkas, and so on.

A useful trick when taking over a new bar is to physically lift and examine each bottle on the bar. Then, when it's requested, you'll just know you saw it somewhere.

The bartenders who come to work later in the day after the bar has opened for business obviously haven't much time to devote to setting up. Of course, if early, perhaps in order to have a bite to eat, the arriving bartender can check with the outgoing person to see if there's beer to be tapped or extra supplies needed. But as often as not, especially in a busy, successful establishment, the replacement will need to go straight to work servicing thirsty customers.

In this position the bartender should go through a "mini-checklist," because there are certain deficiencies that will grind the whole operation to a halt.

Bartender's Checklist
Ice
Mixing glass
Metal shaker
Small shaker
Bar spoon
Sodas
Strainers
Bottle openers
Corkscrews
A selection of glasses
Cut fruit

With the basic equipment available the bartender can go to work. If any of it is missing, the most likely explanation is that the outgoing bartender, in a forgetful moment, failed to put something back where it belonged.

In the first half hour of a shift everything else should be checked with a particular eye to

- Sufficient supplies of chilled wine and beer
- No empty bottles still displayed, masquerading as full ones
- Glaring deficiencies of popular brands on the bar
- The wine list status—any new wines, or listed wines unavailable?

If he's arriving at work in good time, of course, the outgoing bartender will have given a situation report, but once in a while it will be "Hi, bye." If this changeover period is particularly harrowing—and it can be if the outgoing bartender has a lot of register work to do, in addition to getting customers to pay so as to maximize tip income—some rescheduling may be in order. But this can be touchy for all concerned. Far better to streamline the system so that it can all happen fast and efficiently.

So, our bartender is up and running. This may be the "front bartender," only dealing with customers at the bar, sometimes the "service bartender," only dealing with servers who are waiting on tables. In establishments where there is only one bar providing both services, even the service bartender (who will often be a part-timer working a short shift to cover the cocktail and dinner hours) will probably be responsible for the nearest four stools on the bar. Only a large restaurant or club is likely to have a separate service bar out of view of the customers.

There are a few wrinkles that need to be smoothed out to make the service end more efficient. Remember, the whole world wants to eat dinner at the same time, so there is a definite rush hour in most successful bar restaurants.

At the service end the servers will normally put up the requisite glasses, and add the traditional, or specially requested garnish to the finished drink, together with its straw, sip-stick, or stirrer. This isn't written in tablets of stone. Busy glasses will go into short supply, the cut fruit containers will need to be replenished, wine corks will break, and so on. Combined operations are called for.

So popular now is the glass of white or red wine that it makes sense for the servers to have their own supply. A large bottle of white wine is kept on ice on the servers' side of the bar. If there is a run on a special wine currently being featured, then that too can be similarly stored. Nearby a large red is also kept—not in anything like the same demand, but nevertheless popular. The server can just grab a glass, fill it, and serve it.

So popular, too, are the simple drinks of scotch or vodka on the rocks, that again, if the bottles are left within easy reach, a server can pour a drink without distracting the bartender. Some paranoid owners will not allow this. They may fear a loophole in their security system, or that the staff will drink illicitly. All of this is possible. So in bar-restaurants seating over 100 people, paranoid or not, the owners may opt for strict control of liquor dispensing. There will always be weaker brethren who yield to temptation, and clearly the chances of this happening increase with the numbers employed.

In some establishments no drink can be issued to a server without a slip being filled out. These slips are stored and, later, compared with the guest checks (customers' bills) to make sure that they were paid for in the correct way. Sometimes the drinks have to be rung-up on a register or by a cashier near the service bar area.

Occasionally in the United States one sees the French system employed. In many French bars, when you order a drink, the bartender will serve you, then write a check that he presents to you. When you put up your money he gives it to madame la caissière, who is almost invariably from Central Casting with a forbidding look and severe bifocal glasses on the end of her nose. The ceremony does not make for conversation and friendly ambiance, but the main thing from the owner's point of view is that the money has gone into the register.

For many owners, the fact that the bleak and blatantly commercial nature of all transactions in the bar kills all hope of welcoming ambiance, will be so obscure as to be incomprehensible. It must be conceded, however, that in many busy midtown locations the customers are likely to be so intensely concerned with their own business that they won't care whether the bartenders are short, tall, or green with long tentacles, so long as they get their drinks promptly and correctly served. It is when we consider the intensely competitive neighborhood and suburban establishments that the personnel suddenly matter enormously. Usually the cashier is a member of the owner's family. This reduces the chances of collusion between bartender and cashier, but by no means entirely removes it.

These cold but highly secure systems are marvelous, and indeed mandatory in big restaurants or hotels that are part of an international chain, where 20 percent of the people on payroll are employed for no greater purpose than to keep an eye on the other personnel and to supervise transactions. Such organizations have no choice but to implement such safeguards; it is the nature of the dear old human race.

But owners of smaller establishments may not wish to pay too many cashiers and assistant managers, preferring a measure of trust and making the bartenders combine the duties of cashiers—which they are quite capable of doing. Owners and managers who know what they're about will soon detect wrongdoing. A mild warning will sometimes bring people back into line.

After wine and beer, the correct serving of which is discussed in earlier chapters, the most requested drinks are straight vodka and scotch on the rocks—often with a "splash" of water, or soda—plus taller drinks such as scotch and water or soda, gin or vodka and soda, rum and coke, and screwdrivers (tall vodka and orange juice).

At the service end of the bar, for a drink on the rocks, the server puts up an ice-filled rocks glass, and the bartender, or sometimes the server, will put in an ounce and a half of the requisite liquor. If it's gin or vodka it will probably take a twist of lemon peel or a wedge of lime. If customers fail to specify they should be asked, although garnishes are pretty standardized and automatically served in most bars these days.

In general, with these simple drinks the bartender only pours the liquor. Sodas, juices, and garnishes are added by the servers. But if they're busy and the bartender is not, there's no reason why the bartender shouldn't do it. If the establishment is to succeed, floor and bar must work together. They are mutually dependent.

In front of a customer at the bar the procedure is exactly the same, except that the glass is placed on a coaster or bev-nap on the bar. "Highballs" such as rum and Coke, screwdrivers, scotch and water or soda, gin or vodka and tonic, are set up the same way at the front bar, with suitable garnishes: lime in rum and Coke, gin or vodka, nothing in a screwdriver, and nothing in scotch unless, as is common, a twist is requested.

If a customer doesn't request a garnish, it's customary to ask if one is wanted. In the case of Martinis, for example, you say, "Olive or twist?" Sometimes they'll require nothing.

Some fruit will have to be cut every day. Even refrigerated orange slices, lime wedges, lemon wedges, and lemon peels will deteriorate after about 48 hours. Though they'll be harmless, they'll look a bit tired. Bartenders must learn that when a drink takes a wedge of lemon or lime, an orange slice, or a twist of lemon, these fruity additions must be fresh, juicy, good-looking, and zestful because that's their purpose. The nicest Martini will look a bit sorry if it's presented with a dried up squiggle of a two-day-old lemon peel.

Every bar manager should specify how the fruit should be cut. There aren't too many options, but they should be stated anyway. There's a certain strength and discipline about standardization. The sight of a deadly serious, straightfaced bar manager demonstrating the cutting of lemons to grown-up people may sometimes provoke an inner smile, but to some it's as big a deal as landing a 747 in a snowstorm.

The main thing is that the results should look their best. Lemon peels sliced at random are arguably more esthetically appealing than those produced from topping and tailing the lemon. But if you serve 100 drinks a day requiring peel, clearly the production line method will be favored.

With regular customers, if it's a quiet time, slicing up a fresh lime or lemon specially for them is a nice gesture. Remember, citrus slices and wedges should actually be squeezed into the drink with the bartender's immaculately clean fingers.

Cherries and olives are designed for long refrigerated shelf life, but they also need to be checked daily, as they can dry up and shrivel. Standard bar olives are a rather boring vegetable but bar managers should beware of trying to be adventurous in this area. Apart from being more expensive, "real" olives— perhaps imported from Greece—will get strange looks from customers accustomed to the not-very-oily standard green kind. American consumers in general have relatively bland tastes, so it's a case of better safe than sorry. Many a talented chef will come up with a super dish that the boss will regretfully not allow on the menu because it's too challenging. It's the same with drinks.

Mixology

All this discussion of how to run a busy bar at last comes to the mystical area of "mixology"!

A bartender who's asked for an esoteric drink can look it up in the bartender's guide in an instant and make the drink, provided the ingredients are available. As often as not, another member of the staff will recognize the drink and rattle off the recipe.

Sometimes in a busy bar there is a case for inventing an excuse not to make something time consuming. Why should 10 customers wait while one nerd gets a Ramos Fizz—which may well be rejected as not quite right anyway?

It is not unknown for customers to order unusual cocktails, for the bartender to gallantly make them, and for the customers to then complain that they are not correctly made, thus wasting time, energy, and liquor. Often, the cocktail *is* correctly made but the customer has gotten used to an ersatz concoction in some insalubrious dive.

A line that will sometimes get the bartender off the hook is, "Tell me the recipe and I'll make it for you." Still another device is, "Sorry, I haven't got all the ingredients."

None of this has anything to do with laziness, or denying the little old lady out for her Sunday afternoon treat the cocktail that brings back memories of youth. It has to do with business. If the little old lady becomes a regular, of course she should get her Pineapple Rum Royal. Have no fear. You will not encounter affluent-looking potential big spenders who, on being denied the Sazerac of their dreams, will grumpily take their business elsewhere. At least not if your bar staff are doing their job correctly—which is selling drinks. A customer denied a Bronx Bombshell will probably be just as happy with a gin and tonic, provided the bartender's manner is correct. It must be remembered, too, that much customer satisfaction lies in hearing their own voices making silly speeches; it's part of the service bars traditionally provide.

We shall deal only with reality. The most commonly requested drinks on a bar these days aren't cocktails anyway. They are wine, beer, and spirits— preponderantly, by a huge margin, vodka—on the rocks or with various mixers. There is a small group of cocktails still regularly requested and these simple recipes must be known. Then there is a further group of cocktails that are requested from time to time that a bartender *should* know. Finally, there is a small fringe group of cocktails that a bartender could know, but it wouldn't matter much if not. Drinks outside this category can be looked up in the bartender's guide, and if they're not there, too bad.

In fact, most drinks containing spirits are not really cocktails at all, and require no mixing expertise. Scotch and vodka are often drunk plain or "straight" on the rocks, with twists of lemon or wedges of lime or lemon. Scotch on the rocks with a splash of water, or tall scotches and soda, gin or vodka and tonic or other mixer are also very popular. These tall drinks are called "highballs," but the term isn't used much now. However, the eight-ounce glass in which such drinks are served is still called a highball glass.

You will sometimes be asked for a gin, scotch, rye, or vodka "Presbyterian." This means a mixture of soda water and ginger ale in equal parts. Because the tonic water dispensed by soda guns is so sweet, many drinkers like it diluted with plain soda water. This is sometimes called "sonic," as in "Vodka Sonic."

It is important to remain flexible in dispensing drinks. Customers will often request slight variations on the theme. For instance, many people like less ice or more spice in their drinks.

Such requests should be taken in stride. Any comment should be indulgent and helpful rather than scornful. For instance if a customer requests a drink with "very little ice," why not put some ice in the glass, show it to the customer, and say, "Like that? Or maybe a little more?" Such a response will go a lot better than eye-rolling, lip-pursing, and groans of dismay. Remember, serious drinkers often drink at home, where they are able to make their concoctions exactly the way they like them. The standard commercial notion of how a drink should be made often doesn't conform to personal choice; and indeed, many potential customers spend less because they're pretty certain they won't get a drink made the way they like it. Instead of the 5 dollar special Martini, they'll settle for a small beer, or even a nondrink. It need hardly be added that the ability to conform to individual tastes and preferences will build regular clientele and increase tips.

The most requested cocktails are

- Vodka Martinis
- Martinis (made with gin)
- Vodka or Gin Gibsons (Martinis served with onions)

(All of the above are dry Martinis, made with white, dry vermouth. You are much more likely to be struck by lightning or bitten by a snake than to be asked for a sweet Martini.)

- Manhattans (basically a Rye whiskey drink, but various Bourbons and specific brands are often requested)
- Rob Roys (Manhattans made with scotch, often requested by brand)

These can be served chilled but "up" (no ice), or on the rocks.

Vodka Martini or Gibson. At the service end of the bar you can cut a few corners with this popular cocktail. The server will put up a cocktail glass—a four-ounce stem glass with a V-shaped bowl—full of ice and a little water to chill it, which takes only seconds. If the drink was requested on the rocks then a rocks glass is put up and filled with ice from the server's supply. If you are serving it "up" these are the steps:

- Fill your mixing glass with ice.
- Put in a drop or two of white vermouth.
  (If "extra dry" is requested, put less vermouth, or none!) Put in an ounce and a half of vodka—whatever is standard. Using your long bar spoon, stir the mixture until you can feel, through the mixing glass, that it has been completely chilled. With experience you will know how long this takes.
- Using your strainer, pour the liquid into the cocktail glass, which the highly efficient server has just emptied of its chilling ice.
- The server will add onions (if it's a Vodka Gibson), an olive or olives, or a lemon peel, and the drink is ready to be served.

All of this should take no more than 60 seconds. In a super busy place, or any old place for that matter, you can simply keep a bottle of gin or vodka chilled, and pour it instantly from the bottle. This denies customers a view of the ritual of preparation, but if they're sitting at a table it hardly matters.

If customers sitting at the bar ask for Martinis, it wouldn't do to pour straight from the chilled bottle—they like to reverentially observe the steps in the creation of the drink. But occasionally customers will ask you if you have a bottle of Stolichnaya, or other liquor, chilled. If you have, then clearly you can pour it straight from the bottle into whichever glass is requested.

Remember that the cocktail glass can contain four ounces. But you are only dispensing about two ounces of liquor, and aiming to put at least three ounces into the glass—in order to leave a decent space so that the glass can be raised without spillage. So your stirring has to generate some water. Have no fear. So strong is the drink that no one will ever complain about short measure or overdilution. The main customer expectation is that the drink should be very chilled, precisely in order to kill the taste of the liquor, which may sound quixotic, but there it is.

You can throw the ice used to chill the cocktail glass, and that which remains in the mixing glass, into the slop sink or garbage if you like, but it's clean and you can use it to make another drink quite safely. The sooner you exhaust your ice supply, the sooner someone is going to have to interrupt the work flow in order to replenish the bar. If this can be arranged in less busy times, so much the better.

By the way, most bartenders use the handle of the spoon to stir with, holding it in reverse. Maybe this is because the sharper handle penetrates right to the bottom of the ice more easily.

In really mean bars the mixing glass is first dipped into hot water so that as you mix the drink there's lots of "meltage." This way you save on the liquor. There used to be a dreadful fuss made about how little vermouth you put into the cocktail to make it super dry. "Face east and whisper 'vermouth'." "Wave the vermouth cork over the glass," and other such nonsense.

The term "Dry Martini" is less used now because there's rarely any need to distinguish it from the more or less abandoned "Sweet Martini," which would be made as above, but with sweet, red vermouth. However, once in a blue moon you'll get a request for a "Perfect" Martini or Rob Roy. This does not allude to the quality of the proposed drink, which is taken for granted, but to the mixing of sweet and dry vermouth. Instead of only using one kind, you put a few drops of each.

Again, once in a blue moon, a European customer will ask for a Martini, meaning a glass of Martini and Rossi vermouth—a standard drink on the Continent. So, if in doubt, you can always create some amusement by getting the customer to specify. Similarly, innocent Americans abroad who order Martinis in bars other than the hotel bars in major cities will sometimes be a bit perplexed when they get a glass of vermouth.

Martinis are for people who like them stiff and strong but are too genteel to just ask for a shot of booze!

At the front bar, serving a "live customer" as it were, the choreography is a little different. As soon as the customer has ordered the drink, on a coaster or bev-nap on the bar you place either a chilled cocktail glass (if you have a crushed ice display with cocktail glasses stuck in it) or a glass containing ice and water that will immediately start to chill.

You then do exactly what you did at the service bar, except that, if the customer ordered a specific brand, you select it rather theatrically ("Ah! There 'tis!") and perhaps mutter "Tanqueray Sterling" or "Stolichnaya," by way of confirmation as you pour it. As you do this you offer a prayer that the owner didn't come in at dawn and fill all the top shelf bottles with "plonk" (liquor of anonymous pedigree). There's no need to offer the bottle for examination as though it were vintage claret.

Some customers—for whom this golden moment may be the high spot of their day—will watch you avidly, staring like cows in a meadow, observing every move and nuance as you make the drink, and sometimes offering comments. Rookies sometimes find this a bit unnerving. Old hands will exact a peculiar small revenge by doing things that have no relation whatsoever to making the drink, such as twiddling the glass elaborately with their fingers, or putting the bottle to their ear and pretending to listen carefully, with a serious frown of concentration. "Sounds okay, but you can't be too careful these days." If a perplexed customer asks what's going on the bartender says that the alcohol may have been a bit bruised, but it's perfectly okay, thank goodness.

With regular customers you can have fun and enjoy "family jokes," like pretending to be about to pour a detested brand from the same family of liquor. You might amaze the customer by making exactly the correct amount, not a drop too much or too short, or by studiously making a bit too much, then putting the mixer and strainer down in front of the customer with a line such as, "A dividend—made a bit too much—shame to throw it away." A few minutes later the customer will have the privilege of adding to the drink from the mixing glass, if you don't get to it first. Gestures like these make customers feel as though they belong.

How do you know how much to pour when you're doing it right in front of the customer? On the rocks it's easy: you pour until it looks like a normal sized drink, which will be about an ounce and a half of liquor. In the mixing glass you can either check visually, by knowing the correct level that will yield the cocktail amount, or you can count in your head like an old-fashioned parachutist, "One thousand, two thousand." One and a half seconds is the average pour for a Martini or when a similar amount of liquor is required. Especially when taking over a new bar with slightly different mixing glasses and drink glasses, it's a good idea to fill the standard cocktail glass with water, pour it into a mixing glass full of ice, and see what level it reaches. Then you won't waste liquor by overpouring.

If a customer has requested olives (plural) in a straight up Martini, then you can put three or four in a rocks glass and put it alongside the cocktail. Otherwise the small cocktail glass gets a bit crowded. When a twist of lemon is requested there are two ways of making a "classy gesture." The first is to twist the peel in your fingers to break the skin and release the zest. Rub it firmly around the rim of the glass, after you've thrown out the chilling ice, if any, and a second before you pour the cocktail. If the drink is on the rocks then you can do the same thing after you've made the drink. The drinker will enjoy a fresh, pleasant effect at first sip. Alternatively you can squeeze the twist over the top of the poured cocktail, which has much the same effect.

The serious point being made here is that finding a nice bar where they make your drinks the way you like them is the devil's own job. It would be unrealistic not to concede that many bars that do not deserve to succeed by any intelligent assessment make millions from dedicated undiscerning customers. But if you can deliver the goods you may at least do good business with the discerning. Also, the world is full of desperately lonely people. Many go to bars. If you can offer them half an ounce of genuine, if lightweight, companionship, they'll come back for more. You're not required to marry them. Just give them an agreeable hour.

Gin and Vodka Gimlets. These are made in exactly the same way as Martinis, except that instead of using vermouth, you use Rose's concentrated lime juice. Some people may request that the cocktail be shaken instead of stirred. They are garnished with a wedge of lime.

Manhattans. Basically this is Rye whiskey and vermouth. When a Manhattan is requested it means a Sweet Manhattan, using sweet vermouth. Dry Manhattans made with dry, white vermouth are fairly common, too.

You make it either on the rocks or "up" in exactly the same way as you make a Martini, with one small difference. In the case of the Manhattan, you put a little more sweet vermouth, a bit more than the one or two drops of dry vermouth you put in a Martini—about a tablespoonful will do the trick. In a good Manhattan you can taste the vermouth.

The garnish is a cherry, or lemon twist for a Dry Manhattan, unless otherwise requested. Again, particular brands of rye or Bourbon are often specified. Some call these "Call Brands." How anyone can tell the difference between brands of rye or Bourbon once they have been thoroughly adulterated with strongly flavored vermouth is one of life's greater mysteries. Perhaps the customer derives some joy from hearing the magic words uttered.

However, there is such a thing as consumer integrity. If you ask for a cotton shirt and are given a polyester mix there is room for vociferous complaint. Similarly, if a bar customer asks for Dewars, there is no earthly reason for not getting the real thing. May conscience be your guide.

Rob Roy. This cocktail is made in exactly the same way as a Manhattan or Martini except that the principal liquor used is scotch, instead of rye or Bourbon. The sweet version takes a cherry, dry takes a lemon peel, unless otherwise requested. Specific scotches are often specified.

Bloody, Mary, Bullshot, Bloody Bull. These drinks all belong to the same family. The Bloody Mary is a highly flavored mix of vodka and tomato juice. If you like you can make the cocktail in the mixing glass, then transfer it to a drinking glass. On the very rare occasions when the drink is requested straight up, that is what you do, pouring the cocktail into an eight-ounce highball glass, and throwing out the now highly flavored ice that in this case obviously cannot be "recycled" or returned to the ice sink. You don't want your Martinis and Whiskey Sours tasting of tomato juice and Tabasco! Nowadays the drink is usually prepared in the glass from which it will be drunk, because the standard Bloody Mary is served with ice, like 90 percent of the cocktails served today.

You start with a twelve-ounce glass about two-thirds full of ice. If you use too much ice in this drink it will soon start to look rather watery. Into this glass you are going to put spices, tomato juice, and vodka. It doesn't very much matter what sequence you follow, but most people start with the spices. You put in a sprinkle of salt and the same amount of pepper. Some bar managers like to use "Butcher's Pepper," which is coarser with larger grains, but regular table pepper will do. Then you put in about four drops of Tabasco, a teaspoonful of Worcestershire Sauce, and sometimes a touch of unsweetened lemon or lime juice. Horseradish is an optional addition, but most bartenders only use this on request, as not everyone likes it. Then you pour an ounce and a half of vodka, or whatever your standard house pour is (one hopes it will not be less), and fill the glass with tomato juice from a large bottle. People sometimes request "Gin Marys," which is self-explanatory, or a "Danish Mary," which means Aquavit instead of vodka. Finally, you give it a good but careful shake with the smaller metal shaker, squeeze a wedge of lime into it, and serve it with a stirrer.

Often customers will request a "very spicy," or a "not too spicy" drink. They're invariably talking about the Tabasco, which is the strongest sauce in the mixture, so you put a little more, or a little less. At the front bar there's no reason why you shouldn't put the Tabasco bottle at the drinkers' disposal, so that if they are really gluttons for it they can add to their heart's content. Sometimes the request will be for a Bloody Mary without any spices at all, a vodka and tomato juice. Another favorite request is for a Virgin Mary—this is the spiced tomato juice served without liquor. Exactly the same procedure applies at front and service bar.

Tomato juice comes in large cans that are a bit unwieldy, although small individual cans are available too. If, as is most likely, you use the large cans then it's best to decant the juice into glass fruit juice bottles whose tops can be screwed tight, permitting safe refrigeration. The glass bottles have a little more esthetic appeal too. These useful bottles can also be filled with prepared Bloody Mary mix for use at the service end of the bar. Nowhere is it written that this mix should not be used at the front bar too, but some customers do like a bit of ritual.

Many bar restaurants feature the Bloody Mary as part of their weekend brunch. On any day of the week, though, if people are drinking in the middle of the day—not as common a practice as it used to be—a Bloody Mary is a popular choice.

At weekends it is possible to get swamped with orders for Bloody Marys, and there is a good case for making up a batch of the mix in advance, then simply adding the vodka right in the glass. A quick shake and the drink is ready to be served. But some paranoid and insecure owners, or even bar managers, will not permit this sensible arrangement. They view it as an excuse for the lazy bartender. But experience shows that the customer gets a better Bloody Mary when it's premixed than when it's built from scratch, especially on a busy day. The reason for this is simple. If the bartender is allowed to make up a batch of Bloody Mary mix in advance, the preparation can be done at comparative leisure, thus insuring correct proportions. The mix can also be given a good solid shake, insuring thorough mixing of the ingredients.

One bartender experimented extensively with this drink. He made a point of asking *all* his Bloody Mary customers how they were enjoying their drinks. In nine cases out of ten they said they were delighted. Occasionally someone would ask for a top-up with plain tomato juice because the cocktail was a bit too fiery. Others would ask for more spice.

Then the tomato juice suppliers started including a can of their Bloody Mary mix with each case. This came automatically and was billed as being "free." What was to be done with this, the bartender inquired? It seemed a shame to throw it away. With much frowning and huffing management agreed that it could be used. The only occasions on which the bartender received any unsolicited compliments for the Bloody Marys was when this mix was used. It stands to reason. The juice company obviously put a lot of thought into how it should be made, and probably ran some test marketing in order to discover exactly what people generally preferred.

The Bull Shot is made exactly like a Bloody Mary, except that beef bouillon—clear beef soup from a can—is used instead of tomato juice. A Bloody Bull requires the same mixology, but with half bouillon and half tomato juice. Occasionally people will request the drink to be made with Clamato juice, and if you have it, why not?

There was a great to-do in the media many years ago when it was discovered that many famous bars and restaurants were putting *no vodka whatsoever* in

Bloody Marys. Every establishment named was famous, including the then highest-grossing restaurant in the United States. No comment was offered by any of these places. The general supposition was that the owners were being mean and increasing their profits by saving on liquor. The truth is a little more subtle.

Some bartenders like to steal money. The bigger the establishment the wider the potential loopholes. Because of this owners and managers become obsessed with control. Every drop of alcohol has to be accounted for. Every bottle issued is stamped with the house stamp so that the bartenders will not simply bring in and sell their own liquor. (This practice is common among tenant landlords and is done quite cheerfully and openly at Third World airport bars! "Sorry sir, the bar's run out of whiskey. Can I sell you some of mine?")

Even if the bartenders are forbidden to buy drinks on the house they will do so when opportunity allows, in order to drum up decent tips. They may drink themselves, too.

So how is the inevitable shortfall in liquor to be accounted for when the assistant managers come in at the crack of dawn every day and take inventory down to a tenth of a bottle? Well, by not putting liquor in any drink where you think you might get away with it. Twenty Bloody Marys rung up will account for a good deal of vodka that in fact has been given away in drinks on the house, or consumed by the staff.

Whiskey Sour, Rum Sour (Daiquiri), Scotch and Bourbon Sours. This group comprises those drinks that consist of spirits of various kinds mixed with sweetened lemon juice. They are a very simple proposition nowadays. Years ago the bartender was required to combine Frothee (a sort of detergent that made the drinks froth), castor sugar, and fresh hand-squeezed lemon juice. Now the wonders of modern science have given us Lemon X, which combines all three ingredients in a highly satisfactory product with good shelf life.

The generic name "sour" is something of a misnomer because this family of drinks is heavily sweetened—it would have to be if you think about it, plain lemon juice being something of a rare taste. Ninety-nine percent of Whiskey Sours are served on the rocks, so unless they are specified as "straight up" you can safely serve them that way. A basic Whiskey Sour consists of an ounce and a half, or standard house shot, of Rye whiskey, mixed with Lemon X, shaken, and served with a cherry and sometimes a slice of orange. Here are the steps to follow:

• Take a rocks glass and fill it with ice
• Pour in a shot of Rye whiskey
• Fill the glass with Lemon X

- Put the small metal shaker over the top and shake it (only a couple of times—enough to give it a small head of froth)
- Add a cherry and a slice of orange if you have it
- Put in a stirrer and maybe a straw, depending on house policy
- Serve

Any other sour is made in the same way, only with the specified liquor: scotch, brandy, Blackberry Brandy, Bourbon, Canadian Club, Dewars, or whatever. A Rum Sour is called a Daiquiri and is usually ordered by that name. There is also a Frozen Daiquiri that we shall discuss later.

Some bartenders automatically use Bourbon when a Whiskey Sour is ordered. The reason for this is that the darker liquor makes the drink look stronger. It may once have been a valid point. So strong is the lemon taste that the subtle difference between rye and Bourbon is totally obscured.

Here is a secret that some bar managers will not wish to know (or will not wish their bartenders to know). All sours are given an extra zing, which almost invariably elicits joyous comment, by the addition of a small amount of any of the orange-based liqueurs: Cointreau, Triple Sec, or Grand Marnier. A teaspoonful will do the trick. Most owners will be driven to their psychiatrist's couch for an emergency session if they discover that such a practice is common in their bar, but there's no reason why the price of the drink shouldn't be increased by 25 cents to cover this delicious embellishment. Or perhaps bartenders can reserve the gesture for their regular customers.

There are dozens of secrets that many commercial purveyors of alcohol do not know, but which are common knowledge to serious drinkers. For instance, in the avid insistence on white wine and champagne being served absolutely freezing cold, only a few still small voices are aware that, in fact, good wines taste much better about 10 minutes after they leave the refrigerator.

Bar managers must understand that many of their customers are emphatically *not* serious drinkers, and are merely reiterating ritualistic words they've heard others say, and which they believe to be smart. Movie buffs will recall many a scene in which a youngster on the borderline of adulthood is invited to have a drink. Knowing nothing about alcohol, but not wishing to appear juvenile, the person requests a scotch on the rocks, having heard the phrase 1,000 times and aware that this is a fairly standard item. Two sips later the tyro is reeling!

To many customers words like "extra dry" and "Chardonnay" rank with expressions like "heavy duty" in definition. They are often used, but poorly understood.

Tom Collins, John Collins. These drinks are really just larger sours—long drinks served in highball glasses, or even taller in some bars. A Tom Collins is made with vodka, a John Collins with gin. They are made in exactly the same way as the drinks described in the sour section. People will sometimes request a Whiskey Collins or a Rum Collins.

Bar managers need to establish policy in this area. The truth is that a Whiskey Sour on the rocks is a pretty pathetic drink when served in a short rocks glass. Lots of ice cubes, not much liquid—fine for a scotch on the rocks, but highly unsatisfactory for a sour. In many bars nowadays if you request a Whiskey Sour or a Whiskey Collins you will get exactly the same tall drink, not a short one. No complaints have been recorded. Very few consumers go to a bar with the intention of insisting on the mixology rules and regulations of 1953. Fewer and fewer consumers set forth with any intention of having a mixed drink or cocktail anyway! Bar work is busy and demanding enough, there is no point in inventing possible complications—though many incompetent managers devote their lives to this aim.

Margarita. This drink is a cousin of the sour group and, again, seems to work better on the rocks when served tall, in an eight-ounce highball glass (or, in many bars, a 12-ounce "Coke" glass), rather than short. It consists of a shot of Tequila, half a shot of any of the orange-based liqueurs—Cointreau, Triple Sec, or Grand Marnier—topped up with Lemon X, and served with a wedge of lime or lemon according to request. The defining gimmick of this drink is that the glass is rimmed with salt. In bars where this drink is regularly ordered, a saucer full of salt should be kept handy. It must be changed regularly, as the salt hardens and looks disgusting after a day or two. When a customer orders a Margarita it's normal to say "With salt?" If, as happens in 50 percent of cases, the customer declines (salt being a fashionably unpopular item) then you are saved a move.

- Fill a highball glass with ice
- Pour a shot of Tequila
- Pour half a shot of orange liqueur
- Fill the glass with Lemon X
  If "no salt," shake the drink using the small metal shaker
- Wedge of lime/lemon, stirrer/straw—serve
  If salt is requested, then you take another highball glass and
- Run a squeezed lime wedge round its rim
- Dip the inverted glass into the salt saucer
- Rub it around until the glass rim is encrusted with salt

- Give the mixture a quick shake with the small metal shaker
- Pour the whole concoction, ice and all, into the salt-rimmed glass
- Wedge of lime/lemon, stirrer/straw—serve

It sounds like a major production. It's actually easy once you establish the routine. With practice you can do it in your sleep. It is a bit of a bore if you have to make several of them because it generates a lot of dirty glasses. But it's a good profit item. If your base price for a scotch on the rocks is, say, $4.25, then you can price your Margarita at 5 dollars; and many hum-drum bars will charge 6 dollars or $7.50 without blinking an eye.

If the drink is requested "straight up" then you will need to make it in the mixing glass and pour it into a four-ounce cocktail glass, or whichever glass you have stipulated is to be used for such drinks.

There is a connection between Tequila and salt. You will occasionally get customers who wish to inform the world that they've been to Mexico and will request a salt cellar and a little dish of lemon wedges. They then sprinkle salt on the base of their thumb, squirt it with lemon juice, swig a neat shot of Tequila, and lick the lemon salt mixture on their thumb. It looks every bit as inelegant as it sounds.

Frozen Margaritas, Daiquiris. These drinks, popular in summer with the young crowd and not too serious drinkers, are somewhat time consuming to prepare. They are made in the bar blender and can be real show-stoppers at busy periods. That's why it's important to know exactly what you're doing, and be properly set up for them. They are wonderful profit spinners, and if well made will help bring customers back again and again. They involve use of the blender, so if this is out of order (they take a pretty good beating in some bars) then these drinks are off the menu.

To make a Frozen Daiquiri you use the blender as though it were the mixing glass. You pour in exactly the same amounts as for a normal drink, then fill the blender three-quarters full with ice. Put the blender back on the machine, make sure it is fitting snugly and correctly (or you may have a dreadful mess), and switch on. Conversation at this point will come to a temporary halt because of the noise. After about a minute, switch off and inspect the contents. By now they should be thick and creamy, with no chunks of ice left. If you leave it too long it will be too watery. Pour the mixture into the tallest glass you have and serve it with a straw.

Strawberry and Banana Daiquiris are made as above, except that you add either a small handful of strawberries or a few slices of banana into the blender.

Equipment, the size of ice cubes, and portions will vary from place to place.

The bartenders must know what the finished product is supposed to look like according to house format and then adjust to it. For instance, so much creamy ice is generated by some blenders that you only need to put in a half strength drink to get the full effect.

A Frozen Margarita is made exactly the same way. However, in "Tex Mex" bars, the Frozen Margarita is a house specialty, and often a machine is installed into which buckets of the top secret house mix have been poured, making the production almost instantaneous and easy. These machines are much the same as those that dispense frozen yogurt and low-calorie ice cream. You simply put the glass to the nozzle, turn on the tap, or press the rim of the glass against a lever until the glass is full, and serve.

Piña Coladas. Like their cousins described above (Frozen Margaritas and Daiquiris) tall and exotic Piña Coladas are popular in summer with young and not too serious drinkers. They are made in the blender and can also be somewhat time consuming. Since only about 20 percent of the final drink is anything but creamed ice, they are an excellent profit item for which a fancy price can confidently be extracted.

The ingredients are cream of coconut, pineapple juice, and rum blended to a creamy consistency with ice. It is best to have a jar of the mixed coconut cream and pineapple juice made up in advance.

The instructions for making this drink are given on the can of cream of coconut, which is probably just as well as it is hard to think of anything else in the world that uses this intriguing ingredient outside the world of candy and confectionery. Here you will see that the recommended proportions for making two eight- or 10-ounce Piña Coladas are two ounces of coconut cream, four ounces of pineapple juice, three ounces of rum, and two cups of water. The standard container of cream of coconut holds 15 ounces. "Coco Lopez" is a popular brand. The small cans of Dole pineapple juice contain six fluid ounces.

Your bartenders should not get bogged down in these precise measurements. After making the drink a couple of times bartenders know the rough proportions, and of course they can be varied for different effect. The main thing to remember is that a little of the mixture goes a long way and that almost invariably a bit too much will be made because the ice, when crushed in the blender, expands greatly.

If a bartender gets an order for two Piña Coladas there's no reason why he shouldn't make them in accordance with the proportions given above. But this leaves him with an opened and half-used can of cream of coconut and ditto for the pineapple juice. It's time saving and more economical to have these two items premixed.

The best container for this kind of thing is the glass quart juice bottle—an all-purpose container. Into it you can put a whole 15-ounce container of cream of coconut and two small cans of pineapple juice. This is a bit more juice than officially recommended but this is a forgiving cocktail. This will give you almost a bottle full of the mix, enough to make about 15 cocktails, though chances are you'll usually make a bit too much and some will be thrown away.

Having put the mixture in the bottle, you should put it in the blender, at your leisure, and give it a good mix. Then you return the mixture to its bottle and refrigerate it. Lo and behold, when you come to use it next you will find that the ingredients have separated, with the pineapple juice on top and the cream of coconut on the bottom. However, a vigorous shaking will mix it again and it will be ready to use.

Remember, you will only get two full drinks out of one blender load, so if the order is for more you really have to be organized. Also, these frozen drinks use a lot of ice, so if you get a run on them you will almost certainly need a resupply.

Here is the drill for making one drink:

- Fill the blender three-quarters full with ice
- Add a shot (one and one-half ounces or so) of white rum
- Vigorously shake the prepared mix
- Add about three ounces to the blender
  (It looks too little, but there'll be plenty after blending.)
- Fit the blender snugly and switch on for a full minute
- Take a look and poke around with your bar spoon to make sure all the ice is crushed.
- Serve in a tall glass with a straw—cherry optional

The first time bartenders make this drink they may find it tiresome, and they will almost certainly make too much. But thereafter it's a breeze. A common error is to blend the mixture a bit too much so that the resultant drink is of too liquid a consistency.

Wine Cocktails

Kir. This drink, named after a famous former mayor of Beaujolais, consists simply of a few drops (or more, according to taste) of Crème de Cassis, a cordial made from blackberries, added to a glass of chilled white wine. A twist of lemon squeezed and rubbed around the rim of the glass gives this drink an extra zest. Some people like it tall with ice and soda, or on the rocks, but normally a straight Kir is served in a regular wine glass. It is very sweet, but not cloyingly so. The blackberry taste hides any shortcomings the wine might have (usually), and indeed it is not too fanciful to imagine that this may be its purpose.

Kir Royale. This is as above except that the ingredients are champagne and Chambray or raspberry liqueur, again with a twist of lemon, and sometimes served on the rocks. It's served in the house champagne glass, which is often a regular wine glass these days. The price will depend upon the type of champagne used. If you pour imported champagne as a standard item on your bar (a rare and classy touch) then clearly the drink will be on the expensive side, but if you use an inexpensive domestic brand then a normal cocktail price should be adequate.

Mimosa. This is one-half orange juice and one-half champagne. It is priced according to the quality of champagne used and served in a regular champagne glass.

It finds its niche most commonly as an accompaniment to weekend brunch, which is now such a popular restaurant feature. A free Mimosa or Bloody Mary is often part of the all-in-one price.

The English sometimes call this Buck's Fizz. Another English champagne concoction that is surprisingly delicious is Black Velvet: one-half Guinness Stout and one-half champagne.

Champagne Cocktail. There are so many different versions of this concept, all with their own undoubted charms, that the buck must be passed to bar managers to state the house recipe. Of course, customers will sometimes have their own ideas that the bartender can probably accommodate. The standard recipe consists of pouring champagne over a cube of sugar that has been soaked in Angosturas Bitters. The first variation is that the Angosturas is replaced by brandy. After that it's a free-for-all, and often very elaborate, too. Harry's Bar in Venice features a champagne cocktail made from peach juice and champagne, called a **Bellini.**

Some small voices may inquire the point of messing about with this glorious wine. Why not drink it neat? But some domestic champagne really does need a bit of cheering up, especially, as is common, if it tastes a bit of chemicals or acid. Furthermore, some of the great names in real champagne demonstrate a disappointing inconsistency in the quality of their nonvintage wines (though rarely, it must be hastily stated, in their declared vintages).

Vermouth Cassis. This is usually served on the rocks and consists of two ounces or so of dry vermouth (that's the white kind—Cinzano, Stock, and so on) with an ounce of Crème de Cassis and a twist of lemon. Sometimes it's requested tall, and sometimes with club soda or seltzer.

White Wine Spritzer. This is two ounces of white wine served tall on the rocks and topped up with plain club soda or seltzer. A twist of lemon and a stirrer are standard. In Victorian times this was a very popular drink called "Hock and Seltzer." It is almost invariably chosen by someone who wants a light drink, so they will not usually thank you for putting in too much wine. Red wine spritzers are allowed. Sometimes vermouth and soda is requested and it is served in exactly the same way.

Dubonnet Cocktail. Though this cocktail is now firmly relegated to the "could know" division it is mentioned here because it is the only remaining wine cocktail. It consists of a shot of gin or vodka, as requested, shaken and served on the rocks or "up" in a cocktail or Martini glass. A twist of lemon should accompany it. On the rocks, of course, it gets a stirrer, but not when served in a cocktail glass.

Apart from this, *all* the cocktails described above belong to the must know category. Bartenders will definitely be asked for them from time to time.

The following cocktails are fairly regularly requested during what might be kindly described as "amateur hours," which last usually from 5 P.M. Friday until 10 P.M. Sunday night, but are almost continuous in the weeks leading up to Christmas.

Black Russian. Invariably served on the rocks, this is simply two-thirds vodka to one-third Kahlua. No garnish, unless requested, and a stirrer.

White Russian. As above, again served in a rocks glass, but with a dash of milk. Kahlua drinks are listed on the back of the bottle. Remember that Tia Maria, which is the original coffee liqueur, can also be used, though it is somewhat more expensive. Adequate "generic" coffee liqueurs now exist and are perfectly acceptable.

There is a small family of tall drinks that involve vodka and fruit juices.

Screwdriver. This is a shot of vodka in a highball glass filled with ice and topped up with orange juice. Tropicana from the carton or a local equivalent is fine. Most bartenders disdain the "home-style" that includes little polyps of orange because they tend to cling to glasses. Fresh juice poses the same problem.

Greyhound, or Salty Dog. As above except with grapefruit juice.

Sea Breeze. Add a shot of cranberry juice to a Greyhound.

Madras. As above except with orange juice and cranberry juice.

Tequila Sunrise. A screwdriver except that Tequila replaces vodka with a little Grenadine float on top.

These drinks are dangerous because they are sweet and fruity, which disguises their alcoholic power. That's one of the reasons such drinks were invented. There is a world of taste difference between a vodka Martini and a Tequila Sunrise. One is sweet, fruity, fun, and of an intriguing color. The other is colorless and tastes vaguely medicinal. They are equally powerful.

Youngsters often come unglued with sweet and fruity cocktails because they can't taste the alcohol and are only made aware of it when it takes effect, which is too late. Because they are innocuous looking these fruity drinks are favorites with alcoholics, of whom all bartenders will meet a few from time to time. Some bartenders have been known to reduce the amount of alcohol served in them, safe in the knowledge that, as long as the first drink served was of normal power, the subsequent dilution will not be noticed.

This is good for the bartender's conscience and the bar's "PC" (percentage profit), but is actually an invidious gesture from the health point of view, since most alcoholics will simply continue to drink until they achieve whatever stage they are aiming for. If it takes 20 Screwdrivers as opposed to the regular 11 or 12, then so be it. Tyro bartenders who can be bothered to notice are frequently amazed by the vast quantities of liquor taken on board by some of their customers.

Singapore Sling. Said to have been invented by the author Somerset Maugham at the Raffles Hotel in Singapore, this drink is a simple variation on a common mixture. Pour a shot of gin into a highball glass filled with ice. Top up with Lemon X, give it a quick shake with the small metal shaker, then float a little Cherry Brandy on top. Cherry, slice of orange if available, stirrer/straw, and serve. As long as you remember that the basic spirit involved is gin, the rest is easy. Crossword buffs will already have noticed that both words of this drink's name contain the letters that make up the word "gin."

Planter's Punch. The recipe for this delicious tall summer drink is on the back of the Myer's Rum bottle. Pour a shot of Myer's (that's the dark rum in the distinctive bottle) into an ice-filled highball glass. Top up with Lemon X, shake and serve with a cherry and a stirrer or straw. A pleasant variation on this (one is usually plenty, by the way) is plain Myer's with orange juice—a very satisfying drink.

Long Island Iced Tea. When someone orders this absurd concoction you may discretely look at the customer and wonder what kind of a consumer you're dealing with. Most often you'll be looking at a youngster who's out for fun. Quite often you'll be looking at an idiot who wants to get drunk fast. Sometimes people just ask for an Iced Tea. When they do you the bartender must ascertain whether they're looking for caffeine or alcohol, since both are served at most bars, at least in the summer months.

The joke about this drink is that it actually tastes a bit like regular Iced Tea and has more or less the same color. Because of the numerous ingredients, bar managers can safely stipulate a price of not less than twice that which would be expected for a basic mixed drink such as a off-brand scotch and soda. Many bars charge more.

It is only fair to warn the customer of the price. This may sometimes usefully discourage a customer whose presence is in any case of dubious desirability. Some unscrupulous bartenders have been known to greatly exaggerate the expected fee, in groveling apologetic mode, with the precise hope and intention of dissuading trouble.

Into an ice-filled highball glass (or even taller) you pour half a shot of each of the following: Gin, Vodka, Tequila, Cointreau, and White rum. This, you will notice, covers the spectrum of white spirits with the exception of Crème de Menthe. That's how you remember the recipe.

Top up with cola, straw/stirrer, serve. And the best of luck. Just one of these concoctions will put its consumer comfortably beyond the laws concerning safe driving alcohol levels in most countries.

Kamikaze. Named, in questionable taste, for the warriors of an Oriental nation who set forth in crudely constructed aircraft that were really flying bombs designed only to land and explode, never to return, this cocktail falls into the same idiosyncratic fold as a Long Island Iced Tea. Its aficionados may be regarded with the same dubiety.

In an ice filled six-ounce rocks glass mix the following: one shot vodka, one-half shot Roses Lime Juice, one-half shot of Triple Sec, Cointreau, or Grand Marnier (orange liqueurs). Add stirrer and serve. No garnish unless requested.

Zombie. The original recipe for this beauty is as follows:
Into an ice-filled tall glass (12 to 14 ounces) pour one shot of white rum, one shot of dark rum, one shot of pineapple juice, one shot of orange juice, one-half

shot of lime juice, one-half shot of papaya juice (optional), one-half shot of apricot brandy, and a one-half shot of passion fruit syrup or orange curacao. Shake or blend and serve, with either a pineapple spear, orange wheel, mint, or all of the above. That is, after you float a jigger (a one and one-half ounce shot) of 151 proof rum on top.

Maybe there was a time when all of the above drinks could be lovingly attended to, but that time is long gone. Today's Zombie is a tall drink with a shot of 151 Rum (high proof) topped up with pineapple and orange juice. We're looking at something strong and fruity. The subtleties are wasted. The average customer requesting this kind of drink wouldn't know what half the ingredients were. But in this area, that's not uncommon. At this point we have left the world of responsible moderate drinking and entered the world of idiocy. Every business has this area.

In the business of alcohol, which can be so damaging, somebody has to keep their feet firmly on the ground, and especially the people who are at the dispensing end of the game. Several recent cases have established the precedent in law that the person serving alcohol may well be liable for the consequences thereof. Naturally, this has increased insurance costs across the board.

Rusty Nail. This is a simple drink, usually ordered after dinner. Into a rocks glass full of ice pour a shot of scotch and half a shot of Drambuie, which is a sweet scotch-based liqueur. Give it a stirrer and serve. Rarely, someone will order the drink straight up, in which case you reduce the quantities, shake it with ice in the mixing glass, and serve it in a cocktail glass.

Stinger. This is another drink for after dinner. You make it exactly like a Rusty Nail, except instead of scotch you use brandy or cognac, and for Drambuie you use white Crème de Menthe. Again, people often request that it be shaken, sometimes even when it's served on the rocks.

Brandy Alexander. Any bar manager who works on Mother's Day should warn his bartenders to stand by for strange drinks ordered by moms of all ages who haven't tasted alcohol since that naughty glass of eggnog on Christmas morning. Brandy Alexander is actually a very tasty drink. Bailey's Irish Cream is probably a better choice (certainly from the bartender's point of view!), but of course it doesn't have the flavor of chocolate.

To make a Brandy Alexander properly you need heavy cream. Many try to fudge it by using half-and-half, milk, or even a squirt or two of the canned whipped cream. The results are disastrous and they only get away with it because the customer doesn't know better.

Mix one shot (one and one-half ounces approx.) brandy or cognac (any will do), one-half shot of dark Crème de Cacao (chocolate liqueur), and two table-spoons of heavy cream. Either stir it in a rocks glass or shake it and pour it into a cocktail glass. Add a sprinkling of powdered nutmeg if available.

If the drink was requested "up" then you will have used your mixing glass and large metal shaker. They will now be creamy. If you rinse them in your working sinks that water will no longer be suitable for washing other glasses. Either send the offending items to the kitchen (but that can turn into a production comparable to the announcement of World War III) or wash them carefully on the bar, dispersing the creamy washing up water into the slop sink, not the wash and rinse sinks you use for other glasses.

All of the above probably sounds like hard work. It really isn't. Once you've made a proper Brandy Alexander you can make them in your sleep. Bartenders must not be intimidated by detail. They'd better not be, because there's a lot of it to learn! It's basically an easy job. Sometimes explanations seem to involve a lot of words, but it's always easier in practice. The stress factors in bartending do not come from the intellectual torture of remembering how to make Sazeracs. As in most jobs, they come from commuting and putting up with the rest of the human race.

Imagine describing how to tie a shoelace to a man from Mars. It would involve an awful lot of words, wouldn't it? But if you've tied it once, you can tie it again. Anyone can be a bartender. We are not talking brain surgery.

Grasshopper. This is a cousin of the Brandy Alexander. Mix one shot white Crème de Cacao (white chocolate liqueur), one-half a shot of green Crème de Menthe, and 2 tablespoons of heavy cream. Either stir it in a rocks glass, or shake it and pour it into a cocktail glass. The same complications relating to the use of cream in the mixing glasses apply here.

Sidecar. Once in a while you'll be asked to suggest a cocktail by a customer who's looking for a "change of pace." A drink that never fails to delight is the Sidecar, and it's very simple, too. You shake an ounce of sweetened lemon juice (Lemon X will do fine) with an ounce of brandy and an ounce of one of the orange liqueurs—Cointreau, Grand Marnier, or Triple Sec. This is served "up" in a four-ounce cocktail glass.

There are something like 5,000 more cocktail recipes extant. It is unlikely that you will ever encounter more than a dozen of them. Most have died the death years ago.

Bar Trends

There is always a fast traffic in "kids' bars"—rather stark bars, often offering a huge television screen but no food, catering to the affluent 21 to 28 age group.

Now you see'em, now you don't—they often only last six months before the young crowd's attention is diverted elsewhere. Then they have to reformat in order to appeal to a broader age range.

Because this is an audience with a new interest in alcohol many owners and manufacturers twist and turn to invent new drinks, especially of the gimmicky, high-profit kind. To put it plainly, the attraction of these drinks is that they provide a means of ingesting alcohol and enjoying its effects without actually having to endure its strong acquired taste. The naughtier or cuter the name the better. Thus you might currently be asked for Sex on the Beach, Silk Panties, Blow Job, Orgasm, Screaming Orgasm, and many others. These recipes do not appear in the regular bar guides. Why should they? By the time the book's printed the fashion will have passed.

Again, if your establishment is absolutely inundated with demands for weird drinks, your bartenders must learn the recipes and make them willingly. Bar managers fortunate enough to find employment at Planet Hollywood will need to instruct their bartenders in the fabrication of such drinks as "The Terminator—a cyborg's mixture of vodka, rum, gin, Grand Marnier, Tia Maria, Kahlua, sweet and sour (lemon juice), a splash of cranberry, topped with draft beer." They'll also need earplugs.

No bar is in the business of turning away customers. Large groups of giggling youths may well decide to move on somewhere else if a bartender regretfully informs them that he can't make "Woo-woos" and he doesn't know the recipe. Chances are, just as you get organized the crowd will move on, but that's life.

Then there are drinks that are regionally popular, unsurprising in such a vast country, and these must be learned. Mercifully, those restaurants and bars that used to make a major feature of strange drinks, usually heavy on the garnish and decoration, served in a Hollywood-type goblet with lots of Lemon X, but precious little alcohol in spite of their vigorous names (Scorpion, Whiplash) are largely a thing of the past.

The future trend is fairly easy to guess. The health industry will not go away. Countries that are not traditionally wine suppliers are getting into bold, massive, well-organized stride in their search for world markets. The repertoire of regularly ordered cocktails is likely to shrink steadily from here on out. Old hands can already be heard occasionally reminiscing about the not-too-distant past when the three Martini lunch was a normal feature of city business life.

The Efficient Bartender

A very important talent in a bartender is speed. Especially at peak periods, the pace can be quite demanding. It's often the case that there's not quite enough work for two, but a bit more than one can comfortably handle. The boss doesn't want to pay two salaries if possible. The bartender doesn't want to share tips with a colleague if it can be avoided. As discussed elsewhere, a happy compromise is often achieved by having a part-timer come in to work half a shift, covering the busiest time. Whichever way you set up your bar, there will occasionally be a need for speed.

The secret of speed is twofold: (1) know your job so you don't panic when the bar suddenly fills; (2) be correctly set up, with all supplies and equipment in place.

Knowing the job is simply a matter of experience and practice. Bartenders must learn to prioritize their moves instantly. It will help, where a bartender also services the floor of the restaurant, if the floor staff are aware of how the bar is set up, and know how to order their drinks correctly. It's up to the bartenders to show them how—as gently as possible.

Bartenders do have enormous ogre potential in the eyes of some servers—a threat only equaled, but usually comfortably surpassed, by the monster in the kitchen, the chef. Of course, a friendly atmosphere will help reduce problems and stress.

It can be time wasting when servers do not call their drinks properly. Thus, "A Grolsch, two Martinis, a gin Martini up, a vodka Martini down, a Whiskey Sour, and an Amstel" may cause bartenders to gnash their teeth a bit because if they are moving fast, grab a bottle of Grolsch beer from the distant refrigerator, and come back to start fixing the cocktails, they will then have to return 10 yards up the bar to extract an Amstel.

Servers must learn how to group their drinks. First the cocktails that require mixing, then the straight pours (for example, scotch on the rocks), then the beers. Orders grouped in this fashion will save valuable seconds when you're steaming along at the peak hour. A cocktail that requires blending can be whizzing around for a minute while the bartender attends to the other drinks. While the bartender is shaking cocktails, the server may reach for the straight pours, and serving the beer last will ensure that it gets to the table with its head intact, if it's draft, or still cold if it's a bottle.

Draught Guinness is a show-stopper because a pint takes a full minute to draw. White froth comes out of the spout and slowly turns to dark brown liquid. (Don't worry, regular drinkers know this!) You can draw two-thirds of it, let it settle while you make other drinks, then come back and top it off with its trademark inch of white froth, forming a perfect "head" on top.

Sometimes amusing, but more often irritating, scenes can occur when working with inexperienced servers, who perhaps don't speak English well (and quite possibly have no serious intentions of learning). With a bored frown they'll start reading from the list they've written, clearly not understanding what they're reading, but just saying the words. One server, who eventually became a first-class performer, amused everyone by asking the bartender for a "Monkey on the Rocks." The bar bible was thumbed, old hands consulted, and much speculation led nowhere. Eventually someone had the bright idea of checking with the customer to see if he knew the recipe. The item requested was "Mount Gay" rum.

Patience is required with rookies, especially when they have no aquaintance with, or interest in, alcohol. Remember, some of your younger recruits will come from backgrounds where they've had no exposure whatsoever to alcohol, nor will they have any experience of sitting down to a meal. The faintest suggestion of ritual, formality, or request will reduce them to panic. If they clearly are never going to break out into the real world it is best not to waste time trying to train them.

Bartenders can waste everyone's time by not informing their managers and the servers when things run out. If, for instance, the bar runs out of Heineken beer and Miller Lite, this may not be revealed until a waiter suddenly requests a Heineken. Of course, this should never happen, but it does. Delivery problems, sickness, manager's vacation, wrong inventory—there are a hundred reasons why things go wrong.

"What beers *have* we got?" the waiter or customer will demand. A prominently posted beer list, or a beer section on the menu is a good idea here, but such lists must be kept up-to-date. The customer reaction will either be bland and philosophical, or purse-lipped and sarcastic. You may have lost a repeat customer—though, well handled and turned into a joke, you may seize an opportunity to win one.

The whole stress-creating drama can be avoided by the bartender checking the bar, or being warned by predecessors or managers, and prominently posting a notice at the end of the bar. "86 Heineken and Miller Lite. All others okay."

The term "86" is applied to anything that is not currently available, be it the daily special or carrots. When used with regard to a person ("He's 86'd"), it means he isn't allowed in the bar. The origin of the term is obscure, but it was probably an arbitrarily selected codeword such as are often used in the bar and other businesses. The purpose is to eliminate the necessity for wordy and repetitive speech at busy times. For instance, when a waiter brings a check and money to the bartender to pay the bill, the change is often intended as the tip, or as part of it. Often these tips are placed by the bartender in a special jar, discretely placed somewhere in the servers' area. Instead of explaining this, if the waiter just says a codeword—"Airport," or anything (except a much used word that might create confusion), then the message is delivered. For the ultimate in codewords or jargon, tune into air traffic control next time you fly. It is often incomprehensible to the layperson, but the aviators understand it.

A "walk-out" is a customer who walked out without paying. A "stiff" is one who didn't tip, and so on.

In a bar where a selection of wines by the glass are featured it will pay to check to see what you've got at the commencement of business. Running around trying to find the new alternative for the old Chardonnay, and the last six bottles of Macon Village that you just know you saw somewhere can waste a lot of time and lose sales opportunities.

A little discipline with the bar equipment and supplies is essential, too. Bottles emptied should be immediately replaced from the back-up cupboard— no sliding along to the next station and borrowing its Dewars or whatever. The empty bottle will still be waiting for you the next time you grab it.

When a bottle is replaced the pourer should be checked and replaced if it is beginning to deteriorate. The cork variety do start looking a bit "gungy" after a while. If little bits of black rotting cork spread through a bottle of Absolut vodka, the customers will start rejecting their drinks. Time and vodka will be wasted. Sometimes you have to throw out a whole bottle, and that is emphatically not the name of the game.

Mixing glasses, strainers, and openers must be returned to their designated stations promptly. Ideally you shouldn't even have to look; your hand should fall on the required item like a racing driver's on his gear shift. Other jobs require this discipline. Every surgical instrument taken into an operating room must be accounted for after the procedure is completed. An aircraft mechanic's tools are mounted on a board, and after a service or repair, every screwdriver and wrench must be returned to its place. This is a safeguard against a heavy tool suddenly announcing its wrongful presence in the turbine at 40,000 feet. Things may not be as drastic on a bar, but the air can turn blue sometimes as a busy bartender seeks the one ingredient or tool needed to complete an order. Really smart bartenders have their own openers in their pockets, and a secret reserve of bar spoons, stirrers, and so on in a hiding place known only to them.

Trivial though it may seem, one of the worst show-stoppers is the burying of the ice scoop either in the bar sink or the ice machine itself. That's why some scoops are attached to chains, but this can be a cumbersome arrangement. "Scoops out!" must be the cry when ice is poured from the bucket into the sinks.

The scoops have a purpose: they're for putting ice into glasses. Some sloppy workers put the glass straight into the ice. This not only doesn't look very classy, but is also dangerous. If a glass breaks, then small bits of glass may lurk anywhere in the ice sink, and they will be almost invisible for obvious reasons.

Cheap glassware, such as is generally used in bars, shatters into more pieces than you can shake a stick at. If a glass breaks in the ice, then the whole sink must be emptied, all the broken pieces of glass extracted or flushed down the plug-hole, and a new load of ice brought in to replace it. If this happens at a busy time—and some workers get sloppier when the pace picks up—then service will suffer badly.

When drinks are finished the glass often contains some residual ice, a squeezed wedge of lime or lemon, or even a cherry or olive, and the straw, be it large or of the smaller "sipstix" type that also doubles as a stirrer. This debris must be disposed of carefully. Whether you wash your glasses on the bar or send them to a dish-washing area, the debris must be removed before washing commences. If you just throw it into the "slop sink," eventually the sink will block. Now, the slop sink is usually fitted with a sort of grill or even gauze over the plug-hole so that it's quite safe and reasonable to throw ice or squeezed fruit into it. For esthetic and hygienic reasons the accumulated fruit should be removed regularly. But straws and sipstix especially have an uncanny way of going down the plug-hole. At the point where enough have accumulated, you have a blockage.

Especially in old installations, the dreary performance with fizzing "Draino," wires, and plungers is a common sight. If the bartender can't fix it then a plumber will have to be called in, and whether it takes five minutes or 55 minutes, you pay for the full hour.

Make no mistake, this easily avoidable blockage situation can be a total show-stopper. In some establishments, the man who comes regularly to clean the pipes that conduct the draft beer from cellar to bar, will also "snake out" the other pipes.

Another common brick wall that bartenders can run into is a jammed register. Anything can cause it. If it's a newfangled computer type, the reason is most likely that the wrong commands are being given. There will be a delay while the one manager who knows how the thing works is called up. More than one person must know the entire workings of such machines, or the accident is just waiting to happen.

Even the dear old-fashioned kind of electrically-operated register can seize up for no apparent reason once in a while, reliable though they generally are. They will appear to be working all right but when you ring up "Liquor: $4.50" the machine will display "Food: $113.37," and record this on the tape, too. Awareness and general alertness should take care of this. Get the serviceman to check to see that the opening instrument is in your bartender's drawer, and show the bartenders how to open the register if it should ever jam.

A day of improperly recorded business is not the end of the world. But if you can't make change for the customers then things will slow down horribly and you may even have to close. This is not a happy option in marginal businesses where one day's operation in the week represents the profit picture, the other six days' takings being absorbed by running expenses.

Bar managers should constantly review the working system of the bar and be ever alert for areas that can be improved. The best way to do this is to work a shift once in a while, or stand in for an hour while the regular bartender sits down and has a bite to eat. A "hands on" approach will reveal what is user and customer friendly and what is not.

Once business is underway, bartenders must be trained to get into a sequence, a sort of endlessly sweeping searchlight. Is everyone served? Does that ash tray need emptying? Ash trays should be emptied and wiped with a special cloth or paper bev-nap. Once in a while you'll put a lighted cigarette into the garbage and there'll be a small fire—fortunately you have plenty of water on hand. Also, once in a while you'll throw the tip into the garbage as you hastily clear a place after a departing customer. If there's cigarette ash and garbage in the tip cup, chances are there's a tip in the garbage!

When new customers arrive, they should be greeted and served. As soon as the last person has got his drink, then you need to do an immediate check of other customers. They will not have stopped drinking just because you got busy. If your ear is being bent by a nonstop talker the drill is simple: you just walk away. Bartenders get used to it; earbenders, too.

Bottles should be removed from the bar as soon as they are empty—a state that bartenders should rather confirm by attempting to pour the last drop into the customer's glass. This may stimulate further sales, and certainly removes a potential projectile if things get rough.

Once in a while when shaking a cocktail the metal shaker and the mixing glass will jam together. When this happens do *not* bang it against the bar. That is the sure sign of an amateur. Hold it level with your face, shaker uppermost, and strike the mixing glass briskly with the heel of your hand near the join. The two containers will separate immediately.

CHAPTER NINE

The Law, Crimes, and Whom You Don't Serve

Alcohol and the Law

Since its invention the world of alcohol has been hedged about with ritual, myth, misconception, misunderstanding, taboo, and law. Abuse or misuse of alcohol can be disruptive. So strong is the appetite for alcohol—a nonessential item in the grand concept of consumerism—that it lends itself almost automatically to the attentions of the Internal Revenue. Taxes are collected by law.

Thirty strokes of the cane would be a mild sentence for an imbiber apprehended in Moslem Pakistan. In Gibraltar the permitted amount of alcohol for drivers is zero. Since *any* blood test will reveal a small amount of naturally present alcohol, this gives the local police in this tiny British colony carte blanche to prosecute. Motorists who fall foul of alcohol regulations in Scandinavian countries are particularly at risk. Licenses are instantly revoked. For what many would consider a minor excess motorists are packed off to rehabilitation centers for alcoholics!

Strict and irksome as the laws governing alcohol are, the rationale behind them is unquestionable. Drunk drivers kill people. A large percentage of industrial accidents and accidents in the home are attributable to alcohol. In 1993 Scotland's premier duke, the Duke of Hamilton, was found guilty of drunk driving after a horrendous 95 mph car chase in which, fortunately, no one was killed. Four years before he had been banned from driving after his third conviction for drunk driving. This is the grim reality behind sometimes seemingly absurd laws governing alcohol.

Many alcohol-related laws have their roots in reason, though sometimes obscure. For instance, some of the more convoluted laws in the United States may originally have derived from the certain knowledge that large amounts of alcohol were handled by organized crime, a hangover from Prohibition. But for working purposes it is probably best to adopt an "Alice in Wonderland" attitude and simply accept the law as it stands.

Until recently British licensing laws were a cause of perplexity to foreign visitors. Alcohol could be served from 11:30 to 2 P.M. in some pubs and restaurants, but not everywhere in the country. It could be served again from 5:30 to 10:30 or 11:00 P.M. in the evening. Thus, a French visitor who took a late lunch after 2 P.M., could not have a glass of wine with it. Smart restaurants served liqueurs to late diners in tiny coffee cups.

These absurd laws have now been revoked. But it is interesting to note that, so ingrained is the custom, that in many towns the old hours are still observed. The strange licensing hours were originally introduced during World War I in order to increase industrial productivity. Workers too long at the pub at lunchtime did not produce enough munitions. Even that most obnoxious of alcohol laws, American Prohibition, is not entirely ridiculous if you examine the rationale behind it.

A reading of the early life of the writer D. H. Lawrence exemplifies the problem simply. His father had a good job in the late 19th century as a "butty"— a man who supervised four coal miners and was paid by the owners according to how much they produced. He was responsible for paying the miners—a curious system that would find few aficionados today.

Regularly, the Lawrence family lay awake awaiting the return of the drunken and quarrelsome father from the pub. All over the industrial world, from Pittsburgh to Lower Silesia, wives and mothers were embittered by their husbands' insistence on spending up to a third of their weekly wages in bars. So much could have been achieved with the cash made available by moderation. As it was, there was never any money for "extras" or vacations, or for savings. The problem was widespread among the working classes. This is the basic reason for the heavy prevalence of prejudice against alcohol—this, and the danger of accidents. So the law is here to stay, and those who earn a living in the bar business must come to terms with it.

There is of course another, somewhat cynical aspect to the sale and consumption of alcohol that the following historical digression reveals succinctly.

The Catholic Bishop Valancius initiated a vigorous temperance movement in Lithuania in the 1860s. Lithuania was at this time a province of the Russian Empire. He aimed to raise the religious and moral standards of the masses, and ease the hard lot of serfs. Vows of temperance were administered and abstainers were registered. Within two years 82 percent of Lithuania was "dry." But, whereas in 1858 35,000 roubles were raised in one country from excise taxes, six months into 1859, only 500 roubles had been collected. The temperance movement even spread to St. Petersburg and beyond in Russia itself.

At this point the governor of Lithuania banned all temperance fraternities and started promoting drunkenness. The peasants were told that drinking vodka was essential to the health of anyone living in the Lithuanian climate. Barrels of vodka were situated near churches and free drinks were handed out. Eventually the preaching of temperance was banned, and violators of this law heavily fined.

Some believe that "sin taxes are the last refuge of irredeemable politicians." The fact remains that governments recover huge amounts of money from the consumption of alcohol.

The law's inanities are endless. It is illegal to sell an ounce-sized bottle of spirit in New York. Only liqueurs may be thus sold. So a small amount of flavoring is injected into these tiny bottles (a solace for impecunious drinkers who can't afford a bigger bottle) so that they can be sold across the counter in the liquor store.

In most states no alcohol may be sold within statutory distances of churches or schools. "Free pouring" is not allowed in England, which necessitates the use of tiny measures of a gill. The spirits bottles are suspended upside down and a glass instrument called an "optic" is stuck in the neck. This dispenses a gill at a time. To get a decent scotch and soda or gin and tonic, customers in English pubs have to order "doubles" or "trebles."

The laws in all English-speaking countries are bewildering. In some Australian cities only two hours of pub drinking are allowed in the early evening. Everyone works hard to achieve maximum consumption. The traffic police lurk outside the pubs. It is not very civilized.

In Moslem Oman, you can get a drink, as you can in Egypt. In Saudi Arabia, if caught, stand by for a public caning. Only continental Europe offers full service 24 hours a day, and their alcoholism problems are horrendous. Gorbachev drew sneers when he attempted to curtail alcohol consumption, but

Russian orphanages are full of small children whose parents have died from alcohol.

While the world was horrified to learn of Yeltsin's drunken evening that ended with him falling into a river, Russia itself applauded. He was clearly revealed as a "regular guy." Mendes-France, when the prime minister of France, was much mocked when he ordered signs to be put up advising "Never more than a liter a day," and even going so far as to encourage French people to drink more milk. Yet 25 percent of all hospital beds in France are taken up with alcohol-related cases.

Licensing

The method of payment for alcohol deliveries varies from state to state and must be complied with. In New York, for instance, alcohol may not be paid for by cash or COD. It must be paid for by check on receipt of a bill that is a separate document from the delivery invoice handed over for signature by the delivery driver.

When a check sent in this way bounces, the liquor suppliers risk their own licenses if they do not immediately inform the Liquor Authority. At that point, until the Liquor Authority rules otherwise, all delivers *must* be paid for COD.

In most states liquor may not be sold retail, that is, to be taken home by the customer. In some states there are highly convoluted laws concerning what may or may not be consumed at the bar, or at the tables, and a bar manager needs to be thoroughly conversant with these laws.

In some states, such as New York, the stated price of a drink must include the local tax. But this price is included in the grand total to be taxed if the customer also orders food. In other words, a gin and tonic may be $4.25, including tax. But a gin and tonic accompanied by a 5 dollar hamburger at the bar means that the combined price of the drink and the burger, $9.25, is taxed according to local laws. If a customer sits at a table and has a gin and tonic only, then the price will be $4.25, plus tax. This may sound unfair, and probably is.

The rights of children, that is minors under the legal age for consumption of alcohol, vary. In some states they may sit at the bar in the company of an adult, as long as they only have soft drinks. In others, they may not sit at the bar at all.

Bars, like restaurants, must be kept clean and certain regulations observed. In many states these laws are somewhat unrealistic and frequently flouted. For instance, the placing of bottles on ice that is also used to make drinks is forbidden, but almost everyone does it. The statutory temperature for the washing-up water approaches boiling point and no bartender could be expected to wash up in it. One is not supposed to pour from one bottle to another, but bartenders will be reluctant to start a busy shift with three bottles of Dewars, each containing two shots. They will marry them up into a single bottle, and break out two full ones.

The reality is that, if an inspector finds the bar in a dirty, health-threatening state, you will have the book thrown at you in order to extract a maximum fine. If, however, the inspector calls at the behest of an anonymous letter that may clearly be from a disgruntled exemployee or rival business, and finds that in general and on the whole the bar is competently run and in good shape, there's little to fear. A good standard of cleanliness can easily be maintained by having a routine set of tasks. Certain areas or items are to be cleaned every day. Others every week, and so on.

There has been so much "whistle-blowing" nationwide recently that the old custom of popping a 50-dollar bill into the inspector's top pocket is in abeyance, and likely to remain so. Inspector training has been revised also, making health-threatening offenses the main target and relegating the more trivial observations to a realistic perspective.

Many retired health inspectors make a living by giving bars and restaurants an unofficial examination regularly. They point out discrepancies that can be corrected so that if a *real* inspector calls, there'll be no problem.

A strong tradition of employing illegal immigrants exists in the bar and restaurant industry. Immigration officers may occasionally descend and grill all employees found on the premises. Often disgruntled exemployees will instigate this. You may have the opportunity of watching as many as nine armed officers, of various sexes and races, solemnly handcuffing and arresting a 5'2" Irish waitress, as recently happened in New York.

The permitted hours of opening vary considerably, and Sunday hours are often different than the other days of the week. Early closing on Saturday nights is common, too, presumably because it was at one time felt that this impinged on Sunday, and might affect church attendance.

It is worth reflecting on at this stage that the Puritan tradition, which is the basis for much thinking in the United States, does not take an antagonistic attitude toward alcohol. As mentioned elsewhere, one of the reasons the Pilgrim Fathers landed where they did (they were actually heading for Virginia) was because they were running out of beer and wanted to make some more.

Alcohol abuse, however, was not encouraged, Within the Christian world, total intolerance came with later temperance movements and the Methodists. Social disruption, caused by rural migration to cities as a result of the industrial revolution, undoubtedly played a part in changing social behavior. To this day many towns in the strongly Methodist areas of England such as North Yorkshire ("Herriot country" for TV buffs) feature a Temperance Hotel.

Domestic brewing of alcohol is restricted in most non-Latin countries, and possession of an unlicensed still is an offense. A slightly comical feature of school life in England is the annual arrival of the Customs and Excise officer to inspect the chemistry laboratory still and to check its documentation.

In order to get an alcohol license in the first place, an applicant must be of acceptable character and the premises must meet certain structural standards, of which the most important is a bathroom facility and an emergency exit. This is pretty standard everywhere. Laws governing proximity to places of worship and schools vary considerably.

Exits offer opportunities to incoming thieves and outgoing nonpayers. One solution is to put a table, or some light obstruction, near the exit, sufficient to deter easy slipping in and out, but easily and instantly movable in the event of a real necessity to get out. Exits must be clearly marked by illuminated signs. The Maximum Occupancy sign must be clearly displayed.

There are varying degrees of licenses obtainable. In some restaurants only wine and beer are available. A popular trend at the moment is the "BYO" restaurant ("Bring Your Own Liquor"), which means diners can have a really cheap restaurant experience. Good wines can be obtained at liquor stores for far less than a restaurant would be obliged to charge for them, even as "specials." Many restaurateurs would have a fit at the thought of running an operation that didn't have a full license. This indicates the limitations of their thinking because premises that lend themselves to licensing will invariably command higher rents, and there are plenty of coffee shops that do double the amount of business of licensed restaurants in the same neighborhood. McDonald's doesn't do too badly, either.

The Liquor Authority is most concerned with the source of funds for opening a new bar or restaurant, because the industry is notorious for tax shelter and money laundering operations. It's best to put the matter in the hands of a lawyer specializing in such matters.

Sometimes one of the partners may be barred from holding a license because of previous criminal convictions. But this does not necessarily have to be forever, and it is perfectly all right for such an individual to take part in a licensed business, as long as the name of someone of good character is on the documents.

From the law's point of view, anyone who's ever been convicted of financial finagling, or even suspected thereof, has earned an eternal niche on the computer, and they will be regularly inspected by the tax authorities.

A liquor license must be prominently displayed on your premises, usually in the front window. An inspector will check it from time to time. This display also serves the useful purpose of informing the public that they can get an alcoholic drink in the establishment.

The Law and the Customer

How does the law affect customers? Quite simply, no one can be refused service—unless there's a reason. Such reasons are not hard to find. If a customer has clearly had too much to drink on arrival at your establishment service can be refused. If the customer objects, then the customer should be gently and carefully escorted to the door.

These customers should be treated gently, because if you throw them out and hurt them they may come back with armed friends. Also carefully, because they may suddenly pull out a weapon and assault you. Verbal abuse should be simply ignored in the grand tradition of "Sticks and stones may break my bones, but names will never hurt me."

Male members of bar and restaurant staff must be warned that if the bartender or manager requests moral support in these incidents, they are to drop whatever they're doing and assume a menacing posture behind the manager or bartender who's actually handling the case.

Often it isn't this simple. Situations do not always immediately manifest themselves. A charming, elderly lady may come in, sit at the bar, and politely order a Martini. At the first swig she will emerge from her demure shell and with a raucous laugh, yell, "So when are we gonna see some action round here, huh?" The drill here is to coldly and calmly give back the money, rudely and pointedly throw out the drink, and request the lady to leave. If she refuses, then you have to put the male staff on red alert until she's been eased out. The thought that the poor old thing in many ways resembles your Aunt Matilda is entirely a private indulgence and should be suppressed in the interest of business.

Often a customer will just sit and sit getting drunker and drunker. At a certain point—and clearly the earlier the better—the customer should be politely informed that no more alcohol will be served.

"Would you like some black coffee perhaps," a kind bartender may ask. No, the customer wants a drink. "I wouldn't be doing you any favors," the bartender says regretfully. "I'm not asking for favors. I'm asking for a drink," and so on. The mistake here is in commencing dialogue: No dialogue. No discussion. Pronouncements are required. Cold statements of intent. It's a good idea, having made one's statement to simply walk away, thus not offering opportunity for argument. Usually, no matter how drunk they are, customers will get the message.

It is important that alcohol abusers remain the only victims of their unfortunate ways. It is important for bar managers and their staffs to get into the habit of sloughing off potential stress. It's a long shift sometimes. There is a danger of taking out one's frustrations on undeserving customers. Give the cold unfriendly treatment to those who've incurred it, not others. And don't take any of it home.

Managers can help a lot after unpleasant incidents by laughing them off and generally lightening up the atmosphere. A little praise can help too. "You handled that one nicely. What a jerk!"

An occasional voice can be heard inquiring why so many people turn into idiots the moment they enter a bar. Well, the industry has rather brought this upon itself by promoting the promise of good times, wonderful conversation, first class service at incredible prices, with all sorts of things thrown in free. No wonder there is occasionally an idiot response.

Other situations grow. Here is a real-life incident.

A man comes into the bar and orders a Budweiser. He's quiet, slightly odd, dressed all in black with a black beret decorated with several badges. But this is New York, and if you refuse to serve customers because they're slightly odd you won't do much business.

Three beers later he starts doing a little whistling through his teeth. No, the bartender can't turn up the juke box or radio because this is the regulars' cocktail hour and they've made it clear that they want to hear themselves speak. A regular customer doing the crossword flounces his newspaper in pointed irritation. A regular lady customer moves to the other end of the bar. Then the man starts to meow—a very passing feline imitation. More frowns and flouncing from the regulars. Then he starts to bark—a good canine act.

At this point the young bartender approaches the customer and says, weakly, "I'd really prefer it if you didn't make funny noises at the bar."

The customer says nothing. Then he finishes his beer and requests another. Taking a deep breath the young bartender says, "I'm sorry, I'm not going to serve you." Whereupon the customer pulls out a wicked looking knife and lunges across the bar at the bartender—missing, fortunately.

The other bartender sees this, grabs a full bottle of beer and throws it at the attacker's head. He hits him fair and square. The man in black staggers off his stool, drops the knife, shakes himself, and walks out. No one chases him. End of story.

The only observation here is that the bartender should have leaned heavily, immediately when the man started making odd noises. He should have cut him off firmly and decisively. But the bartender didn't understand the potential for danger. How could he? Disturbed people are not always easy to spot. However, the chances of a return match here were small. A deterrent had been effectively launched, and the weapon lost.

And it still isn't that simple. A recipe for real trouble is inexperienced, greedy, and insecure owners who insist on falling upon the necks of every human being who walks into the restaurant without any kind of distinction. This is a social problem for our times that the bar staff have come to terms with. Serious and responsible people will often go around in dirty jeans, a day's growth of beard, and with their hats on backwards. A serious office suit can be dressed down with sneakers and baseball hat to indicate that the wearer is really a regular guy, even if he does just have to mosey on down to the hospital to take care of a couple of triple by-passes, or pop into court and hand out a few sentences. Appearances are deceptive now as never before. Pickpockets wear three-piece suits. Two huge heists were carried out in New York in recent years by gangs of clean-cut men in dinner jackets. So eternal vigilance is required.

In general, bar managers and their staffs should be alert and assess customers constantly, but with a light touch and attitude. There's no point in inventing situations that don't exist. If customers are a bit gruff and unfriendly, there's no need to respond in that spirit. With luck they won't be there long, and often a good bartender can cheer such people into better and more congenial attitudes. Misunderstandings are common. One regular customer was generally disliked because of his peremptory manner. However, he was never impolite. It turned out that his rather sharp manner of speech had nothing to do with his attitude to life, or a desire to be bossy. He had been cured of a bad speech defect and stammer when young, but the end product was a slightly snappy way of talking. But, just once in a while, you have to grin and bear it. The only comfort then is the old saying, "This too, will pass." It always does.

The Law and the Bar Staff

It is not uncommon for owners, or more often their ever-willing and desperately enthusiastic spouses, to make grave errors. As we all know, no self-respecting spouse would ignore a partner's business. You have to share everything and be "supportive." (The industry, by the way, has a very high divorce rate.)

So a common sight is a gushing spouse, saving payroll by acting as host or hostess, dashing down the bar to greet a totally undesirable customer who is quite perplexed by the enthusiasm.

Another real-life incident concerns a busy bar restaurant where the manageress was a total phony, all smiles and action when the owners were around, but heavily into milking the joint for all she could take when they weren't. As part of her smoke screen she maintained a constant harassment of the bartenders, always inventing stories about them, and complaining that they weren't doing their jobs.

Smoke-screening and sabotage by phony employees is not uncommon. On one occasion a dutiful bartender had set up a large drinks order for a waiter in a logical and easy way, so that the waiter would be able to serve them correctly. As the waiter was distracted, the head bartender came over and rearranged the drinks haphazardly.

"Why did you do that? I had the drinks set out just right."

"Never pass up an opportunity to screw up the servers," the senior man said affably. "It keeps the spotlight off us."

This sort of infantile behavior is what happens when you have "adversarial management"—managers who are always looking for trouble, as though to constantly justify their existence and employment. This mentality is very common among NCOs in armies, and where the officers are weak, they will be strong—but the morale of the men will be poor. In business, of course, fancy considerations like "morale" and esprit de corps are not usually entertained. More the pity, they can actually affect the bottom line profits significantly.

Rival colleagues, too, will often seize opportunities to score.

One bartender took a new job and immediately incurred the jealousy of another bartender, an old-timer who only worked three fill-in shifts a week, but felt himself to be in authority and took pride in having the boss's ear. The new bartender found, to his horror, that he had inherited the regular clientele from hell: a bunch of rude, demanding, nontipping alcoholics who always questioned the totals on their checks. With a sigh, the new man set about reducing their numbers.

As each unwanted customer overstepped the marks of reasonable behavior, he stopped serving them and warned them that he would not be prepared to serve them in future. "Who does this new guy think he is?" the jealous man said to anyone who'd listen. "If he keeps on like this, there won't be any customers left!"

Fortunately, the new bartender was able to replace the deadbeats with nicer people and build up a pleasant clientele. No one had any axe to grind. He was making money for himself and for the business.

As a variation on this common scenario, one bartender went to the owner and asked for permission to refuse service to a certain bunch of regular customers.

He explained why: they were rude, mean, and generally obnoxious. Most important, they drove away other customers.

The owner sympathized, and the bartender was relieved.

The next time this crowd came in, the bartender said simply and politely, "I'm sorry. I refuse to serve you."

"Why? What are you talking about?"

"I don't have to explain. I've discussed it with the owner and he agrees with me. Your behavior is intolerable. I won't serve you. Please leave."

"The hell with you. I'm gonna have a word with the boss," said the ringleader of this unattractive group, striding to the back of the restaurant.

"Say, what is the problem with your bartender?" he whined. "Why, me and my friends have so enjoyed coming here and we really would like a drink. I mean, what's his problem?"

The owner chickened out.

"Oh, don't take any notice. You can stay," he grinned, weakly.

Ringleader goes back to the bar. "The owner says you'd better give us a drink."

The bartender felt he had no choice. He simply walked off the job.

In a variation of this plot, the bartender swallowed his pride and endured the abuse. He then systematically stole a hundred dollars a shift until he found another job, at which point, without giving any kind of notice, he simply didn't show for work, and naturally, at a point in the week when this would cause maximum aggravation. This was a case of "don't get mad, get even." Weak owners often destroy their own businesses.

None of these incidents took place in slum dives. They were all in middle-class, respectable, professional, and family-oriented neighborhoods.

But one should not be too impressed by small dramatics. The defeated bar owner referred to above may have been a member of an organization that owned 10 restaurants, six garages, five dry cleaning establishments, four laundries, nine private refuse collection agencies, and much, much more. It's a jungle out there!

Many bartenders today are women. There has been an increase in their numbers in recent years. One spin-off of this may be that male customers will become enamored and misinterpret the pleasantness that people in service jobs are required to impart as part of their jobs. Men often think they've been singled out for special attention because they're considered attractive, and will naturally wish to exploit the situation. Many women handle themselves haphazardly in this area, deliberately giving every man who walks in the impression that he's the handsome Lothario she's been waiting for all her life. Sometimes this is a deliberate tip-grubbing policy. Sometimes it's just a manifestation of deep insecurity. And one must concede that occasionally it's just sheer love of life and the human race.

This is one of the negative drawbacks of the determined informality of American life. Polite formality to Americans is cold, offhand, indifferent treatment. Behavior that would be considered perfectly pleasant in Europe is considered cold by many Americans.

"Gee, he/she's got a lot of attitude," people will say.

Russians, and others, find Americans altogether strange in their manner. What's all this endless smiling, and overexpressive face pulling they all seem to insist upon?

So, once in a while a female bartender may find herself the unwilling object of a man's attentions. It's tough to be cold and dismissive when the lonely guy drops a hundred dollar tip on the bar before disappearing into the night. Not unnaturally some women are tempted to maintain a flirtation.

How can men be gently dissuaded from their obsessions, without insulting their masculine pride? The answer is simple. Day One, you invent a husband, and ideally, for full effect, children. Early in your conversations you refer to them, more than once if necessary, in order to get the message across. This will usually cool ardor. To thicken up the smokescreen of unavailability you can talk avidly about your church affairs, your eight cats and six dogs, your nutrition and aerobic studies, and flirtation with some obscure religion.

It is a pity all women are not given instruction in getting rid of men they don't want, regardless of whether they work in bars or not. Millions of men shake their heads as they retreat from women who have been inviting, but who suddenly seem to remember they have a serious boyfriend, or even a fiancé.

Crime

From the Outside. All bars are tempting targets for criminals. The main attraction is cash. If the place is doing any kind of business there'll be more than a thousand dollars somewhere on the premises by the end of the day. Members of the floor staff will be leaving with a small bundle of tips in their back pockets, sometimes as much as 200 dollars on good days.

It is absolutely necessary to adopt a defensive attitude toward crime in cities and large towns today. Residential neighborhoods are constantly patrolled by alert criminals looking for targets: a distracted motorist, the person returning tired from a trip who puts his briefcase on the sidewalk while he pays the cab.

Every doorknob on the street gets an attempted turn or two during the course of the day.

The high turnover in employees throughout the industry means that there's a constant outflow of information about an establishment's routine, particularly how the cash is handled. Even where this source of information is not available, criminals will reconnoiter premises military style, and sometimes even infiltrate as phony employees.

When the money is being counted and banks set up before commencement of business, the premises should be securely locked. Only known delivery people or salespeople should be admitted. Remember, the relief driver of the fish truck parked outside may be self-appointed.

Another vulnerable time is toward the end of business day when many people are tired, relaxed, drunk, or all of the above, and the maximum amount of money is sitting in the registers.

In many bars, at a certain time, usually after the closing of the kitchen when restaurant personnel are automatically reduced in number, the doors are locked. Only known customers, or selected customers, are then admitted by the bartender who will usually have a buzzer under the bar to open the door remotely. Some bars have a policy of depositing large amounts of money as they are amassed, either by making a lunchtime deposit at the bank or putting it in a safe.

There is a special weakness in the restaurant bar operation that makes it especially vulnerable to exploitation by outright criminals and "wise guys." Everyone who works in a bar is programmed to smile a lot and to be affable and friendly. Thus, an equally affable crook with a big smile can operate without arousing suspicion.

One cannot overemphasize the diligence and intensity of the criminal mind. Crooks will spot new bartenders or managers instantly, and immediately wonder if they can put something over on them.

Here is a true-life incident. A new bartender is half-way through his first shift and it's a very busy period. He wants to give a good account of himself because it's a great job. Everyone's friendly. Staff and regular customers all say "hi" and introduce themselves to him.

In comes a well-dressed jovial-looking guy with a big smile. He extends a hand to the new bartender and says, "Hi, you must be . . ."

"Steve."

"Steve, that's right. Al (that's the owner or someone in authority) mentioned you'd be starting. You won't go wrong—it's a great place. I've been coming here for years. It's our office hangout."

He peers around the bar.

"Say, did you see Joan? The red-headed gal with the great legs? Oh, you don't know her? Or Joe—stocky guy with a big moustache? Damn. I need 20 dollars to pick up some stuff from next door. My wife'll kill me if I forget it again. I don't suppose you could . . ."

"20 dollars? Sure, square me next time you come in."

"You're a pal, thanks."

The jovial regular customer disappears with the money. The denouement isn't hard to spot. No, the other bartender had never seen the guy before in his life. A red-headed girl among the regular customers? Nobody can think of one.

Our bartender got off cheap. He learned his lesson. You never, ever give anyone any cash unless you are absolutely certain they're entitled to it. If you lend money to colleagues or customers, then it's your problem.

If in doubt, a good way to get off the hook is to pass the buck. Someone asks the manager for money, be it for personal use or as settlement of a bill. If there is an element of doubt the manager can turn to the bartender and say, "The boss didn't leave an envelope with the meat money in it did he?" Or, if someone's fishing for a personal loan, "What's the cash situation? Have we got enough to get through the day? I know you had some big payouts already." The bartender will look regretfully in the drawer and shake his head.

Many casual employees, hired in an emergency and certain not to be invited back, will routinely borrow 5 dollars from everyone in sight. They'll never be seen again. Who's going to mount a federal investigation for five bucks? But they may have borrowed 5 dollars from ten people—they're ahead of the game!

Another real-life incident. An old hand bartender sees three young crooks entering the bar. How does he know they're crooks? A lot of experience.

"Yo," said the leader. "Y'all take the Discovery card?"

"No," snarled the bartender. "We don't."

"Y'all take any credit cards?"

"No. We don't."

The bartender's tone was rough, unfriendly, and full of aggression. This was not an accident or fault of character. He was being deliberately cold to convey to the punks that he knew they were punks.

His bartender partner, however, was not quite so savvy. Perhaps he was a younger, kinder, sweeter person.

"Waddaya mean?" he said. "Of course we take credit cards. We take American Express, Master Card . . ."

"NO!" insisted the senior bartender. "We don't take credit cards. You heard."

"Okay," said the punk leader. His tribe left quickly.

"Gee," said the real nice bartender. "What was all that about?"

There came a scream from the lady sitting by the door.

"Oh my God. My bag's gone. My money, my jewelry, credit cards, everything."

"That," the older bartender sighed, "is what it was all about."

The younger bartender's intervention had given the thieves the extra seconds they needed to search, spot, and snatch.

"Have you ever heard me talk to anyone like that before? Didn't something in my voice alert you to strange circumstances? Didn't you think they looked a little unsavory?"

It was too late. Another victim of nice guyism had bitten the dust.

One also learns to be just a little suspicious of professional nice guys. It is a definite lifestyle that one often sees in service industries. Some of the greatest crooks you'll meet—and you will meet them—will be warm and caring, almost invariably with nice wives and really gorgeous kids.

As a final comment on this true story, a few weeks after the incident the warm, nice bartender was peremptorily fired. He proved to be a flagrant and obsessive thief, whose crude methods soon glared.

For ease of description we have juxtaposed an older bartender with a younger one in this real-life story. However, this is just a convenience. There are people who will work in restaurants all their lives and know nothing at the end of it.

The habit that some women have of putting their bags on the backs of chairs in restaurants and bars has created a whole profession. Sometimes customers will get quite testy when they're warned about the practice. Fortunately, when pursesnatchers are abroad someone will usually spot them. It's usually the manager who, as part of the job, is constantly looking all over the bar and restaurant to see what's going on. Busy staff and intensely communicating customers may not be so alert. Larger establishments have security personnel who do nothing but look for potential crime situations.

City people in particular often lose all sense of awareness. One bartender tells of a hilarious (in retrospect) scene in which, to the accompaniment of much screaming and yelling and scuffling, as two regular customers tried to apprehend a thief who'd just extracted a wallet from a lady's handbag, he dashed down the bar to phone the police. Naturally, service had been suspended from the commencement of the incident. As he passed each customer they all ordered drinks! When he eventually explained to customers what had been going on (the thief shook off his would-be apprehenders and ran away) they were not particularly sympathetic. Just one more excuse for lousy service!

Constant exposure to people and public places seems to dull sensitivity. Also, it must be pointed out, the mentality of many restaurant people, owners and employees alike, is that any human being that slouches through that door is or may be a source of profit. Only good management and leadership can maintain alert attitudes and a proper intelligent perspective, and as we all either know or will eventually find out, these commodities are hard to find.

In the same spirit, street sellers should not be allowed to bother your customers. They are *your* customers, not a happy band gathered together at your expense and effort for someone else to exploit.

When closing the bar at night, it is customary to leave the cash registers open. Then, if burglars break in they will not add to your woes by smashing them to see if there's any money.

Finally, the worst nightmare in a bar is armed robbery. If precautions are taken the risk can be reduced, but if it happens, the drill is quite simple: you hand over the money promptly and without question. If a gunman panics he is more likely to shoot. In some bars there is a buzzer system connected directly to the local police station. When it's sounded it means there's trouble. The efficacy of this system, of course, will depend entirely upon the quality of the local police. In some precincts a probable response would be for the police to ring up and say, "You got a robbery in progress down there?"

Any employee who made a visible move in the presence of armed robbers would stand a good chance of getting killed. You give them the money, of which ideally not a large amount is available, and pray.

Remember, too, that the tip cups represent an easily grabbable amount of money—it could be several hundred dollars at the end of a busy day. The containers should be carefully sited, and it should be remembered that exemployees may remember the site and pass the information on.

Some armed robbers, showing commendable workers' solidarity, have declined to steal the bartender's tip cup, but it would be a mistake to assume that such consideration will always be extended.

From the Inside. There is always an element of risk involved in hiring anyone. Even those big establishments with elaborate hiring methods— sometimes involving lie detector tests and drug tests—are no less vulnerable. References can be forged or arranged.

One common scam is performed by the newly hired host or assistant manager. At lunchtime he's sent off to the bank to make a deposit. Twenty minutes later, perhaps looking a bit roughed up and obviously shaken, he returns, minus the money and minus the deposit slip with a harrowing tale of how he was mugged. In fact he gave the money to a friend, for collection and mutual enjoyment later.

As for internal stealing, we shall not dwell too long on it. The methods of doing it are legion. Ordinary routines will certainly reveal theft, even if they don't instantly show what's being done, or who's doing it.

Simply, if 12 bottles of booze have been issued to the bar, then there should be an appropriate amount of money in the register. This must be carefully monitored. Some bar managers post the profit margin on the notice board week by week, and it had better not vary too much.

In assessing the correct income from liquor dispensed, various human factors must be taken into account. Maybe the owner, an alcoholic, does a bottle of Chivas Regal a day? Perhaps the bartenders have carte blanche to buy regular customers drinks on the house if they wish—they may even be encouraged to do this. Like it or not, some bartenders pour a little heavier than others. Decent sized drinks go down well with the regular customers, many of whom will be—like it or not—heavy drinkers and often alcoholics.

Some personnel are particularly bold in the ways they find to steal. Often they will not steal from the house at all, but concentrate on the customers.

One star used to automatically add 2 or 3 dollars (or more according to the size of the bill) to every check he presented. The final total would be shown on the bottom stub that is commonly detached and given as a receipt. As often as not customers did not notice the small addition—he always kept the total amount within the ball park figures that most diners look for or expect. Then he'd detach the stub, pocket the extra, and, when he handed the check to the cashier, he would simply fill in the correct total in the space he'd thoughtfully left himself.

He was caught when a manager, convinced that he was doing something, though he couldn't think quite what, solemnly inspected the garbage and compared discarded receipt stubs with checks presented. Incidentally, the owner of this restaurant eventually went to prison for a year for tax evasion. Be warned, bar managers of the world, you may have "fallen among thieves."

Some thieves will pocket cash and pay the bill on someone else's credit card, forging the signature with blithe confidence and panache. Most of these subterfuges come to light eventually, but their perpetrators are not into long-term investment. Getting fired is no big deal, and until recently there was an abundance of jobs.

The principle of applying a blind eye is entirely a personal one. Some shrug off theft easily, others are enraged by it. A bar owner and his wife once spent a whole weekend sifting through checks and dupes to examine the activities of one of their employees. They discovered a steady trickle of stealing, between 5 and 10 dollars a day, by adding items to a check after it had been completed, then rubbing them out and pocketing the extra. The employee was promptly fired. However, this particular woman was very popular with the customers, and was the only employee they'd ever had who could properly handle one of their bars that became extremely busy at lunchtime.

Were they right to fire her? Might it have been a better idea to diplomatically question her, or mention in passing that some of the checks didn't seem to be quite right, or any old nonsense just to get the point across that they were alerted to some irregularity?

At some point in the chain of command the buck stops.

There is a whole school of humor in restaurant stealing, involving partners who steal from each other and even spouses who steal from each other.

One young bartender was approached by his more experienced partner who said, "See the customer with the moustache? Walk up to him and say '$39.50.'"

"Oh, he just paid," the young bartender replied.

Patiently his mentor said, "Just do as I say."

So, quaking in his shoes, the junior bartender approached the customer, who, it must be pointed out, had had a lot to drink, and said, "$39.50."

The customer blinked. "I thought I paid you?" he said.

The bartender's jaw quivered, but before he could blurt out an admission of the truth the customer had put up 50 dollars—the change was the tip.

"Remember," the experienced bartender said, "always $39.50. Some nights he'll pay three times, but I've never tried four."

Careful choreography and distraction are sometimes used to insure that customers forget the change placed discreetly at their elbow away from the direction in which the customer's interest is concentrated. In dark bars, a regular patrol around the stools will often yield a dropped 20-dollar bill or better.

Perhaps the richest story in this genre concerns a wildly successful large establishment that opened in New York in the 1960s, famous for being decorated with Hollywood memorabilia. It became apparent that a lot of money was not finding its way into the cash register. Ordinary control soon revealed that the bartenders were bringing in their own liquor by the case, and this small factor was easily straightened out. The whole crew was fired and a new bunch brought in. The new bartenders put hardly any alcohol at all in the cocktails, particularly the Bloody Marys. This was straightened out, but there was still obviously a leak.

The management called in a security firm who sent inspectors to spy on the bar. Although these people are supposed to look like ordinary customers, they almost invariably give themselves away because they ask such unusual questions and are clearly testing. They eventually submit nerdish reports that read rather like this:

"At 6:30 we sat down at the bar. The bartender said, 'Good evening, sir,' but failed to smile. We ordered two Beefeater Martinis up. These were correctly served, well chilled, with the specified garnish, on clean bev-naps. The bartender's fingernails were clean. A check was correctly rung up to record the sale, and correctly rung up when we paid. We left a 2 dollar tip. The bartender said, 'Thank you, sir,' but did not smile."

Few people in the industry arouse more scorn than these inspectors. Further, there is contempt for owners and managers who are so hapless that they need to call in spies.

When the inspectors had paid several visits to the Hollywood-style restaurant they filed their report. It included a passage that read, "All four registers were carefully monitored during this period and all checks appeared to be correctly rung up." Management pondered this for a while, but one of them began to frown thoughtfully. Finally he realized what was bothering him.

"What's this four registers?" he inquired. "We're only supposed to have three!"

The bartenders had brought in their very own register, and yes, it was correctly operated. However, all of its takings went into the bartenders' pockets, not the owner's.

Some operators will get hold of a guest check, take it to a printer somewhere out of town, and have a batch made up. They will then intersperse these with the real house checks.

It all sounds as though management and owners are up against a wall of wily professionals, but the bottom line remains the same. If 20 steaks are issued to the kitchen, then 20 steaks must be accounted for. If a case of vodka is issued to the bar, then it must be accounted for. Simple routine inventory control is the key to reducing theft.

A gray area here, of course, is the fact that staff may keep the inventory apparently in good shape by pouring short drinks. There's nothing to be done about this unless you are going to have elaborate quality control and spot check regularly. Fortunately, cocktails are less fashionable than they used to be. An almost alcohol-free Whiskey Sour or Bloody Mary (as discussed elsewhere) is one thing—the average customer won't detect it. But the more commonly ordered drinks—various spirits on the rocks, or with mixers—will draw attention eventually if they contain no alcohol.

There'll always be a small amount of skullduggery. There is a certain type of person who doesn't so much seek a job as an opportunity to handle cash, in the belief that some of it may stick to the fingers. People with a strict moral sense will not do well in the restaurant or bar industry. There are too many gray areas, and if they are too easily outraged then they are in for a stressful time! Furthermore, owners themselves often do not always set a good example. One of the most famous bar owners in New York City regularly pads her bills. If the customers spot the embellishment, it's simply deleted with a shrug. Only the owner prepares the bills. Madame sits at the end of the bar with a beady eye for eight straight hours six days a week. At her elbow sits a large cupful of sharp, yellow pencils with erasers, like arrows in an archer's quiver.

Some owners entirely forbid the use of pencil. Checks can be reworked, crossed out, or voided and a new check issued, but that which has been written must remain.

Another bar owner bought a job lot of white wine at a knock-down price. It was awful, undrinkable stuff. The customers complained endlessly. The wine was not thrown out. Orders were given that it was to be used only in Kirs and Spritzers. Thus 500 dollars of ghastly wine was sold for around 10,000 dollars.

One bartender found himself employed in a smart restaurant where the Italian cuisine was delicious. There was only a small amount of money in the register and no tape. But it didn't matter much because the regular customers never paid anyway. There was enough change to accommodate the few casual "drop-ins."

The regulars, all of whom seemed to be on close terms with the apparent owner, used to show up in a sort of uniform of soft butter yellow leather jackets and Gucci shoes, invariably with beautiful molls on their arms, even though the men were almost invariably ugly and overweight. Often, many of them had just come back from Las Vegas, and were on their way to Miami.

"That'll be 20 dollars sir," the bartender said on his first shift, to a customer who'd just shared a half bottle of Bardolino with his doxy, and was preparing to move to a table for dinner.

The customer smiled. "Don't give me no tab, pal, okay? Put this in your cup." He promptly handed over 50 dollars.

No salary was discussed. The bartender didn't insist on discussing it because he figured it would be the regular going rate anyway, and tips matter more. Once a week the owner would approach the bartender and say, "You make any money this week?"

Naturally the bartender would shuffle his feet and roll his eyes regretfully, whereupon the owner would absentmindedly peel off around 400 dollars from his huge roll and hand it over. "Ya doin' a great job, kid."

The establishment obviously filled some niche in the accounting system of an organized crime operation. One day the bartender showed up for work and found the door locked. Nobody knew anything about the owners. They'd "vanished forever, like mist on the heather."

One bartender reported for work only to find the restaurant burned out. He then realized what the Chinese chef had been trying to explain to him for the last few weeks. The chef had been arriving at work to find the kitchen full of gas, with a lighted candle on the table.

So drafty was it (one assumes) that insufficient gas had accumulated to create an explosion—which was just as well, since two old ladies lived in the apartments upstairs. At last, it appeared, the restaurant owner (whose brother-in-law was an insurance executive) had got it right, and the place had burned. In this case, the forensic scientists from the Fire Department declared the fire to be of suspicious origin, and the insurance claim was denied.

Some areas of the industry are simply dens of thieves. May conscience be your guide.

CHAPTER TEN

Bar Health and Hygiene

The oldest joke in the business isn't at all funny, really.

Customer: "What's this fly doing in my drink?"
Bartender (peering): "Uhm, looks like the back-stroke to me."

Public Health

The public—your paying customers—place great trust in the restaurant and bar industry to take care of health and hygiene. Hell hath no fury like that of a health inspector who discovers flagrant contempt for people's safety. And quite rightly too!

The areas of food hygiene abuse are well known. An unscrupulous operator will repeatedly display cooked meats and sausages without regard for their proper treatment. Few food items are more deadly than the humble sausage. Such items should only ever be in one of two conditions: piping hot or refrigerated. All properly trained food handlers are imbued with the maxim, "If in doubt, throw it out."

One of the serious and honest reasons many bar owners refuse to supply free food at the bar—even nuts or chips—is that they regard the practice as unhygienic. Food that is expressly ordered, paid for, and consumed at the bar is entirely another matter. Having been consumed, the debris is removed and the bar cleaned up—as opposed to having chunks of remolded cheese and much-fingered biscuits sitting around for hours on end.

It's cocktail hour, put out the chilis. Put out the bread, the chicken wings, the buffalo wings, and so on. And let them sit there all night.

Most diners don't know that the cute-looking basket of assorted bread rolls put on the table by the ever-smiling bus person has been hastily assembled "back-stage" from half a dozen returned baskets that may have received a good mauling from the general public before.

How many hands have ferreted around the apparently pristine nuts that appear in the presented bowl? How many clients' hands have shaken those hands? How many hurried trips to the bathroom with minimum attention to personal hygiene have occurred? How many subway grab-handles grabbed? How many Bassett Hounds walked, and collected after, during the course of a busy day?

Dips? Have fun at your next soirée watching and seeing how many people dip their chunk of cauliflower, bite it, and dip again.

Fortunately, most of us are pretty clean these days. But the lazy and the untrained are always with us and eternal vigilance is the price of good hygiene.

The average bar mop, if clinically examined under a microscope would be revealed as filthy, even if it looks clean. In Europe, glasses in bars are often washed, rinsed, and wiped. The wiping renders them immediately filthy again. If a noncotton cloth has been used, you can even see the loathsome fibers clinging to the usually imperceptible imperfections in the glass.

The American system—wash in hot water, preferably with motor brushes, rinse, drain, and reuse—is much safer. If a final rinse in running water can be arranged, then your customers are getting nonrisk glasses. Even a "clean" glass will not correctly accommodate draft or bottled beer if there is any build-up of detergent adhering to the glass. That's why so many customers, if they're regulars, ask the bartender to give the beer glass a good rinsing in fresh water before pouring their beer.

The greatest enemy in this area is lipstick. Some of it is not only kiss-proof; it's bomb-, detergent-, brush-, and boiling water-proof. There is only one defense—visual checking. Of course, often a good bartender will inherit the sins of a previous lazy one. But good bartenders are defensive and always assume the worst possible scenario; namely, that when they take over the bar, all the juices are about to explode, every glass is smothered in lipstick, and so on. Furthermore, they always check to see that they have at least a half a dozen glasses on hand in every category that they've inspected carefully and that they know to be squeaky clean.

Bar towels and mops should be changed daily, or when clearly overused. This can mean three or more times a day when it is busy. A good supply of reserve mops and towels should be on hand at all times. You never know when a customer is going to have an accident and need several clean towels for mopping up.

A bartender's hands are very much on display. Every time a drink is put down they are open to inspection by the customer. Nobody wants a crystal clear Martini to be marred by the effect of a row of black fingernails. Some bartenders, very wisely, make a huge fetish of their personal appearance. If men, they are always immaculately turned out in dazzling white shirts (often with old-fashioned arm bands to keep their sleeves up). Their shirts sometimes have French cuffs with sparkling cuff links, and on at least one of their fingers they will have a large dazzling ring that, not uncommonly, will be in the form of a coiled snake, with two ruby chips for its eyes.

Women bartenders are a little constrained in their dress choice by the practicalities involved. You can't teeter around on high heels, and you certainly wouldn't want your silk blouse to be splashed with tomato juice, or the explosion of a long-neglected ketchup bottle when the top is removed for the first time in weeks.

A word of warning on the subject of perfume, cologne, and aftershave. Many people like to freshen up during the course of the day with a quick splash and a squirt or two of cologne. This is an excellent idea because it really is quite refreshing. But care should be taken to see that no heavenly smelling perfume lingers on the hands. It will contaminate every drink you pour until it wears, or is washed, off. Agreeable though Chanel No. 5 or English Leather may be, they are not what drinkers wish to smell when they raise a glass of Chivas Regal to their lips.

It's true, high standards of personal appearance will be largely wasted in your average "Woo-woo" and "Sex on the Beach" cocktail bars, but in the kind of establishment that seriously intends to stay in business and make large amounts of money for all involved, it is definitely to be encouraged.

All bottles should be dusted or wiped regularly. Some bottles have an interminable shelf life, usually because they are only used in such tiny quantities that it simply takes weeks for them to be used up. Examples of this are Dry Vermouth and Grenadine. After much handling involving the dispensing of a drop or two, their labels come off or look tired. Their appearance is not pleasing at all, and must be hidden from view.

Once in a while you get a bottle with a damaged label, or something that renders it unsuitable for public display, but which is still perfectly okay to use. Such bottles can find a happy home at the service end of the bar.

Where glasses are washed at the bar, the water must be maintained at the highest possible temperature and changed regularly. A dripping tap and a stand pipe can effect a regular flow, but even so, from time to time it's a good move to simply drain the sink and refill it with fresh water. Care must be taken in the selection of detergent. There are nonstreak versions available now that work very well.

From time to time all food and liquor establishments require the attention of the exterminator. Bottles must be protected from antiinsect sprays. In some places a grand ceremony is made of this. The exterminator arrives at some unearthly hour shortly after closing, in the small hours of the night. The day's accumulation of dirty tablecloths is then used to cover all areas of the bar that are subject to handling, working, or consuming with special attention to the bottles. Remember, bottles that have been opened and fitted with pourers are more or less open bottles and therefore vulnerable to impregnation from ghastly insect-killing chemicals.

The day after such a visit, more "creepy crawlies" will be seen than normal, such is the effect of the treatment. Bartenders must be swift to remove such offending creatures from the presence of customers. But insect control is fairly straightforward, and once a building is controlled, there's no reason for it to deteriorate.

Heavier equipment is used to kill rodents. Glue traps are placed all over the bar and restaurant. These unpleasant devices are very efficient, but it's not exactly delightful when you have to start your day's work by administering the coup de grace to an englued rodent—either by dropping him into the toilet or simply throwing him into the garbage.

Just as responsible armies will keep meticulous records of the mines they've laid, exterminators must remember where they left the traps, and remove them before the commencement of business. If they don't, horrific things can happen. No nicely dressed lady with an exciting luncheon appointment will wish to see an expiring mouse in a glue trap. Still less will she wish to be bitten by a glue-wrapped rat when she stretches her elegant legs under a table—as happened in a headline-making case in New York in recent years. This is not, by any means, the sort of publicity most restaurants or bars would deliberately seek.

Strictly speaking, bottles should never be inserted in ice that is also put in people's glasses. Where this is practiced (and given the constraints of space in most establishments it's hard to avoid) at least the bottle must be clean.

In all of the above discussion, the single most common and important issue is the cleanliness of the glasses. This is the area where most bars will offend from time to time. If customers are served drinks in loathsomely greasy or lipstick decorated glasses, they are entitled to wonder what other shortcomings of hygiene the establishment may have.

Although this is unlikely to be the province of a bar manager, it should be mentioned in passing that all establishments nowadays have a responsibility to the environment. Environmental agencies are quick to act when examples of air pollution (perhaps from kitchen exhausts) or improper garbage disposal are found. Vigilance here can save huge fines.

Personal Health

Most jobs pose certain health hazards. Even the soft office worker is at risk from back trouble through too much sitting, eyestrain from too much perusing of memos, and (some suspect) from the rays that emanate from cathode ray tubes. Coal miners suffer from the dust they breathe, firemen are at risk from the asbestos they may encounter, and so on.

The bar and restaurant industry has its problems too, both physical and mental. It also has public responsibilities. A good bar manager will take an interest in the staff's health and anticipate problems before they occur.

Overwork, with all the inevitable spin-offs, is the main enemy. The eagerness of a bartender to grab every shift available, and work "doubles" when required may look heroic at first glance, but it can be disastrous.

A "double shift" is one of those human experiences that defy definition. Eight continuous hours of lifting, bending, and dealing with colleagues and customers is enough for most. But 16? And for day after day? The mind boggles.

The determination to pay off that lawyer who managed to gain custody of the child in the recent divorce, or to pay off that new car, or whatever, may seem admirable. Some may question whether the bar business is about "proving oneself," or making as much money as possible, or just earning a decent living. But, for a majority of Americans, the job is *life,* and so one has to accommodate this.

Most of us automatically genuflect at the mention of hard work. It is part of the Puritan conspiracy. Few contemplate the challenges of "hard think."

In many ways hard work is an easy solution. ("After the death of his wife he threw himself into hard work." "He worked hard, and in 10 years had saved enough to . . .") The reality is somewhat different. Tired bartenders are no good. They will not sell the establishment, they will not sell themselves, and they will not sell enough drinks. They may lose more customers than they gain.

The classic "overwork" syndrome is when a bartender works three double shifts in a row, and then calls in sick on day four, thus throwing the whole establishment into disarray, as managers run around trying to find a fill-in at extremely short notice. Here is where a list of part-time bartenders is essential. Many a struggling poet or "resting" actor will be glad to fill the breach at short notice. Every bar needs backup personnel. The more the merrier.

It is generally agreed that for anyone working in a moderately busy bar, four shifts a week ought to be the maximum. Many establishments nowadays will not allow anyone to work more than four shifts a week. However, there are also a large number of restaurants—usually French—where everyone works six days. The place is closed on Sundays and for all of August. If employees don't like it, they are free to work elsewhere.

Night workers are especially at risk, not only from physical fatigue, but also from stress that can lead to depression and even personality disorders. It is simply unnatural to go to bed at 3 A.M. or later several nights a week. Many people choose such hours for private reasons, of which the most common are that they are studying or pursuing another line of work in which they are not yet established, such as acting, writing, or setting up their own business. Clearly such people need some energy left to "do their thing" during the day.

The existence of the Circadian rhythm, the body's 24-hour built-in clock, has been confirmed, and tinkering with it is known to be unhealthy. Night workers above all should give serious thought to working less than five shifts a week. They are the most at risk.

One bartender changed his schedule on orders from his boss. He'd been working four nights and a day.

"I feel like a new man," he said. "I felt my whole personality changing. I was always tired. I had no interest in anything—reading, seeing friends, no sex interest, no nothing. It was drudgery. I felt permanently jet lagged. I got sick of the sight of my pasty face in the mirror. . . . I'm earning less, but feeling better."

Bar employees who find themselves on this treadmill are likely to be tempted to try various stimulants to get them through. Coffee and alcohol are all around, and real discipline is required to limit intake. Fortunately, most people have a natural capacity which, once satisfied, does not require further intake. Those who lack this natural appetite regulator, or who damage it, are in danger of becoming alcoholics, of which the industry, naturally, has its fair share.

When you see a bartender whooping it up at midnight, laughing, joking, doing Hollywood tricks with the glasses (throwing them in the air and catching them behind his back, for instance) and generally behaving as though he were just having a ball, there's only one question to be asked. What's he on? Uppers? Downers? Heavier items?

By contrast, the part-time day bar manager or bartender who toddles along to the local golf club to work the lunch hour, and perhaps makes 20 drinks on an average day, with a bit of a rush on weekends, clearly is less stressed. A further blessing in this sort of situation is the familiarity of surroundings and customers. A full work week is unlikely to generate any serious stress. These kinds of jobs are often covered by the retired or semiretired.

It is interesting to note the attitude of the airline industry to this problem. Their personnel are forbidden by law to exceed a certain number of hours. This is mainly for air safety reasons, but also to safeguard the health of employees. Concord crews, who fly at great height and are therefore exposed to more radioactivity, have an absolute maximum number of hours they can fly the aircraft. They are fitted with a gadget that registers the amount of radiation they have absorbed, and once the maximum is reached, they're transferred. In order to service an airline, however, a huge payroll is incurred. Because an aircraft simply must have a minimum number of personnel to service it, there are always people on stand-by.

It is unlikely that any restaurant or bar could ever afford such an arrangement. Payroll—even in an industry in which many employees are on minimum salaries that are supplemented by the public's generous and entirely voluntary tips—still looms large in the list of overhead.

Many years ago it was discovered in London that the suicide rate among night workers for the Post Office was significantly higher than the national average. This was before computerized equipment reduced the requirement for large numbers of personnel to man the telephone service and so on.

A survey yielded no definite clues as to why this should be so. However, any number of observations were bandied about. One was that the unnatural hours caused depression because the workers didn't have a normal social life. Another was that the sort of people who sought night work were predisposed in some way to depression. The only tangible benefit from the survey was to acknowledge that night work was unnatural and potentially harmful. This in itself was a useful finding.

To grasp the full extent of reality, however, most bartenders are paid an hourly rate, not a yearly salary. Further, they only get tipped when they work. It is common in England for the whole week's tips to be pooled and divided among the employees, so that, arguably, some people receive tips when they weren't actually at work. But this is not general practice in the United States, and it doesn't sound like the sort of system Americans would welcome. Therefore, a bartender who elects to work only four days when he has the opportunity to work five is voluntarily kissing a fifth of his potential income goodbye. This is no big deal to the 24-year-old student or actress, who is probably only looking for living expenses and a bit of pocket money anyway. But what about the 44-year-old with the mortgage, family, school, medical expenses, alimony, and so on? The only safeguard is to at least take time off regularly. If you've worked your five shifts and are offered a sixth, decline, whatever the pressure. Bar managers should not allow their employees to overwork.

Furthermore, the industry is notoriously insecure. A restaurant that has done good business for 20 years will suddenly close: the rent is doubled, or the large enterprise that provided most of its customers will disappear, or whatever. The fickle public may suddenly move elsewhere for no discernible reason.

It should be noted that continuous work can be healthily survived in short bursts. Many a bar or restaurant worker will gladly work 10 days straight before Christmas. There's a lot of money being spent, and once New Year's Eve is gone, there may well be a lull that will provide an ideal period in which to take off an extra day or two.

Some inexperienced employees take on a great deal of strain by being too indulgent with the customers. There are bullies abroad, and they will sniff out a weak bartender for oppression. Many retired men and women have nothing better to do than to make scenes in shops and bars.

This problem is best resolved when bartenders get a grip on their own personality and decide how much they're going to put up with. A certain detachment is absolutely necessary, especially as, by the nature of the situation, you will often have to serve people who may not be the sort you'd like to share your desert island with, but who are perfectly harmless, paying customers.

But you don't have to serve people who are rude and obnoxious. It is almost invariably the case that *all* the staff will agree that such and such a customer is a pain, and when this unanimous opinion exists the situation is eased. If a customer is generally rude to one employee in particular, and that employee has done nothing to deserve such treatment, then the customer should be "86'd" anyway, even if other bar staff have had no problems. This is part of the ruthless and continual war against stress that everyone has to wage when their job involves dealing with the public.

It occasionally happens that for various personal reasons a manager will discipline an employee in front of a customer. This is really bad for business. Such employees should be taken aside and talked to gently and privately. When a manager misreads a situation, or handles it badly and clearly takes the side of the customer against the employee, morale will suffer. Self-righteous customers will feel themselves empowered to be even more demanding or outrageous.

Stress reduction should be high on the list of every manager's agenda. You should try and spot it in advance, long before it arrives. It helps to understand the underlying reasons for fatigue. Everyone in the industry complains about it. "I work five shifts. My first day off is just spent in a haze of fatigue. I sleep late, then take at least two cat-naps before I go to bed again. Next day I'm beginning to feel rested, and may even get up and do things. The day after that, I feel great. But then it's time to go back to work." You will hear these sentiments recited so often that in the end it begins to sound like a ritual dirge.

A bar employee's day is a day of constant interruptions. You will have 100 half-finished conversations. This in itself is tiring. It is the other extreme of monotony. Performing the same task over and over is notoriously tiring. Modern production lines are organized so that people change their tasks regularly throughout the day.

Aviation provides a useful metaphor. A plane used for "island hopping" makes many more landings and take-offs than one used on the North Atlantic run. Consequently, such planes "age" faster and need to be closely monitored for the metal fatigue that will occur sooner than in standard or average operation.

There is nothing to be done about this. Even if your bartenders become morose and taciturn, refusing to talk to the customers, they will still need to discuss things with colleagues. Where a meal break away from the bar is feasible, you will often notice that employees, far from wanting to sit with others for a good old gossip, will prefer to go to a corner with a newspaper and a book. They shouldn't be denied this privilege.

Then there is simple physical fatigue. We have mentioned lifting and bending, and there is plenty of it to be done. Buckets of ice, cartons of beer, the bottles themselves—it all accumulates.

Here defensive methods exist. All bar and restaurant employees should take care to stay in good physical shape, with special regard to potential back problems. Helpful exercises to circumvent this are well known. There is bound to be someone on staff who will know them. If not, there are books describing them. No one should ever try to lift anything that even looks as if it might be too heavy. If you notice the beer delivery people, they are usually very strong, but they have their techniques for lifting. They also wear special belts that will protect against hernias and muscle strain.

The important thing when lifting any object is to square up to it and bend the knees before you even touch it. This may sound like one of those silly military drills, but you will only need one back spasm in order to be converted to it forever.

It's a shame that so many of us learn about back problems the hard way. Proper lifting should be taught in school. A really seized-up back will keep you off work for a week at least, during which time you'll be in pain, and the symptoms will be there for weeks afterward.

"I'm lucky, I only have to see my chiropractor once a week now," you'll hear victims say. The club of those with back problems has a huge membership. All would resign if they could. It's best to avoid joining.

However, although there is such a thing as a spontaneous spasm—a sudden wrench of the back, or even as a result of sneezing without bending the knees—there is also a growing spasm that creeps up on you. Drafts on the lower back, accidentally suffered while sleeping, are strongly suspected of having a bad effect. The problem is that you may endure the draft for an hour before waking up, feeling cold, and pulling up the covers. You should check the position of your bed, particularly for subtle drafts that may be sneaking in under doors or through windows. Throughout the day stretching exercises should be carried out at regular intervals. It looks funny, but it pays dividends. It's important to avoid rigid standing, like a sentry outside Buckingham Palace. (They march up and down at regular intervals, by the way; otherwise they'd go crazy.)

If you are forced into a position for any length of time by the nature of the task at hand, then put one foot up on a beer crate or whatever is available. By the time bartenders have worked a couple of shifts on a bar they will usually know every ledge where they can surreptitiously sit, while remaining attentive to the customers, and every place where a raised leg can find a footing. When the bar is empty, as long as the bottles have been dusted and everything's in order, there's no reason why bar staff shouldn't sit.

Many bars have special flooring—nice bouncy wooden duck boards. These can be removed for ease of cleaning. Where these are not provided for one reason or another, then extra precautions are absolutely mandatory. Most shoe stores nowadays have a good selection of thick-soled shoes of one kind or another. It is important that they should have laces, as these help support the 32 hard-worked bones of the foot. Unfortunately they are not very chic (to some tastes, at any rate), especially for women, but since many women today live in sneakers anyway, this is unlikely to be a problem. It is tough on hostesses, as they have to look smart, and as any woman knows, high heels can be hell.

It is nice to have two pairs, so that each day you put on a dry pair of shoes. President Reagan, when campaigning, often didn't have time for a shower and a change of clothes in the evening, but he found that just changing his shoes was refreshing.

There are various sorts of inserts that can help, too, of which the best are silicon liquid filled. They really help. Then there are elastic stockings, which support the calf. Again, though acceptable for men, some women may find them demoralizingly unchic. "Jobst" is a well-known brand name for this product. The elasticity wears out long before the material, so it makes sense to order backups. An extra pair of socks worn on top of these is very comforting, too.

All of this may sound very fuddy-duddy and old-maidish. But are hemorrhoids and varicose veins really such fun? Ask a million bartenders! Most people don't even know what these two marvelous complaints are—until they suffer them. Few people will reach the age of 40 without experiencing hemorrhoids. Pregnancy induces them, as does too much standing, sitting, mental stress, and constipation. They are pretty well a guaranteed, if unwelcome, hereditary gift. Domesticated animals get them. They are unknown in the wild.

Napoleon and his comrades all suffered from the complaint. It is seriously suggested by some historians that Napoleon lost the battle of Waterloo because an attack of "piles" (the popular name for hemorrhoids) confined him to his caravan (mobile home) at the height of the battle. They swapped ideas as to how the complaint could be combatted: the favorite solution was leeches. But there's no instant cure and you simply have to get off your feet.

The squeamish should turn a page or two before continuing this book.

Hemorrhoids are swellings, like small grapes, which occur around the anal rim. They are usually painful and frequently bleed. For sufferers, bowel movements become miniature apocalypses to be endured once a day or more often. The swellings descend, painfully, from the bowel, often at the most inopportune moments. Once this happens, there is no hope of continuing a normal day—it is equivalent to severe toothache, stomach upset, cold, flu, or hangover.

In a majority of cases, the condition is containable and endurable, though it will recur from time to time—especially at times of stress. Many sufferers eventually have a "procedure" called a "hemorrhoidectomy." This is about as much fun as it sounds. The offending swellings are amputated. Fine, except that all of this is taking place at a "Times Square" area of the body's endless traffic. The only glimmer of joy is that three weeks later the patient feels "born again" and the problem rarely recurs.

The first cousin of this complaint is varicose veins. Once in place they can either be endured or removed by surgery. They can be painful, and even after the operation—sometimes called "stripping"—the condition may recur.

Sufferers who decide to have this operation may care to consider going to Ireland. The Irish, for some reason, are particularly prone to varicose veins. A considerate government has therefore set up a highly efficient branch of its Health Service to deal with this situation in an expeditious manner. Remember, if either of your grandparents were Irish, then you are Irish too! You can claim an Irish passport (which will allow you to work anywhere in the European Community) and have your veins done, too, possibly free. A much smarter approach to these medical considerations is defensive measures.

Bar personnel are more exposed to the ordinary airborne microbes than most. A good gargle with Listerine before turning in will help keep colds away.

Most bar customers are also smokers. This may seem like a sweeping generalization, but check it out. Ventilation varies from place to place. There should be a flow-through of air but, of course, especially in winter, this can break down from time to time. There are machines called Smoke Eaters. They don't do much, but they help. They should be switched on as soon as you open, not when the place is full of smoke.

Bar personnel who are unfortunate enough to work in smoky establishments should remember that, when they leave, they will reek of cigarette smoke. You simply can't go from work in such places to a romantic date—or any kind of date where you want to look and feel your best. When you undress, you can smell it, right down to your socks. This is just one of those facts of life you have to accept and work around.

After all this, the major health problem of bar employees may seem a bit of a comedown: dishpan hands. But if you've ever let your hands get so bad that you had to go to the Emergency Room, and were prescribed steroid creams by a worried doctor who was hoping to keep your hands attached to your arms, you'd know better. Even if glasses are not washed at the bar, the exposure to water is considerable for a busy bartender. Because hands are constantly on display, they must look good at all times. Therefore, a little hand obsession is not out of place.

The worst case syndrome is as follows. Your hands get wet. The skin, nails, and cuticles are softened. Handling citrus juices (constant squeezing of limes and lemons) weakens the skin's resistance. Infection creeps in. When you wash your hands in the morning and clean your nails, you notice that they take an awful lot of digging out. A blackish greenish deposit seems to lurk, especially along the sides of your nails: It's a growing fungus. The drugstore will give you medication to clear it up—the same chemical that kills fleas on dogs or crabs on humans—and it can be contained.

But it takes weeks to clear up, so the best approach to this common threat is to avoid it. Rubber gloves will protect the hands when washing glasses, and also enable you to do a better job because you can work with hotter water. No matter how many times a day you put them on or take them off, it will pay dividends. The best gloves for bar work are called "Bluettes," at around 5 dollars a pair. The house should pay for them!

Again, bar managers should always be on the look out for burnout in their employees. The obvious signs are frowns, and snappy, bad-tempered responses to colleagues as well as customers.

You will usually only see the tip of the iceberg. A not too friendly response that you overhear may not compare with the insults hurled at harmless customers who are unlikely to return, or to employees who will quit, or be miserable and take it out on the wrong people—the customers.

All too often ill-tempered, rude, and often thoroughly inefficient employees become sacred monsters and get away with murder. This implies two things. Either the managers or owners are burned out and don't care, or they are stupid and don't see it. Both situations are distressingly common.

CHAPTER ELEVEN

How to Get and Keep a Job, Hire Personnel, and Increase Sales

One advantage of writing a book as opposed to writing for a newspaper or magazine is that no punches need to be pulled. In journalism, all writing is slanted because the consumer is not only reading the editorials and the news, but also the advertising that provides most of the income for the press.

One magazine writer was fired because in a fashion article he referred to "scruffy jeans." "We carry advertisements for six jeans companies," the editor wearily explained. "There is no such thing as 'scruffy' jeans."

Many companies "pulled" their advertising from television at the time of the Gulf War because they didn't want their glorious product aired alongside the latest casualty figures for American forces. They feared that this might depress sales, rather than improve them. Similarly, no magazine or newspaper wants to feature bleak articles that are "downers," no matter how true they may be, if there is a chance that they may dilute response to joyous advertising of consumer products. Here, we can tell it like it is.

The bar and restaurant industry is one of the worst managed in the whole

175

consumer world. For some entrepreneurs, the central attraction of the industry is that it is one in which consumers are corraled into a situation in which, to put it mildly, their better judgment may be clouded. This cynical view is validated with depressing regularity.

One restaurateur used to say piously to his customers, "If people are kind enough to come in here and give me their business, then I feel I have a responsibility to do my best to give them service and value." A noble sentiment indeed. But in unguarded private moments he often used to say with a sigh, "The problem with the bar business is that in between the idiots coming in, and me taking their money, you actually have to give them something."

It is incredible what low quality people will accept when they think they're in the trendiest place in town, alongside people they wish to impress, and slightly drunk. There is no shortage of businesspeople delighted to exploit this.

Ask any employee, or exemployee, and they will usually have their horror stories, generally in the area of horrific ways in which customers were insulted, ripped off, or given food or drink that by rights should not have been served because it posed a health risk.

The food area is more notorious than that of wines, beers, and spirits. We hear of huge batches of "Chicken à la King" that are swarming with bacteria and smelling of vomit being brought swiftly to the boil and laced with bicarbonate of soda in order to make them servable. Wondrously, we then hear of how delighted the consumers were by the dish!

In the endless catalogue of restaurant horror stories, food long past its "sell by" date is served relentlessly until complaints are made. Only then is it reluctantly thrown out, or recycled. Last week's hamburger meat can still be used in the chili, as long as you're careful to spoon off the rancid fat that obligingly rises to the surface of the cooking pot. Some food cynics aver that the whole rationale behind hot dishes such as curry and chili is the need to disguise the condition of meat that is no longer fresh.

Apart from the endless stories of "what goes in the 'grappa,'" what *doesn't* go in the Bloody Marys, and the horrors of irresponsible wine manufacture, the beverage end of the industry comes off fairly well. Scraping the barrel (as it were) for an alcohol horror story, one has to be content with the report, unproved and unprovable, that the brandy in which Admiral Nelson's body was preserved after his death at the battle of Trafalgar in 1805, was reissued to sailors as part of their free ration of two pints of spirits a day.

Finding a Job

Many bars and restaurants are partnerships, and one of the disadvantages of this common arrangement is that the various partners may require, as a condition of their participation, the employment of certain people. Requirements may include people like "the son," "the daughter," the carpenter or plumber who helped build the last adventure they were involved in, the otherwise unemployable no-good brother-in-law, the new wife, the exwife, the really nice guy (underneath it all) who just needs a chance, and a dozen other selections from Central Casting's endless parade of losers. This is known as "nepotism," and it's here to stay.

When setting up partnerships this is one area in which a clear understanding must be reached. Are there going to be any shoe-in jobs for useless people or must all partners find all appointments acceptable?

Of course, life being what it is, it's never this easy. The eager, willing son of a partner who just wants to learn the business and doesn't care how many hours he has to work, may be a paragon of virtue—for the first month. Sometimes it takes a little while for people to work out their devious routes and plans for making life miserable for others. And, particularly if a business is successful, no partners will wish to jeopardize their position by complaining about closely connected employees. Partners can be hard to find, so one often sees absurd situations.

Similarly, a lowly employee will often perform the function, often voluntarily, of "house spy"—keeping owners informed about every move the staff makes. Fortunately, everyone soon finds out who the stool-pigeon is, and the person is usually treated like a leper. The spy's attention often focuses closely on the bar staff who, for various reasons, seem to attract a certain jealousy. Everyone fantasizes about how much money they're making, how much they're stealing, and the delicious, illicit meals they enjoy. Fixed salary employees are often jealous of the server's and bartender's tips, which clearly provide a bonus that is in fact the whole reason for taking the job. Also, bar managers and bartenders often have personality and achieve popularity with the customers, and this means they are in a less menial position than others.

Sometimes, it must be admitted, bartenders are held in such awe—often by their employers—that they let it go to their heads a bit: coming in late, only hearing the orders they choose to hear, and so on. They have huge repertoires of snappy one-liners, and set international standards for cool aplomb. From time to time they'll be observed checking their profiles in the mirror. The world roars with laughter when they get their comeuppance.

In summary, although we must address the business of finding and keeping a job, and hiring others, in an adult and businesslike way, we must accept that the bar and restaurant industry is often a bit like the strange Wonderland in which Alice found herself after she drank from the bottle and went down the hole. Sometimes people have to be endured, as in many other lines of work.

There are agencies that specialize in providing bar and restaurant workers.

Some of them are hired to provide the whole staff for a new enterprise, or are automatically called by regular customers when new personnel are needed.

These agencies seem to come in two kinds: the good and the utterly ridiculous. The latter heavily outnumber the former. We are talking cottage industry, very often one man and a dog in a tiny office with a telephone and a Rolodex defines an employment agency at the lowest level. At this lowest level, agents eke out a precarious living by providing lower-ranking workers at short notice. You will see their waiting rooms full of people snoozing as best they can, the tabloid newspaper long read and discarded, too much coffee and soda drunk, too many cigarettes smoked, as they wait for the call to wash dishes or bus tables for a shift. Unfortunately, huge, well-run firms like Manpower don't have large departments dedicated to the hospitality industries.

Many agents advertise their services in the newspapers. They often blatantly state that they have jobs available when they don't. This is the process known as "building an inventory" of personnel. Finding the vacant job is often much harder than finding the person to fill it, but they need to have at least 10 names and telephone numbers to call if a client suddenly calls in requesting help.

This is a common situation in cities. Suburban establishments often have great difficulty finding staff and have to resort to all sorts of means to entice them. Seasonal establishments in resort areas, for instance, often hire students for the summer or ski season and offer them accommodations and transport as part of the incentive.

The good agents will understand both sides of the fence and all the realities of the game. They will also run their businesses efficiently, answering their telephones, calling people up, being at their desks, and knowing the answers to the questions. The bad ones simply work on the principle that, if they send a body to a job, they get a commission from the employee and the establishment. Therefore, the name of the game is to keep people moving and the hell with whether either the business or the employee gets what they want. A similar attitude is encountered with leasing agencies who relish heavy turnover in apartment buildings, because every newcomer must pay them a fee.

When reporting for a new job as a bartender, bar manager, or other restaurant-related work, it's always a good idea to sniff out what happened to your predecessor, if any. If your predecessors have been so numerous that no one can really give you a good answer to this, then you are probably in the process of taking a high-turnover job. If this is the case, then the reasons will soon become apparent.

Some establishments are perfectly happy to see a different face every day, and it is hard to sympathize with such indifference. Others automatically fire all employees every three months. The theory is that by then they will have discovered all possible methods of stealing and have become security risks! The cynicism demonstrated in these places is sad and profound, but it is here to stay.

It is a good self-protective attitude not to build great hopes on any new job. Consider everything as being probationary. The employee is on probation—so is the company. Job hunters should be on the lookout for anything which they will definitely not be able to put up with. Noise level, smoke level, stairs, traffic fumes, all that sort of thing should be considered.

The opening of a new restaurant and bar always generates curiosity and excitement. Though new places will obviously need staff, it must be noted that the first few weeks and months of any such operation are notoriously stressful and fraught with all sorts of possibilities for things to go wrong. Staff will quit in disgust during this shakedown period.

The problem is that many wrong decisions are not revealed as such until they're put into operation. Many professional restaurant managers are imbeciles. Their real talent is being able to impress new owners with their abilities—often after years of distinguished failure. Also, especially in businesses with many partners, there will often be a lot of pointless and witless input from people who know nothing about the business, but who consider themselves knowledgeable and creative. Spouses can be deadly in this area.

The optimum time for taking a job in a new restaurant is probably not less than three months after it's opened. Of course, if you need a job, and are offered a job, it would be wrong to refuse it on these grounds. It's even possible to emerge as the hero of the hour, if your wisdom reveals the true path to success. But be warned: the proof of the pudding is in the eating. It is not uncommon for restaurants to open and close in three months flat when it becomes clear that it just isn't going to work.

The "Help Wanted" section of the newspaper will often feature jobs in the industry. The problem is that many people read these ads so that, when you arrive at the appointed hour, you may find as many as 40 or more candidates vying for the same position. A hapless, inefficient manager may be doing the interviewing and hiring. He may have his own particular axes to grind. He may only want pretty women, or pretty boys. An ever observant, jealous, and suspicious spouse may preclude the hiring of either, or both, of these two categories. Someone who's really stupid may be wanted, so that they won't pry too much into private wrinkles and rackets, such as they may be.

The psychology of hiring can be very convoluted, and anyone who thinks the best person for the job is the one who gets it had better grow up. Weak managers and owners are often intimidated by the thought of hiring someone who clearly knows what they're doing. They may actuallly view someone who clearly knows what they're about as a threat to their own position, not an asset to the business. That old cliché, "The kind of person I hire is the person who wants my job," is a huge joke among realists. When managers are working in an agreeably sloppy way, yet making a profit, why should they hire efficient zealots?

Others will only hire people from whom they are sure they can exact total humility and obedience. Quite often they will only hire people whom they judge to be eminently exploitable. One large chain of restaurants in New York notoriously requires its managers to work 12-hour days. Naturally, the sort of people they hire are those who, for one reason or another, need any work they can get.

Bad managers will often interpret sensible suggestions as threats to their egos, rocking the boat rather than making life easier. Also, if 40 people are being interviewed for a job, and you are number 35, you may be sure that by the time the hiring manager interviews you the faces will have begun to blur. The interviewer may have already made a decision and continue to see the remaining applicants only out of politeness. You will invariably find that the later interviews are much briefer than the early ones.

If you have to sit through 30 or more interviews, drinking your coffee from a cardboard cup, reading the newspaper for the fourth time, and starting to get a bit of a headache because it's so stuffy but you don't dare leave in case you're called, you will consume a lot of irrecoverable time. It is most likely that this time will be wasted. True, someone has to get the job, but general experience shows that newspaper advertisements are a very poor means of finding work in this industry.

Your time spent waiting to be the 35th person interviewed for a job would be better spent on your two feet pounding the sidewalk. This is the proven best method for finding employment, because knowing what you look like is a vital part of a manager's decision as to whether you are hired or not. The advantages are numerous. You can start seeking work near home. If you're lucky you won't have to travel far to work, and this can be a tremendous blessing in the age of the two and a half hour commute by car or subway.

In this industry, because you are dealing with the public, personal appearance is important. Sometimes it's carried to a ludicrous degree with a proliferation of shy Lolitas in miniskirts irritating the women diners because their male companions are so distracted, or Mel Gibson and Tom Cruise lookalikes strutting their stubble. In such establishments this entertainment may be part of the apparatus for distracting the customers from the pork posing as veal, the Virgin Marys posing as Bloodys, and so on.

Two notorious playboy brothers in New York set up ice cream parlors all over the city with the real intention of providing a source of teenage girls for their private delectation. They had inherited their father's huge fortune and the ice cream parlors were just a front. Oddly enough, though they sound like medieval Hun invaders, they were not bad fellows, but they were not serious businessmen.

When you set out to find a job, it's a good idea to determine to go to *every* place you pass—unless it's instantly evident that you couldn't get a job there or definitely wouldn't want one. Some low-key establishments with a very bland outward appearance are absolute goldmines.

Your visiting time is limited. Stay away at rush hours when no one has time to talk to you. Just before lunchtime, or better yet, the quiet afternoon period are best.

You've got to be dogged and a bit hard-nosed. Some managers will brush you off rudely. Others will have fun at your expense. Most will listen politely and tell you on the spot that there's nothing doing, or to look in again, or to come back at another time when the manager who does the hiring comes in.

Never build hopes, because even the most polite and friendly manager or employee may just be soft-soaping you to get you out quickly and pleasantly. As often as not, after an exhausting afternoon, you grit your teeth for one last lap and go back to see the manager who was supposed to be in at 5 P.M. He's late. When at last you see him he looks straight through you and brushes you off with a "nothing available."

Don't waste your time seeking work on the telephone. It never works. Of course, if you hear, or see a notice that a place is recruiting, then you can politely call to inquire the best time to attend for an interview.

The better the job, the smaller the turnover, so it's a good idea, even when you're reasonably employed, to do a little job exploration from time to time. Often you'll get a job on your third or fourth call over a period of months or even years. But one should never lose sight of the impermanence of life. Very few things are forever. Employees who set themselves up assuming that they are going to be employed for life in the same restaurant or bar are foolish. This is another of those traps that make so many workers put in too many shifts—from fear that suddenly there won't be any shifts available at all because the joint has closed down.

One bartender got a job after three years of calling. He lasted only one week, because of instant personality clashes with the other staff and customers. A bar manager who usually worked within 10 blocks of his apartment once found a job on the same block less than 10 doors away, five minutes after setting out to look for work. On another occasion he had to look a little further and it took him 20 minutes. But on other occasions it took weeks and months to find something, and it required some traveling too.

The average executives in the United States have five jobs in their working lifetime. The figure for bar and restaurant employees is much higher. Places fail; employees get bored and simply want a change. Many artists use the industry, as is well known, as their backup job while awaiting the big break in show biz. The close association between theater, TV, and cinema and the bar and restaurant industry is very obvious if you go to the movies. Bar and restaurant scenes abound, partly because such places are natural venues for interaction between people and thus make good dramatic arenas, but also because the writers are so steeped in the industry folklore that they can never resist referring to it. Many films are set in bars. The arrival of immigration officials at a restaurant kitchen is a stock joke, as is the chase through the kitchen or dining room.

It's a good idea to have a short concise resumé ready to hand out when you go job hunting. This should detail work experience, but in a selective way. Five years as bar manager at the Plaza obviously looks a lot better than six months here or six months there over a period of 10 years.

Some hapless but honest managers will tell you not to bother leaving your resumé. Others will take it and put it in File 13 (the Round One). But a few will put it on the spindle, or in the file with the others and, when occasion arises, give you a call.

Many large personnel offices select personnel simply by reaching for the next application on file, without reference to qualification. In other words, a highly unsuitable person might be called in for a job while two or three papers deeper into the file is an application from a dream employee. If this smacks of bad or at least unimaginative management, that's exactly what it is, and it's depressingly common.

If nothing else you've got your address and telephone number on file. Job hunters really need an answering service or machine in case of callbacks. Some managers are fickle or busy, or both. They'll call once, they'll call twice, then they'll call the next candidate.

A sad feature of bar life is seeing an ideal, attractive person who applies for work being sent away, and for someone much less suitable to be hired within the day because some emergency situation has arisen. Timing is important. There's a big luck factor, but the harder you work, the luckier you get.

Although most people tend to approach all establishments with an equal amount of enthusiasm, occasionally you will see a place that is mouthwateringly attractive. Acquaintances may give you the tip that it's just your kind of place. Then it's worth doing a little spying, or to put it more politely, reconnaissance, to help you in your job application.

There's no law against going to the establishment and having a drink or dinner, either alone or with a friend. If you do this, do not intimate that you're job hunting. Look your best, be affable, say enough to the staff with whom you come into contact to register pleasantly—a mild flirt may cause amusement and will usually do no harm. If you go with a friend, choose a pleasant and attractive one. Do not go in the rush hour, or your face will just be part of the blur. Leave a decent tip—no need to go crazy.

The object is that when next the staff see your face, on that happy day when you come in looking for a job, their vestigial memory of you will be a positive one. By talking and listening while you're having a drink or dining you may discover all sorts of useful trivia. You hear the owner is crazy about everything French—and you speak French, don't you? The owner is an exbaseball player, an ex-Marine still on reserve, a skier, an amateur musician—anything you can find out about the owners or managers who will be hiring you may prove valuable. Anything that can help you to strike a personal rapport is useful.

On the professional side, you can discover down-to-earth useful things by noticing the equipment used, and the wines and beers featured. If you're experienced you may even spot a problem area or two. When you go to seek work, you should let slip some of this information. Just a few observant comments will do, no need to read the Bill of Rights.

"I see you use those IBM 747 registers—they're very good I find, once you've trained everybody to use them!"

"I see you have a good selection of draft beer. What a money spinner that is!"

"I see you have a good selection of wine. I was just on vacation in Bordeaux and went around the Chateau Plonk. . . ," or "Boy, those Lithuanian wines are coming on, aren't they? The price is right, too!"

"I stopped by my friend Joe's the other day—they have a really nifty bar food menu. Must be doing 500 dollars a day on snacks at the bar. Of course, they're well set up for it."

You can even rehearse your observations. They are designed to give an instant impression that you know your stuff, to convey commitment, responsibility, and professionalism.

Too many giggling youngsters try to get work in the spirit of "Look at me, ain't I cute? I'm so sassy I'm like joy to be around. But I know how to work, too."

It's not uncommon nowadays for people to come into a restaurant or bar looking for work, chewing gum, with their Walkman earphones hissing, and smoking a cigarette with their baseball hats on backwards.

"Hi. Hiring?"

It works well on the TV sitcoms. It will actually work well if you strike a chord with some motherly or fatherly soul. ("Oh, he/she is so cute. These kids today are just like . . .") But this approach is best restricted to the zanier areas of major cities.

As regards using your personality—and some have more than others—there are important things to note. There are no negatives or disadvantages in anything. If you actually have no personality, you may place yourself streets ahead of the competition in some establishments. If you're short, tall, bald, or have thick blonde hair, or if there are any striking aspects of your appearance or character, then the main thing to watch is that such factors work for you, and to make it clear that you have no chips on your shoulder.

This is a delicate area in the current obsession with seeking political correctness. Put it this way, you should try to put yourself across as a regular person, not as a central casting Transylvanian. If you have an accent (as so many of us do in this country) then let it be a charming one. If your ethnic background is famous for assassins and romantics, then make it clear which of these glorious traditions is the one you favor.

All of this advice is set against an imaginary scenario of intelligent people pursuing intelligent lives in regular businesses. But there's a strong idiot factor, too, and you'll do well to get used to it. Many managers live a pathetic existence where they look forward no further than the end of their current shift. Because of this, the place that told you at 5 P.M. today that, unfortunately, they had no vacancies, will be going crazy for a bar manager or bartender by 9 A.M. tomorrow. During the evening shift someone quit, was summarily fired, or dropped dead. If you're up to it there's even a case for going job hunting dressed and ready to go to work on the spot. It's amazing how often you can run into something.

Office temps have to observe this discipline when they're looking for work. Their agent will call at 8 A.M. to make sure they're up, dressed, and ready for work if the opportunity should arise. All of this smacks rather uncomfortably of those folk memories of the days when 100 men showed up at the factory or dockyard gates, 20 were put to work, and the rest were sent home. It used to be that bad in the bar and restaurant business. Old hands will tell you of the famous slogan that often appeared on the schedule: "If you don't work Sunday, don't show on Monday."

This is the way it goes in the United States. In most European countries nowadays, its almost impossible to fire anyone, and each employee gets six weeks paid vacation that they must take. The other side of the coin is that the payroll flexibility of the U.S. economy means it can adapt to recession better by "right-sizing"—a dread term for those who lose their jobs.

As a bar manager you will probably be responsible for hiring the bar personnel. A word of warning here about this rather nebulous job title of "Bar Manager." It has different interpretations.

The best and happiest interpretation is that the incumbent is really the head bartender, and works perhaps four full shifts behind the bar. Because of extra supervisory, office, and accounting responsibilities pay will be more than the statutory rate.

Bar managers will also receive privileges like paid vacations, being able to select the schedule that suits them best, and the pick of the menu. If they're doing the buying, and we're talking quantity, they may even get a nice little present or two from the salespeople that might be a t-shirt and a key ring, two tickets to the game, a case of wine, or a useful sum in an envelope.

This "kicking back" is part of life. When it gets ridiculous the law will step in, but there are legal precedents in which judges have shrugged their shoulders and refused to see anything criminal in it. It becomes criminal when it creeps up into the area of unfair trading practices and the antitrust laws.

However, there is another version of bar manager that is, frankly, a sucker's job. This is where managers are on salary, with no bartending duties, and go to work in a suit. They have an office, set the schedules, keep the books, take inventory, do the ordering, and generally oversee the running of the bar. However, they may find themselves earning half as much, or less, than the bartenders they supervise, and this "sticks in the craw." Having found such a sucker, owners and senior management will be reluctant to demote the bar manager to a better-paid position!

Sometimes the hours will be long. Jobs that are not union protected, or influenced, are open to exploitation. Thus, a house that does not employ union members will observe local union rates of pay and conditions, accepting them as a guideline, and also as a means of denying the unions any axe to grind.

Assistant managers are particularly vulnerable. They can be required to work long hours. A nasty twist is the "split shift." Your hours are midday to midnight; but, they say generously, you're off from 2 to 4 P.M. What can one do with that period? Usually nothing, unless it's a resort job and you're right on the beach. Split shifts constitute the worst and hardest hours imaginable.

However, life is hard and sometimes there may be a good case for taking such a less than ideal position. First of all, sometimes you need a job. Second, there may be management promotion opportunities that will enable the bar manager to move up and earn more. Likelihood of promotion is something a person in such a position should be careful to assess. If there isn't any, then it's time to hit the sidewalk and get those resumés out.

Hiring

If, as bar manager, you are responsible for hiring personnel, you'll be looking for bartenders, male or female, and perhaps what are sometimes called "barbacks"—youngsters who cut the fruit and fetch the ice before the princes and princesses themselves come strutting into the bar. If there are cocktail waiters they're usually part of the wait staff, and hired by the maitre d' or general manager.

It is important to know exactly what you want in your bartenders. When an establishment first opens it's often hard to get a feel for who the regular clientele are and what they'd like to see. Once established, bars take on a life and identity of their own and it's easy to see what works and what doesn't.

Until this point is reached you can experiment and have different types of people working for you. An experienced, grown-up, fatherly kind of guy, an outgoing youngster, a sassy wench, a motherly type, or whatever. It must be said that the personality of a bartender in an upscale, busy city bar may be irrelevant. If the customers are mainly busy businesspeople or belong to the "smart set," they probably won't be in the least bit interested in discussing ball scores with the bartender, or swapping stories about the idiocies of young officers in Viet Nam, or detailing their problems with spouses or jobs. They'll be far too interested in attending to their own business or social affairs.

In such places, far more emphasis must be placed on the technical expertise of the bartender. Such a clientele will probably be international, or certainly well traveled. When they order a dry sherry before dinner, they'll expect it to be chilled, of a decent quality, and in a suitable glass. If they order a glass of champagne it had better not be flat. And if they ask the bartender what time the afternoon Concorde arrives from Paris, they'll require a better answer than, "Search me, Mac."

For anyone with a bit of interest in life, or a "people person," jobs like this are fun and pay well. Workers of this caliber are hard to find, but once on board they are likely to stay and perform consistently well. For a working man, a job with a take-home pay of a thousand dollars a week for work that is not physically heavy, and carried out indoors (as opposed to the construction site) is manna from heaven.

For the ordinary middle-of-the-road kind of bar, however, the personality requirements are perhaps greater. The bartender must be the kind of person who can *build* business, and many professionals sell themselves on this skill. Many even have a following and, on joining a new company, will solemnly write to their clients from former bars on the house-headed writing paper, saying things like

Dear Mr. Smith:

I hope you remember me from the dear old "Green Cockatoo." Pity the block had to come down, but that's life.

I'm now at "Porgy's"—right across from the subway—and I'm there Tuesday thru' Friday till midnight so, if you're in the neighborhood, look in.

You'll be delighted to hear we have Old Plunket on draft!

From a small nucleus, a huge clientele can grow.

The broad personality type you are looking for is an easy-going, genial, slow to anger kind of person who can adapt easily and quickly to varying characters. A suggestion of steel inside the velvet glove will not come amiss, as often bartenders have to assert a certain authority, as we have discussed. Part of the job, it's true, is to suffer fools gladly, but there must be an awareness of when behavior is out of line. The rule of thumb for defining this point is simply when other customers are negatively affected, or when an employee is addressed rudely.

However, one of the talents that good bartenders need is for acting. Many develop a professional facade that works very well, possibly for years. Often problems lurk beneath the surface for ages only to emerge at a time of great stress. That's when you find out that your cuddly bartender has a record of violence, or is an alcoholic who just fell off the wagon, and not for the first time, or whatever.

A certain reserve should always be maintained in one's judgment of people in business situations. It isn't like personal relationships such as family, marriage, or ordinary social friendship, and there may be a real need to dissimulate in order to, quite simply, stay in a job and earn a living.

You should learn not to be afraid to hire inexperienced people. If they are clearly disposed to learn, you can strike gold with youngsters.

In such a commercial situation it would be humbug to talk too much about "leadership" and "example," but it is important to be pleasant and polite to employees. A bar is an arena where an atmosphere of pleasant friendliness should be present at all times, if it is to do good business. Many owners and managers are anything but pleasant and polite. The price they pay through employees who are surreptitiously seeking revenge, and exacting it by stealing money in subtle ways, will probably never be known. Professional bartenders are steeled to take a certain amount of abuse. The tougher ones also know how to make it up to themselves, and do so without compunction.

How to Increase Sales

Bar managers must be ever on the lookout for ways of increasing profits. They should be alert for "post-offs"—special prices from their liquor dealers. This isn't hard, since as soon as a "post-off" is featured they'll be on the phone to tell you about it!

Job lots of wine should be approached with great care. It's sometimes dreadful junk. A regular exception to this of course is end of line sales where the wine is no longer being made, or for some other reason is not going to be catalogued, and the warehouse needs the space. But it's wise to taste first. Wine drinkers are discerning consumers, increasingly so, and bad wine will be rejected, which is bad for business.

Unfortunately, such is the poverty of imagination in the industry that the single most common method of procuring profit is to give small portions. If you can get 30 scotches on the rocks out of a bottle, surely you can stretch it to 32, which is another 8 dollars or so in the kitty. And will anyone notice if you top up the Smirnoff vodka with the much cheaper Vladivostok (answer: almost certainly no—may conscience be your guide).

Many owners are entirely paranoid about "portion control" and will fire bartenders suspected of being too generous. Others have a fit if the service bartender gives the server Dewars when asked for Dewars. Since customers can't see what they're getting, why not pour the cheaper "well" scotch, with which the premium bottles are filled up in the dead of night anyway?

All these charming and often practiced tricks will succeed eternally where there is a "captive client base." In other words they have nowhere else to go, or the location insures a constant consumer flow in such circumstances that it really doesn't matter much whether people ever come back again or not. This is the bitter reality of the tired old cliché about the three most important things in the retail business being "location, location, and location." The greater the flow of potential consumers through the neighborhood, the less entrepreneurial imagination has to be brought to bear on the profit picture.

However, it is interesting to consider certain locations as one wanders around the world. At Grand Central Station in New York, where you'd think they could get away with murder (and some joints do), there are at least two landmark bar restaurants that have a very regular clientele, in addition to the multitude of transients. The staff all make excellent money and, because they usually train in a subsidiary role for at least a year before being allowed to become full-blown bartenders or waiters, they stay for ages.

(It's tough getting a job in places like this, because of the infrequent turnover, but opportunities do occur. These are the sort of places where it pays to pop in once in a while and maybe get on "hello there" terms with the managers.) Then, if you stroll uptown a bit, to some of the plush and expensive hotels, you'll see bars that are always empty, even at the cocktail hour. Many local workers will be dashing off to the burbs where they live, that huge band of non-New Yorkers who work in New York, but couldn't tell you the way to the Metropolitan Museum.

Midtown in any city is not a neighborhood; few people live there. In other words we're looking at a lot of concrete, but not many bodies, after five o'clock. Ninety percent of the lunch business is either looking for the cheapest coffee shop or sandwich bar on the block, or brown-bagging it. The three Martini lunch is no more in New York, except in approximately five plush steak houses—the kind where the Martinis come in goblets, and everything on the menu, from salad to vegetables has to be ordered à la carte. Everything is on the computer. Fat, jovial businesspeople of a certain type slap each other on the backs as they consume huge plates of protein and—a big item in these places—onion rings.

So why is our midtown bar not doing any business? Well, take a look and ask yourself if you'd like to have a drink there, if you have half an hour to kill while waiting for a friend, or whatever.

The place is very well lighted, with lots of glass and plastic. It is the other extreme from the Stygian darkness of the traditional American dive. It looks a bit clinical and instinctively you know somehow that it's going to be expensive. The bartender, with a face as impassive as the moon, stares out of the window. The waitress has the same sort of face. However, because you are following a train of thought for exploration you decide to go in and have a drink. Nobody greets you. The bartender's manner is peremptory—a vague syllable somewhere between "sir" and "hi." The faintest embellishment to your order will provoke a frown and a barely restrained snarl. Having sympathy for one whose private miseries may exceed your wildest dreams, you leave a decent tip anyway. But you don't get any thanks.

There's nothing repellent about the location. Some places, even city corners, just never make it as restaurants for reasons no one can quite understand. Why is the southwest corner bar always full while the northeast corner—where the staff are jolly and the drinks are good—always empty? No computer program exists to explain why such situations exist.

Our rather dull and depressing bar is mainly that way because of the lack of imagination of its owners and managers. If it's a huge international corporation (as it probably is in this kind of area) they may not even be well acquainted with Western culture. They will probably employ many executives from grand schools of hotel and catering, with degrees in food and beverage control, but they won't know what makes a bar attractive.

Often, management is so wrapped up in computer projections of "throughput" and net profit, that they simply lose touch with the hands-on human aspects of this business, which are in fact the key. We are now in an age in which it's not uncommon for a waiter to tell a customer who's just decided to order something as an afterthought, "Sorry, sir, I can't get into the computer right now. Be with you soon as I can." This absence of a sense of reality is also reflected in the fact that many commercial chefs, though highly trained, don't really know what food is supposed to taste like. They satisfy the market because most American tastes are bland and easily satisfied, and food made by someone else always has a certain novelty value.

If they were to put in an outgoing and gregarious staff they'd be well on the way to success. If they reduced the plastic and glass and replaced it with junk memorabilia, that would help too—it's amazing how little one has to do to convey "character." As to whether they would be advised to put in pool tables and a juke, that's too subjective. Sometimes you do, and sometimes you don't, depending entirely on what your target market is and what the traffic will bear, or requires, in your neighborhood.

It is generally true that some kind of background music is desirable in bars. This should not dominate the proceedings—unless your establishment is dedicated to music, as in a piano bar, or talent show. In the electronic age a majority of people find the presence of a TV screen comforting, even if the sound is down. Sports bars that feature games on enlarged screens currently enjoy great success.

The whole question of noise, the major pollutant of our times, is a wretched one. The brutal truth has to be faced that most people like it. Look around you. The proof is everywhere. Some might modify this observation to say that most people are so inured to noise that they no longer notice it, and this may be true. It is acknowledged that the hearing of young people is now affected by earphones, ghetto blasters, and disco sounds, and that finding normal hearing for medical research is increasingly difficult.

It has been proved that people eat and drink faster in noisy places. Of course they do. No conversation slows them down. Managers must simply have an eye to the tastes of the majority of their customers. Places that are blasting noise will undoubtedly not attract people who wish to talk to each other, though they may be attractive to those who have little or nothing to discuss.

One bartender took a job in a student neighborhood. The draft Budweiser flowed, the kids hooted and hollered as they admired each other's t-shirts, and so on (the usual scene of American intelligentsia at leisure). The juke box was on loud all the time. Many speakers insured maximum coverage.

One day a young woman came in, sat at the bar, and ordered a cocktail. In the brief intervals between records she spoke to the bartender.

"Have you worked here long?" she inquired.

"No, I just started."

"What do you think about the noise level?"

"I don't like it, but maybe I'll get used to it."

The woman looked at him sympathetically and said, "I'm a doctor, studying to be an ear specialist. The noise level here is dangerous. You should wear earplugs. Even then, I can assure you that in a short time you will damage your hearing. You will start losing sensitivity at the higher registers and you won't actually notice it until it's bad, and probably irreversible. Sorry to be the bearer of bad tidings!"

The bartender needed the job because he needed the money. However, he took the eminently sensible view that no job is worth it if it is health-threatening. He bought plugs and swiftly set about finding another job.

Flowers are always nice. Linen, furniture, and glassware should be as attractive as is feasible. Some restaurants are hilariously wrong. One successful establishment has fresh flowers every day (they have to be paid for by the customers, by the way), beautiful young men and model hostesses who actually wear different dresses every day, advertising certain designers. There are no tablecloths however. Instead, as each party departs and the table is reset, a great roll of nasty, noisy, cheap-looking paper is produced and spread over the table. It is ugly. But few notice, so perhaps one shouldn't be too critical in the assessment of what is appealing and what is not.

A bar manager can only enhance a location; you can't put Times Square on Beacon Hill, you can only make it inviting. A little stage work helps here. Let the hostess or manager or maitre d', or whoever the job title belongs to, try to get to the entrance as soon as they've seated a party or directed them to the bar. While the host is busy, the waiter whose station is nearest the bar can greet people. When the floor staff are nowhere in sight (an all too common phenomenon) the bartender—in those common but not universal situations where the bar adjoins the entrance—can take over the greeting.

"Hi, folks. Nice to see you. Dolores will be with you in a second," will do just fine at busy times.

In the same way, at the bar, a potential customer who has received a greeting will be more likely to stay and patiently await an opportunity to place an order than one who is ignored. You buy time and increase customers by being punctilious about your "greeting drills." Being ignored is exasperating for would-be customers.

One very busy lunchtime restaurant usually had a line by 12:30, and a busy manager listing names. Sometimes when the line was long, people would look in, pull a face, and go somewhere else.

This used to reduce the owner to physical pain. "You're losing them, you're losing them," she'd whine, actually wringing her hands, like a general who suddenly sees his army being massacred.

Bartenders must be reminded that they're salespeople. "I don't want to hear about the drinks you've sold," one manager used to snarl affectionately. "I want to hear about the drinks you're *going* to sell."

So, when a beer bottle is emptied its removal should automatically be accompanied by the query, "Would you care for another, sir," (or, "One more time, dude?" depending on the nature of the joint).

Similarly, although it can be rather rude and pointed to remove a glass that has been drained, it is polite to look at it and say gently, "Would you care for another?" Some very old-fashioned people consider it rude to be invited to have "another" anything, but the question need only be modified to "Would you like a drink" in the presence of Park Avenue or New England matrons.

When regular customers are spending lots of money and you judge them worthy of a drink "on the house," make sure the customers know they're getting a drink on the house. Don't just set them up discreetly. Say, "That's on the house," and make sure they hear you. Clearly, past a certain point of festivity, such gestures will be wasted anyway, so don't bother making them. Similarly, the customer who asks for a strong drink may get an extra drop or two in the first drink, but may get a little less in the sixth.

Scrounging boozers will sometimes brazenly ask for a drink on the house. Depending on their manner and your assessment of the situation, you may well go along with it, treating it as a good joke. But there's a hard-nosed kind of professional adversary who'll say things like, "I'll take a shot of your best brandy on the house." The answer to this must be direct confrontation and assertion of authority. Unless you're intending to quit any day and the person usually leaves a good tip, of course!

One young drinker in a small town was heard to say, "I don't understand alcohol. When I go to 'Joe's Bar' I can drink 10 gin and tonics and walk home sober as a judge. But when I make myself a drink at home, two is my maximum." It was a while before the penny dropped. Joe was pouring them short. Young drinkers aren't looking for a blast of alcohol into the system. And in a gin and tonic, unless you put a really large shot of gin in the glass, all you'll ever taste is the tonic anyway.

Wine sales can be increased by suggestion. For this to be effective the bartenders must be able to talk about them. "I don't know, lady, I don't drink," is not an appropriate reply to a customer who asks whether the featured Chardonnay of the week will satisfy her requirements. It isn't hard to learn a bit of reassuring patter; that's all wine talk is, anyway. "Very dry, but with a nice fruity taste," "a deep dark satisfying taste, sort of blackberry and chocolate." With practice you'll discover what works best.

You can have "loss leaders" too, which really means that you feature a wine for which you could honestly charge 5 dollars and let it go for 4 dollars a glass. You are only reducing your profit, not foregoing it. Once the pump of consumption is primed, your customers may order more and more of everything on offer.

A running competition with a small cash prize for the waiter who sells the most wine sometimes works well.

At the tables, the simple exposure of a bottle of wine as part of the standard setup may stimulate a sale. In the same way, the goods you offer must be clearly listed and displayed where possible. Part of the bar display can include either a list of beers and/or sample bottles of the range you offer. Thus, at a glance the customer can say, "Whoopee! Kronenburg Beer!"

Featured waters and nonalcoholic drinks should be displayed too, space permitting.

The debate over the benefits of "Happy Hour" is endless. The theory is, if you reduce by half the price of drinks between 5 and 7 P.M., you will sell more than double the amount you might expect to sell at the ordinary price. True, but those extra drinks will not have been sold at the normal profit.

How many drinks would you sell at normal prices? The only way to reach any decisions in this area is to experiment, and watch the figures very carefully over a period of weeks. It must be accepted that cheap drinks and free food may attract a down-market crowd, and if your existing clientele is on the whole rather middle class, then Happy Hour could be a big mistake.

The real but unadmitted rationale to Happy Hour is simply the crude notion that, where large numbers of consumers gather, sales must be generated. "Let's get some bodies in, let's see some human traffic."

Nothing is written on tablets of stone, but once a regular clientele has been built up, it's unwise to tinker too much with the operation. People get used to a certain pattern, and they'll come back partly out of a sense of security—they know what they're in for.

It really should not be hard to imbue bar staff with the urge to sell more. Most of their remuneration is from tips. The more they sell the more they make. It's almost like being a salesperson on commission.

Pricing

We are still in Wonderland here. Two restaurants on the same block each sold imported draft beer. In one the price was $2.50 a pint. In the other it was $4.75. Oddly there was hardly any resistance to this price, except from out-of-towners, so inured are consumers to inane prices in bars.

The operators of the cheaper bar owned the building. In the more expensive establishment, they paid exorbitant rent, and eventually went under because of this. Need one say more about how prices are determined?

Managers should be aware of the prices the local competition are charging. This, and your overheads, are the determining factors in the prices you charge.

Every bar should have a price list handy and update it from time to time. But bartenders can easily carry prices of most items in their heads once they know a "base price." If a gin and tonic from the well is, say, $3.95, then a "call brand" (a Dewars and Soda as opposed to a Scotch and soda) will usually be $4.25. They should avoid any discussion of prices with customers. So they're ridiculous, what else is new?

CHAPTER TWELVE

A Shift with the Bartender from Hell—and with One Who's Read This Book

Here he comes, Boris, the bartender from hell, dragging his butt up the avenue, eyes downcast in the direction of shoes that could use a shine, a wash, or something. A cigarette dangles from his lips and he has a good wad of gum working. He looks about 28 going on 50.

He greets no one, neither customers nor staff. They, being more polite, greet him, but their friendliness falls on stony ground. He hangs his coat up somewhere in the back, in the dubious area where employees' clothes may be hung, at slightly lesser risk than that for the hapless customers who are fated to drink or dine, or both, in his establishment.

He takes his time about it. After all he's only 20 minutes late.

"Be right with you," he tells the bartender who's champing at the bit, in the ninth hour of his travail, waiting to get off.

Boris has to go and sit down for a while, and have some soup or coffee. He's dreadfully hungover from the previous evening's overindulgence.

At last the king of the night ducks under the transom, still fixing his tie. His white shirt is not exactly dazzling and there's a ketchup stain on his chest.

"So what we got here?" he asks the departing bartender.

"There's Doctor Smith."

"That jerk? Wish he'd drink some place else."

"And Mrs. Rodriguez . . ."

"Oh God, is she bitching about us not having any Macon Village again?"

Two customers come in and sit at the bar. Boris ignores them and continues his conversation.

"So we got everything?"

"No, we just ran out of draft Bass."

"You wanna go down and tap a keg before you go off?"

"No, sir. It's my wife's birthday, and I would have liked to have been out of here half an hour ago."

"Oh . . ."

One of the newly arrived customers catches his eye.

"Could we get a . . ."

"Be right with you, sir."

Boris suddenly notices two dirty glasses on the zinc draining board awaiting their wash.

In a panic-filled voice he says to the outgoing worker: "Say, I hope you're not leaving me with glasses to wash."

The day man returns and washes the glasses. He is mildly angry, but congratulates himself on having made an extra 20 dollars in the last 20 minutes while awaiting the arrival of the king of the night.

The day bartender leaves. Boris stubs out his cigarette, cracks his gum, and at last turns to the new customers.

"Yeah?"

"Two scotch and soda, please."

He picks up two glasses and wooshes each one through the pile of ice in the sink. Then he puts them on the bar, sticks the nozzle of the soda gun and the scotch pourer into the glass at the same time, and squirts. He puts the glasses in front of the customers, omitting the bev-nap, even though there is a convenient pile at his elbow.

"Eight dollars," he yawns.

The customer pays up. The bartender opens the register, sticks in the 10 dollar bill, and hands the customer his change without a word. He doesn't ring anything up. To uneducated and uninterested ears, the opening ring signifies payment. And they are more interested in their own lives than the intimate workings of bars, anyway. Our hero's just made his first 8 dollars of the evening. The customer leaves a 2 dollar tip. Boris puts it in the cup absent-mindedly, without a word. A waiter at the service end of the bar has been asking for drinks for five minutes now. At last the bartender goes down to the service end and fixes the drinks.

"And a pint of Bass," the waiter requests.

"Outta Bass."

"We had a delivery this afternoon. There's two kegs down there."

"Yeah, but . . . Give'm Watneys."

"They're regulars. They come for the Bass."

"Screw 'em. They won't know the difference."

There's a new and nervous young server requesting drinks.

"Hi, I'm Suzie," she says cheerfully.

"Yeah, well where's your glasses? You put up the glasses, I pour the drinks, okay? I mean have you ever worked before? I just can't stand working with inexperienced people."

The drinks are served at last, with many a snarl and much huffing and puffing.

Someone requests a Whiskey Sour "up." Muttering under his breath, the bartender sets up the glass, sticks a cherry in it, and shakes the mixture. But when it's time to pour it he can't separate the metal shaker from the mixing glass.

He bangs the unholy conglomeration of glass and metal against the side of the bar. Bang, bang, bang—everyone looks to see what's going on.

You would think he'd give the servers better service, especially as they're required to tip him five percent of their tip earnings—a very common house rule. The rationale is that the bartender has to sacrifice some of his own tippable service time in order to assist the servers in theirs, so this effort should be rewarded.

A server returns several dirty glasses to the bar to be washed. One of them has contained a cream drink. Boris looks at it in some disgust, then throws it into the garbage. It will take too much time to wash.

Down at the other end of the bar Doctor Smith requests another drink. The bartender reaches for the Tanqueray bottle. It's empty. So he walks down the bar and reaches for the other one, on the center station. The empty bottle stays in place.

"This isn't my shade," says Doctor Smith pushing his glass across the bar. A great red daub of lipstick glows fiercely.

"Oh," says our unembarrassable bartender from hell. He replaces it without a word of apology.

There's a lull.

Boris pours himself a stiff one. Almost immediately he feels better.

One of his cronies comes in. They have a deal. This customer drinks all he wants and leaves 20 dollars, which goes automatically into the tip cup—a good deal for everyone concerned, except, of course, the establishment.

There is now a suspension of service for a straight eight minutes while they rehash the previous night's ball game. The evening gets busier.

A waiter requests a bottle of Beaujolais.

"Out of Beaujolais," Boris yawns.

"There's six cases in the basement."

"No kiddin? Wanna bring one up?"

"I have a full station."

"Tough."

In this particular bar there is no manager to take charge of such small problems. The manager is the owner's mistress. But she's two-timing him and also in the process of setting up a business of her own. So she spends all her time on the telephone, ignoring the restaurant and its customers.

Boris has another drink to keep his crony company. Then he's feeling a little peckish so he orders up a nice lobster for dinner and eats it right on the bar. Naturally, the polite customers don't want to interrupt a working man when he's eating, so service is still pretty spotty.

By ten o'clock his shirt has come out at the back. No one is disposed to tell him because they know they'd get no thanks for doing so. It's quite a busy night so he rings up a few drinks to make it look good.

Around twelve midnight Boris is so sloshed that anything goes, and the waiters are having to make their own drinks with whatever they can reach. Howls of wrath would greet any attempt to get behind the bar.

The last customer leaves around 1 A.M. The bartender is now alone in the bar. The remainder of the staff has gone home.

He switches the TV to his favorite channel and sits at the bar enjoying a nightcap. Feeling tired, he puts his head on the bar and has a little snooze. But he's forgotten to lock the front door. When the robber comes in, he doesn't even have to pull out his gun. He just takes the money from the register and the tip cup, stuffs it into his pocket and walks.

The next evening goes better, mainly because it's Boris's day off.

Around 6:30 P.M., half an hour before he's due to go behind the bar, or "stick," our bartender from heaven can be seen striding jauntily to work.

Let's call him Ken.

Well known in the neighborhood, he greets people left and right. When he walks into the restaurant everyone gets a smile and a greeting. He goes straight to the kitchen and orders himself a sandwich. Thus, he can eat his main meal later, when things quiet down a bit.

He checks the reservations. Any big parties or special requests? Then he has a word with the day bartender, who is relieved to see the end of his shift now comfortably in sight.

"Do we need anything?"

"We need ice, but the busboy had to leave so . . ."

"No problem, I'll bring up a bucket. Anything else I can do down there?"

Ken notices Mrs. Rodriguez at the bar.

"Good evening, Mrs. Rodriguez, how nice to see you. Are you meeting your friend? In that case I'd better make sure I have a bottle of that San Diego Chardonnay on ice. I remember she raved about it last time she was in."

Downstairs, our heavenly bartender looks around. Plenty of ice in the machine. Ah, that Chardonnay—might as well take up a couple of extra bottles to be on the safe side.

Ken looks into the beer room. Goodness! There can't be more than a teaspoonful of Bass left in that keg, judging by its weight. Heavens, let's tap a fresh one right away.

On returning to the restaurant he meets Suzie, the new server.

"Suzie," he says, "relax, the job's a breeze. Any problems, let me know."

Noticing that the hostess is otherwise occupied, he greets a party of businesspeople.

"Good evening, gentlemen."

"Do you serve steaks?"

"Sirloin steaks in two sizes, $14.00 and $10.50. All the trimmings, and I just tapped a keg of Bass. How many are we? Suzie, can we squeeze these four gentlemen in somewhere? Enjoy your dinner. What's that? Four pints of Bass? Coming up."

The mixing glass locks into the metal shaker. With one deft tap of the heel of his hand, Ken frees it, and pours the drink.

"What a delicious cocktail!" the customer says.

"It's one of my favorites. The secret is a tiny dash of Cointreau to give it a little zing."

"My, I'd never have thought of that!"

In a quiet lull Ken checks the bar and makes a short list of things required, which he will leave for the manager.

His very presence is a cheering and stress-reducing factor. What a guy!

He is never unknowingly rude. He knows the full gospel of trivia that customers want to hear. The origin of the expression "Let them eat cake," the number of Arabic words in English, and why bloomers are so called. His jokes span the generations: a Churchill story here, a Reagan story there, right up to modern times. He knows the sizes of large champagne bottles—magnums and jeroboams—and what it is that gives gin its flavor . . .

No special request bothers him. He rarely says, "I don't know" with glazed eyes. Sometimes he'll say, "I don't know, but I can find out."

Every tip Ken picks up is exorbitant. Guys who order one Martini will tip him 5 dollars, more than the price of the drink. This, plus the extra tips generated by his judicious buying of drinks "on the house" for selected customers, means that he actually goes home with more money than Boris.

A few weeks later the owner has a bit of a domestic problem. His sister-in-law's fourth husband has just retired from the Fire Department and would like a job.

Our owner is a strange sort of fellow. He wears 2,000-dollar suits that look as though they were made for scarecrows. His shoes never match his other clothes. Sometimes he comes into the restaurant very early and tops up the premium bottles with cheap liquor, unbeknownst to the bartenders and managers. He inherited five restaurants, a gas station, and a pasta factory, but most of his small empire is long gone. All his businesses failed through hapless mismanagement. Only this restaurant remains. It has a long lease at a cheap rent and is in a super location. Were it not, it would die in a week.

Once he complained to the manager about the size of the meat bill.

"We've been selling a lot of steaks," the manager pointed out.

"Oh," said the owner, barely comprehending.

His relative by marriage has made it known that he would like to be a bartender. So much pressure is brought to bear that the owner agrees to fire one of his bartenders.

Anyone who has developed any kind of a feel for the bar business through reading this book will know who gets the chop.

GLOSSARY

Ale Malt beverage (beer) made by top fermentation at lukewarm temperatures.

Aperitif Wine or fortified wine served before a meal.

Aroma Fruity or floral scent of a wine.

Backbar Rear structure of bar for storage, glasses, equipment, and displays.

Backup Reserve supplies.

Bar back Junior bartender, "go-fer," and runner.

Barspoon Long-handled teaspoon for mixing drinks.

Bar sugar Superfine sugar for making drinks.

Bartender Person who mixes and serves drinks to bar customers and fills table waiters' orders for drinks.

BATF Bureau of Alcohol, Tobacco, and Firearms.

Beer Fermented beverage made from grain, water, hops, and yeast.

Bitters Herb-flavored spirits used as drink flavoring.

Blood alcohol content Percentage of alcohol in the blood, used as a measure of intoxication.

Brandy Distilled spirits made from fermented grape or other fruit juice.

Build To mix a drink in a glass.

Cognac Brandy made in the Cognac region of France.

Cooler Bucket for serving bottled wine or ice; refrigerator; tall, iced drink.

Cordial *See* Liqueur.

Corked (Wine) spoiled by a defective cork.

Dash   Generally, one-sixth of a teaspoon.

Decant   Pour wine into a carafe so that the sediment remains in the bottle.

Distilled spirit   Beverage made by distilling a fermented liquid.

Down   Served with ice, "on the rocks."

Draft beer   Unpasteurized beer pumped up from a keg, not bottled.

Duck boards   Springy, removable wooden boards on the bar floor.

Dry   (1) Term used for areas where sale of alcohol is illegal. (2) Not sweet.

Eighty-six   Code expression denoting shut off, or out of stock. E.g., "He's 86'd"—Don't serve him; "86 the roast beef"—There's no roast beef left.

Flag   Slice of citrus fruit on a pick, used as a garnish.

Float   Carefully pour cream so that it floats on top of a liqueur.

Front bar   The part of the bar utilized by the customers.

Gig   A bar job.

Gin   Neutral spirits flavored with juniper berries.

House brand   Liquor served when the customer does not specify a particular brand.

House wine   Wine served by the glass or by the carafe.

Jigger   Small glass or metal measure for liquor.

Jug wine   Inexpensive wine packaged in large bottles.

Keg   Half-barrel of beer (15.5 gal.).

Light beer   Beer with lowered alcohol and calories.

Liqueur   Flavored and sweetened brandy or other spirit.

Metered pour   Alcohol-dispensing system that controls drink size.

Microbrewery   Small, independent beer-making operation.

Mixing glass   Glass container for stirring drinks with ice.

Mixology   The art of mixing alcoholic drinks.

Nonalcoholic beer   Malt beverage containing less than 0.5 percent alcohol.

On the rocks   Served over ice in a glass.

Par   The standard stock of the bar, to be replaced daily.

Pickup station   Section of bar where table servers give orders and receive drinks.

POS   Point of sale, system in which cash register is a computer input terminal.

Pourer   Metal or plastic bottle insert to facilitate pouring drinks.

Proof   Measure of alcohol content (each degree equals 0.5 percent alcohol by volume).

Rack   Knee-high container holding the most used bottles.

Rail   (1) Recessed section of bar top where bartender pours drinks. (2) Brass foot rest for customers.

Rim   Decorate the edge of a glass with salt, sugar, etc.

Rum   Spirits distilled from sugar cane or molasses.

Setup   The basic standard arrangement of the bar for business. Also, necessary equipment for certain drinks or meals. E.g., Mr. Jones is having dinner at the bar. "Set him up" with cutlery, napkin, and condiments.

Shake   Mix a drink with ice in a shaker.

Shelf life   Length of time a product can be stored without loss of quality.

Simple syrup   Liquid sweetener (one part sugar to one part water) for drinks.

Slice   A thin segment of a lime, lemon, or orange.

Sommelier   Wine steward, who buys and sells the restaurant's wines.

Sparking wine   Bubbly wine containing carbon dioxide.

Stick   The bar.

Stir   Mix a drink with ice, using the long bar spoon, in a mixing glass.

Straight up   (Cocktail) chilled but served without ice.

Strainer   Drink strainer with a flexible spring that fits over a glass or cup.

Stripper   Hand tool used for making citrus peel strips.

Tap   Beer faucet. *See* Draft beer.

Teetotal   Does not drink alcohol.

Tequila Spirits from the Tequila district of Mexico, made of fermented juice of the blue agave plant.

Third-party liability Liability of a server of alcoholic beverages for damages caused by an intoxicated customer.

Twist A slice of lemon peel, twisted to release its flavor.

Up (Cocktail) chilled but served without ice.

Vodka Neutral spirits treated to remove flavor and aroma.

Wedge Quarter-moon segment of a lemon, lime, or orange.

Well Knee-high container holding the most-used bottles.

Wet Denoting an area where the sale of alcohol is legal.

White spirits Colorless spirits, including gin, vodka, rum, tequila.

Whiskey, whisky Spirits distilled from grain.

Wine Fermented grape or other fruit juice.

Worm Spiral part of a corkscrew.

INDEX

Printed in the United States
204037BV00002B/139-525/P